"Us Indians Don't Want Our Reservation Opened"

Documents of Salish, Pend d'Oreille, and Kootenai Indian History, 1907-1911

"Us Indians Don't Want Our Reservation Opened"

Documents of Salish, Pend d'Oreille, and Kootenai Indian History, 1907-1911

edited by
Robert Bigart
and
Joseph McDonald

published by
Salish Kootenai College Press
Pablo, Montana

distributed by
University of Nebraska Press
Lincoln, Nebraska

Publication of this book was made possible through the generosity of the Oleta "Pete" Smith Endowment Fund of the Montana Community Foundation.

Cover design: Corky Clairmont, artist/graphic designer, Pablo, Montana.
Cover illustration: Sam Resurrection. Source: Séliš–Qĺispé Culture Committee, St. Ignatius, Montana.

Library of Congress Cataloging-in-Publication Data:
Names: Bigart, Robert, editor | McDonald, Joseph, 1933- editor.
Title: "Us Indians don't want our reservation opened": documents of Salish, Pend d'Oreille, and Kootenai Indian history, 1907-1911 / Robert Bigart and Joseph McDonald.
Description: Pablo, Montana : Salish Kootenai College Press, [2021]. | Includes bibliographical references and index.
Identifiers: LCCN 2021007499 | ISBN 9781934594292 (paperback)
Subjects: LCSH: Salish Indians--Montana--History--20th century--Sources. | Kalispel Indians--Montana--History--20th century--Sources. | Kootenai Indians--Montana--History--20th century--Sources. | Indians of North America--Montana--Government relations--1869-1934--Sources. | Flathead Indian Reservation (Mont.)--History--20th century--Sources.
Classification: LCC E99.S2 U8 2021 | DDC 978.6004/979435--dc23
LC record available at https://lccn.loc.gov/2021007499.

Published by Salish Kootenai College Press, PO Box 70, Pablo, MT 59855.

Distributed by University of Nebraska Press, 1111 Lincoln Mall, Lincoln, NE 68588-0630, order 1-800-755-1105, www.nebraskapress.unl.edu.

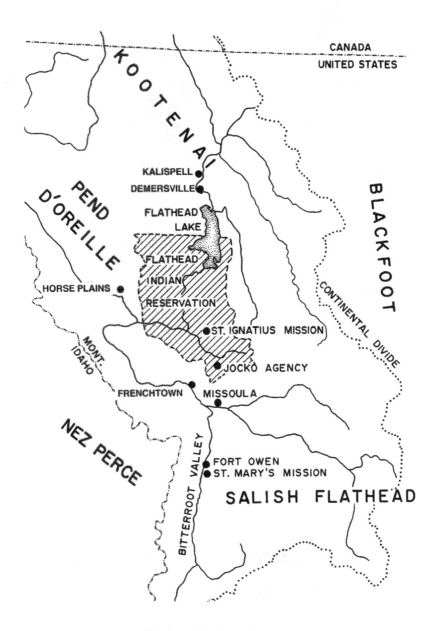

CANADA
UNITED STATES

K O O T E N A I

KALISPELL
DEMERSVILLE
FLATHEAD
LAKE
FLATHEAD
INDIAN
RESERVATION

PEND
D'OREILLE

BLACKFOOT

HORSE PLAINS

CONTINENTAL DIVIDE

ST. IGNATIUS MISSION

MONT
IDAHO

JOCKO AGENCY

FRENCHTOWN
MISSOULA

NEZ PERCE

BITTERROOT VALLEY

FORT OWEN
ST. MARY'S MISSION

SALISH FLATHEAD

**Flathead Indian Reservation
Showing Tribal Territories
and Surrounding Towns**

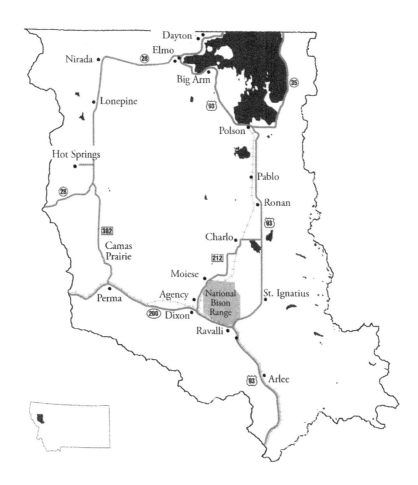

Flathead Indian Reservation, Montana

Map by Wyatt Design, Helena, Montana.

Table of Contents

Detailed Table of Contents

Introduction

The written records of Salish, Pend d'Oreille, and Kootenai Indian history between 1907 and 1911 were dominated by the continued complaints against allotting and opening the reservation. A long string of letters and a series of delegations to Washington, D.C., left no doubt that the Indian leaders and tribal members opposed the opening. Tribal members recognized that the allotment policy was driven by the greed of white men and the desire of whites to get tribal assets at bargain prices. The tribes were being robbed, and they were not willing to be quiet about it.

Most of the complaints that made it to the Indian Office files were from, or initiated by, Sam Resurrection. Presumably Resurrection was more eloquent in Salish than the English translations indicate, but there was no mistaking his point that the allotment and opening of the reservation were vigorously opposed by the Indians.

To make matters even worse, in 1908 Senator Joseph Dixon secured funding for the Flathead Irrigation Project. The project would destroy most of the private irrigation ditches the Indian farmers had dug over the years and make the tribes pay for the construction of an irrigation project which mainly benefitted white homesteaders. The tribes fervently protested against this use of their assets — the land — to reward Dixon's political backers.

The allotment and opening of the Flathead Reservation devastated the new tribal economy based on livestock and agriculture. The opening signaled the end of the open range grazing on the reservation. This forced the large cattle owners to sell most of their stock, and it forced Michel Pablo to dispose of his herd of buffalo. The roundup of these buffalo for shipment to Canada was a major event on the reservation and attracted international attention.

At the same time as the tribes were fighting against the theft of their lands, they had to deal with Montana state efforts to control tribal hunting rights on and off the reservation. State hunting regulations tried to protect wildlife, but they were structured to favor white sports hunters over Indian and white subsistence hunters. Most tribal members tried to adjust to the state laws, purchased licenses, and observed the new hunting seasons and limits.

Some of the white game wardens were prejudiced against Indian hunting. This, combined with language and cultural differences, led to the death of four Indian hunters and a game warden in the Swan Valley in 1908. The conflict over tribal hunting rights was not resolved until later in the twentieth century.

As always, the newspapers covered reservation crime which ended up in the white court system. Most of the crime was Indian on Indian and resulted from alcohol. Some of the "illegal" activities originated in Agent Fred Morgan's crusade to force Indians to observe Christian marriage rules and end gambling on the reservation.

Tribal celebrations — especially the Arlee Fourth of July powwows — were described by newspaper reporters and attended by many white spectators. Between 1907 and 1911 a number of tribal businesses advertised or were publicized in the written sources. Other sources gave glimpses of everyday life on the reservation, but most of the routines of daily life were hidden from the historical record. There was no mistaking, however, tribal efforts to protect their assets from theft, and their insistence on having a say in the government policies that affected them.

Cautions, Biases and Selection Strategies

The documents of Flathead Reservation history in this collection were selected because they offered valuable information about the tribes. However, because they were written records, they also reflect the biases and bigotry of the white men and women who wrote many of the records. Some of the documents in this collection were written by Indian people, but most records that survived give the government's side of the story. The readers need to look beyond the bigotry to see the specific incidents being described.

The editors have given preference to statements by individual Indians or chiefs or descriptions of specific activities. The documents chosen needed to be readable and make sense on their own. Normally historians often rely on many small, short references in diaries or newspaper articles which do not tell a full story.

The documents have not been edited to remove all bigoted words or references. However, an offensive term describing Indian women has been rendered as "s...." An offensive term for Black people has been rendered as "n......"

The editors have tried to insert "sic" as infrequently as possible. It is usually only used when we felt the reader might be confused about whether the mistake was in the transcription or in the original manuscript.

The most important sources for tribal history are the oral traditions of the elders. The written sources contribute towards telling history, but they do not give the history. Hopefully, the documents reproduced here will supplement the oral tribal histories currently being collected and written by the Séliš–Qlispé Culture Committee in St. Ignatius and the Kootenai Culture Committee in Elmo, Montana.

Frustration and Complaints Over Opening the Reservation

The most persistent and prolific tribal leader opposing the allotment and opening of the reservation was Sam Resurrection. At about the age of nine, Resurrection apparently died but came back to life during his wake. As a result, he received the name Sam Resurrection. Chapter one of this collection contains a sampling of the many letters Resurrection sent to Washington, D.C., complaining about allotting and opening the reservation. Presumably Resurrection was much more eloquent in Salish than in the English translations of his letters. At the end of the twentieth century, tribal elders remembered Resurrection positively for his efforts to have tribal voices heard, despite his failure to prevent the opening of the reservation. Resurrection did have a problem with alcohol and was repeatedly arrested in Missoula for being drunk. (Chapter 1, August 1908, and August 1909)

In 1910 Resurrection was approached by a Baltimore attorney named Robert F. Leach, Jr., who promised to represent the tribes if he was paid a $5,000 retainer. (Chapter 1, April 1910) The records do not indicate how the Leach affair turned out, but the events do indicate the desperate tribal efforts to prevent the opening of the reservation to white homesteaders.

In addition to Resurrection's complaints, tribal leaders made other protests against opening the reservation between 1907 and 1911. In January 1907, Antoine Moiese and Allicott traveled to Washington to express tribal opposition. (Document 2) On October 6, 1908, Chief Charlo repeated his opposition through a letter written in braille by Pierre Pichette, a young, blind tribal member. (Document 22) Even in December 1909, Chief Antiste and five other Kootenais protested against opening the reservation without the consent of the tribes. (Document 35)

To add to the tribal complaints about the opening, in 1908 Senator Joseph Dixon secured appropriations for the construction of the Flathead Irrigation Project. The project mainly benefitted white homesteaders on the reservation, but was to be paid for with tribal funds from land and timber sales. Many tribal farmers had private irrigation ditches that were destroyed during the project construction. Dixon's plan to use tribal funds to pay for the irrigation construction caused continued turmoil on the reservation and was not finally resolved until 1948.

Not satisfied with having opened most of the reservation to white homesteaders and voters, in 1910 Dixon proposed to allow tribal members to sell three quarters of their allotments to white farmers. Antoine Moiese and other tribal leaders unsuccessfully protested the law allowing the sale of sixty acres of the eighty-acre irrigable allotments. (Document 42)

Finally, in 1911 the principal tribal chiefs hired Richard C. Adams, a member of the Delaware Tribe in Oklahoma and one of the founders of the Brotherhood of North American Indians, as their lawyer to pursue claims arising out of the forced opening of the reservation and unfulfilled treaty promises. (Document 75) Henry and Alexander Matt, Antoine Moiese, and Baptiste Kakashe joined the Brotherhood to gain national support for the struggles of the Flathead Reservation tribes to oppose the allotment policy. (Document 78) More information about the 1912 activities of the Brotherhood on the reservation can be found in the 1912 to 1920 volume of this documentary history series.

Impacts of the Allotment Policy

Aside from depleting tribal assets, the opening of the reservation also meant the end of open-range grazing. The cattlemen had to reduce their herds to the number of animals they could pasture on their family allotments. One of the biggest impacts was on Michel Pablo's buffalo operation. Pablo was not able to sell the buffalo the American government, so he sold them to the Canadian government.

Between 1907 and 1910 the buffalo were rounded up and loaded on railroad cars at the Northern Pacific Railroad station at Ravalli on the reservation. The buffalo roundup attracted enormous publicity and international attention. Samples of the coverage by local newspapers are included in chapter two of this collection. Many tribal members worked on the roundup, but only a few were identified by name in the newspaper coverage. Chapter two ends with the first plans to kill the wild buffalo bulls that could not be loaded and sent north.

In 1910, Pablo's buffalo herd became entangled in Montana state's efforts to control hunting on the reservation. That year the state declared the outlaw buffalo to be wild animals and subject to state hunting restrictions. Finally, in December 1910, the Indian Office insisted that the buffalo were not wild game but Pablo's personal property. (Document 62) Lincoln Ellsworth, an off-reservation white sportsman, left a detailed description of his successful October 1911 hunt for a buffalo bull in the Little Bitterroot area of the reservation. (Document 74)

Fighting Off State Efforts to Control the Reservation

While the tribes were fighting against federal efforts to open the reservation to white homesteaders, they also had to contend with Montana state efforts to control hunting on the reservation. In addition to declaring Pablo's buffalo to be wild game, the state moved to require tribal members to have hunting licenses and observe state hunting regulations on the reservation. Kootenai Chief Thomas Antiste filed a written objection to the state move to control on-reservation hunting. (Document 54) Tribal hunting rights on the reservation were affirmed by the federal courts in 1915. It took until the middle of the twentieth century to establish tribal treaty hunting rights off the reservation.

A particularly gruesome incident in state efforts to control tribal off-reservation hunting resulted in the 1908 death of four Indians and a white game warden in the Swan Valley. Various accounts of the incident have been published over the years, but this collection only includes a sampling of the biased newspaper coverage. (Chapter 3) The Séliš–Qĺispé Culture Committee has recorded extensive oral material about the killings and plans to publish a book on the subject. For a shortened version of their research see Salish–Pend d'Oreille Culture Committee, "The Swan Massacre: A Brief History," in Upper Swan Valley Historical Society, Inc., *The Gathering Place: Swan Valley's Gordon Ranch* (Condon, Mont.: Upper Swan Valley Historical Society, Inc., 2017), pages 62-93.

Criminal Enforcement on the Reservation

The written documents preserve some accounts of crime on the reservation. In 1909, a new agent, Fred C. Morgan, began a crusade to strictly enforce church and government regulations controlling marriages and gambling on the reservation. By many accounts, the previous agent, Samuel Bellew, had been lax in enforcing the law. On January 30, 1909, Special Indian Agent Thomas Downs was ecstatic in his endorsement of Morgan's more rigorous stance. (Document 24) Morgan fought with Baptiste Kakashe who wanted to take Jackson Sundown to Washington, D.C., as his interpreter. Sundown was not legally married and Morgan asked the Indian Office to refuse to meet with Kakashe and Sundown. (Document 25) In March 1909, Charlo filed a series of complaints against Morgan. (Document 27) A year later, Louison complained when Morgan fired him from his longtime position as tribal judge. (Document 47) Duncan McDonald, however, was chairman of the Flathead Business Committee and supported Morgan's policies. (Document 52) In July 1911, Kootenai Chief Thomas Antiste complained about Morgan's refusal to allow allottees to freely sell their land. (Document 68) Complaints against Morgan's administration continued past 1911, but, in many cases, Morgan was being blamed for carrying out Bureau of Indian Affairs policies dictated from Washington. D.C.

Other crimes making it into the newspapers included murder, mostly involving alcohol. All of the cases found in the 1907 to 1911 period included Indians killing other Indians. (For example, see Document 1; Document 3; Document 15; Document 19, Document 26, and others.)

Tribal members were arrested in Missoula for being drunk. (Document 7; Document 8; Document 10, and others.) In the summer of 1908 a series of arrests were made of tribal members accused of bootlegging alcohol on the reservation. (Document 20; Document 21) In January 1910, William Deschamps was arrested for bringing whiskey on the reservation to treat a serious case of tuberculosis. He received a pardon and was sent home to die. (Document 36)

In one case in 1908, Bazille Matt and Alvina Luddington wanted to get married. Alvina was under age and got pregnant. Her father refused to consent to the marriage and had Bazille charged with statutory rape. (Document 14) Sometimes family difficulties made it into the legal sphere.

Fourth of July Celebrations

The 1907 Fourth of July celebration at the Jocko Agency was an especially gala event. A trainload of Missoula white people visited the affair. The Secretary of the Interior James R. Garfield was the most prominent visitor. James R. Garfield was the son of James A. Garfield who negotiated with Chief Charlo and the Bitterroot Salish in 1872. (Document 6) The 1908 Fourth of July celebration was attended by Helen Fitzgerald Sanders, a white writer who wrote a long description of the celebration. (Document 18) The Missoula newspaper also contained a long article describing the Indians who joined local whites in the 1911 Fourth of July celebration at St. Ignatius. (Document 67)

Indian Businesses on the Reservation

Between 1907 and 1911 mixed blood tribal members invested in a number of reservation businesses. The first national bank in Polson in 1909 included Wm. Irvine, Charles Allard, Jr., and Mike Matt among its investors. (Document 29) Charles Allard, Jr., and J. O. Dupuis invested in Polson's second bank in 1910. (Document 44) That same year Mike Matt also had stock in the new bank in Dayton. (Document 43)

Between February 1910 and January 1911, John Matt advertised his locating business helping white homesteaders find unoccupied land to claim on the reservation. Matt had previously served on the appraisal committee that classified the "surplus" land which was open to white settlement. (Document 41)

Some tribal members started retail businesses. One of the Courvilles was part owner of the Plains Meat Market in 1908. (Document 23) Mike Matt was part owner of the Dayton Mercantile Company in 1910. (Document 43) Zephyre Courville had stock in the Sanders County Mercantile Company in Plains. (Document 48) Michel Pablo owned a general merchandise store in Ronan named Pablo & Potvin. In 1912, the Pablo store was installing steam heat and electric lights. (Document 77) Pablo's store was destroyed in the 1912 fire which wiped out most of the Ronan business district.

Others had service businesses. In 1909, Charles Allard Jr., established the Flathead Stage and Express Line between Ravalli and Polson. (Document 28) T. G. DeMers operated a hotel in Plains. (Document 33; Document 51) Arthur Larrivee developed housing lots in Dayton in 1910. (Document 43) One of the Stingers was part owner of an automobile stage between Ronan and Ravalli in 1911. (Document 70) Harry Burland had a blacksmith shop, automobile garage, and auto sales at Ronan between 1911 and 1917. (Document 71) A Stinger and a Morigeau were co-owners of the Central Hotel in Ronan in 1911. (Document 72) Ed Deschamps was the proprietor of the St. Ignatius Pool Hall in 1911. (Document 76)

Other Glimpses of Reservation Life

A few written sources gave brief glimpses of other aspects of reservation life. In 1908 several baseball games played between reservation teams were reported in the Missoula newspapers. (Document 17)

Chief Charlo's death and funeral in January 1910 were covered in detail. (Document 37) At the end of that month, Martin Charlo was elected to succeed his father. (Document 40)

Finally, one of the Flathead Agency employees wrote an extended account of his trip to Carlisle Indian School in March 1911. He chaperoned twelve Flathead Reservation students from Jocko to Pennsylvania. (Document 66)

Conclusion

Between 1907 and 1911, the Flathead Reservation boiled with opposition to allotting the reservation and selling the "surplus" land to white settlers. Sam Resurrection and other tribal leaders were not able to stop Joseph Dixon's plans, but they expressed their opposition loudly. Dixon based much of his political career on transferring Indian assets to white voters at bargain prices. The Flathead, Blackfeet, Fort Peck, and Crow Reservations all suffered from his theft of tribal assets. In the twenty-first century, the Flathead Reservation was still suffering from the impacts of his policies. But in the twenty-first century the Flathead tribes had far more political, legal, and economic power to defend and preserve the tribal community than it did between 1907 and 1911.

Chapter 1

Sam Resurrection

1907-1919

Sam Resurrection

1907-1919

Editors' note: Sam Resurrection was the most prolific Flathead Reservation leader during the 1907 to 1919 period who complained bitterly about the allotment policy forced on the tribes. Only a sample of his letters and news coverage have been reproduced here. He made repeated trips to Washington, D.C., and Helena, Montana, to petition for a revocation of the policy. The written sources give a distorted representation of Resurrection's abilities. Sam Resurrection was probably much more eloquent in Salish than in his letters written in English. Resurrection signed almost all of the constant complaints during the early twentieth century against the forced allotment and opening of the reservation. Even though the government ignored his protests, he never gave up his crusade to have tribal voices heard. Tribal elders at the turn of the twenty-first century remembered Resurrection positively, despite his failure to halt the allotment and opening of the reservation. The newspaper coverage treated his campaign against allotment as a joke and emphasized his problems with alcohol. The tribal history based on oral sources being compiled by the Séliš-Qlispé Culture Committee in St. Ignatius, should help correct the biases in the condescending letters from the Commissioner of Indian Affairs and the Flathead Indian Agent, and the bigoted reporting of contemporary white newspapers. See the biographical sketch of Resurrection in Salish-Pend d'Oreille Culture Committee and Elders Cultural Advisory Council, Confederated Salish and Kootenai Tribes, *The Salish People and the Lewis and Clark Expedition* (Lincoln: University of Nebraska Press, 2005), pages 126-127. Some periods have been added to Resurrection's letters to make them easier to read.

The 1855 Hellgate Treaty did include an article allowing the President to assign lots to individual tribal members or families who would locate permanent homes. The article also referred to the 1854 Treaty with the Omaha which allowed the remaining land after allotments were made to be sold to non-Indians. The transcript of the negotiations for the Hellgate Treaty, however, did not indicate that this article providing for allotments was explained to the Indian chiefs. Resurrection's letters made plain that the tribal leaders believed that allotment without the consent of the tribes was a violation of the 1855 Hellgate Treaty.

After 1910, Resurrection and most tribal members were upset when the state of Montana moved to control the hunting and fishing on the reservation. They were even more upset when they learned that the construction of the irrigation project on the reservation was to be paid for with tribal money. They had not asked for the project and were especially insulted when it turned out their tribal funds were being used to pay the expenses of the opening of the reservation, the operation of the Flathead Agency, and to fund the irrigation construction. Most of the benefits of the irrigation system went to the white homesteaders.

According to some 1910 correspondence in the Commissioner of Indian Affairs records at the National Archives, Resurrection was approached by a Baltimore, Maryland, attorney, Robert F. Leach, Jr., and told that Leach could prevent the opening of the reservation if the tribal members would raise $5,000 to pay for his legal work. Leach (1873-1946) was a graduate of the University of Virginia and later in life was State's attorney for Baltimore City. No record has been found to show how the Leach affair worked out, but the episode did indicate the desperation of tribal leaders as the reservation was opened to white homesteaders in 1910.

Source: Sam Reslection to Theodore Roosevelt, December 8, 1907, from file 7,667/1907 Flathead 054, Central Classified Files, RG 75, National Archives, Washington, D.C.

Dec. 8, 1907

Theodore Roosevelt
Washington D.C.

I wrote to you once and was telling you how the reservation was in the early days. We were all Indian decendents here in this state, and there was no white man to speak of, and when the whites came, you all smuggled up the country away from us poor indians. Its now almost 6000 years since the world was created. Its now 460 years since the whites first saw the indian tribes. When you whites and we indians first met together, we never did have any counsils about the lands before. When you first saw us all of us indian tribes were all well to do in those days. And now we know that since all you white settlers came in this state, you all Killed off all the wild games and fowls for us and now

Sam Resurrection
Source: Séliš–Ql̓ispé Culture Committee, St. Ignatius, Montana

today there is hardly any thing left. When Stevens came to give us a reservation to settle down on is now about 50 years ago. there was three tribes together, the Flatheads, Kootinies, and Penderollies. And then Garfield came about 30 years ago, and said that what Stevens said about the reserve was right and that it was for your life time. During the celebration of the fourth this year, we saw Garfields Son and another, and they never said a word about the reservation. Only said that he was glad to see us having a big time.

Us fullbloods and mixed bloods on this reservation are one and the same to us and we like your blood the same as our own. There is now only one person that is throwing the reservation open, and we never had a talk about it and if we did have a talk over it, we indians would know how it is, and there would be no kicking about it.

And what people who claim to have blood here, and have come from the outside dont look at us, and we dont look at them, but the one that have always lived with us, treats us right. Well us indians dont want our reservation opened and so that is all.

Good day
Sam Reslection
Cheif Flathead Indians

Source: Sam Reslection to Theodore Roosevelt and Commissioner of Indian Affairs, January 12, 1908, from file 76,667/1907 Flathead 054, Central Classified Files, RG 75, National Archives, Washington, D.C.

Arlee, Mont
Jan 12th 1908

Mr. Theodore Roosevelt
President
Washington DC
and
Commissioner of Indian Affairs
Washington D.C.
Dear Honar.

I thought I would drop you a few lines to tell you what we all think about our Resevation, and what we all say about it. Before you gave us this place for our Resevation we was all mixed up with the Whites. we used to travel all over the Country, and you gave us this place to stop and we all thought that this Resevation belongs to us, and why is it that the whites wants to take it away from us.

We all know that you are the Head man of all over the World, and you know your self how long ago when you came across the Ocean and get in with the Red Skin and then we were all mixed up with the Whites?

And why is it now the Whites want to take our Resevation away from us?

It is about Fifty Years ago when you send a man to give us a Resevation his Name was Mr Steven, and when Mr Steven got here he had a talk with the Indians. at that time we had three Chiefs the Chief of the Pondera was Alexander-no-Horse, and the Coutaina Chief was Michel-Ball-Head and the Flathead Chief was Victor.

And when Mr Stevens was here at that time he told the Indians that this place will be you Country and live here till you all die and so we all believe him, and then the second man you send here his name was Garfield. When he got here at that time the old Chiefs were dead all ready. We had Charlo for our Chief and Ignace Paul for the Coutana and Mr Garfield ask the Indians. What did Mr Stevens said to them and the Indians told Mr Garfield that Mr Stevens gave us this place for our Resevation for ever, and Mr Garfield told the Indians that Mr Stevens was right.

And now Why is it that our Indian Agent Samuel Bellew and Joe Dicksen and the Fathers want to get our Resevation Threwed open. And we all Indians believe on Mr Stevens of what he told us and here is another question I would like to ask you. What become of that Grazing Tax money. In the First place our Indian Agent Samuel Bellew Says that you told him that we would draw money for Ten Years. The first time we got Five Dollars $5.00 each and the Second year we got Ten Dollars $10.00 each and since that we never got a cent from him. it is two years now, and how is it about the Wood at Evaro. What they are sawing does that money goes to the Indians? This Agent Samuel Bellew does not help us poor Indians at all. All the Chiefs and poor Indians are doing the best they can to get him out of this Resevation. Samuel Bellew does not suit the Poor Indians.

I Wrote to you Three times and this last time I got a letter from you. — there was no Enveloupe. did it Came that way with out no Enveloupe. And why is it that Chief Charlo got a letter from you and the Letter was Opend? and Antoine Moise the same way? and Pierre Big Hawk the same way? I always thought it was against the law to open letters.

Well I will Close my Poor writing in sending you my best regards to you. hoping to meet each others some time and will you please as to be so kind to answer my poor Writing.

Well good bye. will you please send the letter to me at Arlee P.O. Mont.

Very Respectfully
Sam Reslection.

Source: Patee Ki-Ki shee, Chas. Molman, and Sam Reflection to Jannie A. Garfield, July 20, 1908, and Acting Commissioner of Indian Affairs to Patee Ki-ki-shee, August 1, 1908, from file 51,017/1908 Flathead 308.1, Central Classified Files, RG 75, National Archives, Washington, D.C.

July 20th 1908

Hon Jannie A. Garfield
Secretary of the Interior
Washington D.C.

Well I wrote to you since last year. I did received no Answer from.

I want to ask you somthing about my letter I got from Washington, D.C. All the letters I get they be open be our Agent here.

We have had four Agent. Mr. Pete Ronan Mr. Joe Carter Mr. Smead Mr. Samuel Bellew.

Well since from that we found out that our Country was made to pe [be] open. Be them four Agents.

The time Mr. Joe Carter was the Agent well [Louie?] Mr. Froish tail. He sent me some money and did find it. This is 11 years ago. Two years ago I went to Butte And saw Mr. Froish tail he ask me if I got $64.00. I says no I didnt.

And the time Mr. Smead was the Agent. So I went to him ask him for some oil and said I got 35¢ worte of oil here. He sell it to me and 25¢ matche.

Now it is four years ago Mr. Samuel Bellew is here. First time was law. Since from that we got more law. When the chifes goes to him and say here there is some stilling going on. About horses. He turns his face and sayes that is not my business.

I write you my friend.

The first whites the Flatheads seen were Louis and Clarke 103 years ago. when we first saw the white people we made friends and have ever since been friends. After seeing Louis and Clark 50 years later we seen Mr. Stevens. When we three tribes Mutoo chife of the flathead. Alexander Chief of the Pondrail. Michell Chief of the Cootna. Frank also Chief of the Pondrail.

Steavens told us three tribes that if we would make this our reservation it would be ours as long as these was one of us living.

After that Garfield visited us. Garfield asked us three tribes. What kind of a treaty did we make with Steavens. We told him that we had it understood that this was always to be a reseive. Garfield agreed with Steavens. We believed these two gentleman from Washington.

Now reservation is to be opened up and we are only allowed 80 A. If us three tribes would know this reserve was to be opened up we would have been willing to have had let half go. we would be well satisfied with half.

This Petition given by the promant chivnes [chiefs] of Flathead.

Yours Truly
Patee Ki-Ki shee
Chas. Molman
Sam Reflection.

* * * * * * * *

Mr. Jannie A. Garfield

Arlee, Montana, July 18, 1908

The following named are ones that object to opening this Reservation. This is signed by the different parties:

[Followed by four pages of 130 names of tribal members written in the same hand.]

This Petition given by the promant chives of Flathead.

Batise Ki-Ka-Shee
Charles Mool-man
Sam Reflection.

* * * * * * * *

Department of the Interior,
Office of Indian Affairs,
Washington.
August 1, 1908.

Subject:
Opening Flathead
Reservation.

Patee Ki-ki-shee
Jocko, Montana.
My Friend:

A letter signed by you and Charles Molman and Sam Reflection dated July 20, 1908, objecting to the opening of the Flathead Reservation, has been sent me by the Secretary of the Interior to be answered.

You sent me a petition of 134 Indians in which you ask what kind of treaty Stevens made with the Indians, as you told him that you understood that your land in Montana was to be reserved for your people and that you now learn such is not the case, as the reservation is to be opened up, and you will only receive your allotment. You say that if the three tribes had known the reservation was to be opened, you would have been willing to let half go and would have been well satisfied with the remaining half.

When Governor Stevens made his treaty with the Flathead, Kooenay, and Upper Pend d'Oreille Indians on July 16, 1855, conditions were altogether different from what they are today. The lands that were given to you were of small value, and the settlers were few. Now, however, the people have increased in numbers, and they must have land in order to live and support their families. You and I must bow to the laws which Congress in its wisdom sees fit to enact.

On January 5, 1903, the Supreme Court of the United States, which is the highest judicial body in our country, said that —

> The power exists to abrogate the provisions of an Indian treaty, though presumably such power will be exercised only when circumstances arise which will not only justify the government in disregarding the stipulations of the treaty, but may demand, in the interest of the country and the Indians themselves, that is should do so.

On April 23, 1904, Congress decided that it was for the best interests of your Indians that the land in the Flathead reservation should be allotted to them, and that all lands left over should be opened to settlement by white people upon the proclamation of the President, and that of the money received for these lands, one-half should be used for paying the expenses of the allotment and sale, for constructing irrigation ditches, for purchasing stock, cattle, farming implements, and other articles which will aid you in farming and stock-raising and in the education and civilization of your people, the remaining half to be paid to all people having tribal rights on the reservation.

You will see, therefore, that while Congress believes that your lands should be opened so that their productive value can be utilized, it has directed that all the money received for the lands shall be used for the benefit of the Indians and has therefore taken nothing away from you.

This law of Congress is supreme, and you must accept that which it believes to be for your best interest. I have nothing to do with the making of law, and when Congress decides that certain things must be done, it is my duty to do them. I have therefore, under this Act, caused the lands to be surveyed and to be allotted to the Indians of the Flathead Indian reservation, and when the allotments shall have been finally completed the lands must be opened to settlement in accordance with the law.

I want you and your people to accept the new conditions which Congress, to further your interests, has established; and I would like you to aid me in this matter by getting all the Indians to see that the proposed change is necessary for their best interests and that each Indian with his own farm and his own improvements, by adopting the white man's way of life, will be better off and happier.

> Very respectfully,
> C. F. Larrabee
> Acting Commissioner

Source: "Sam Resurrection Is Angry," *The Daily Missoulian*, August 16, 1908, page 12, col. 4-5; "Sam Resurrection in Jail," *The Daily Missoulian*, August 18, 1908, page 2, col. 1; "Sam Resurrection Is Released from Jail," *The Daily Missoulian*, August 22, 1908, page 10, col. 4.

Sam Resurrection Is Angry
Flathead Veteran Has Many Grievances Which He is Anxious to Adjust.

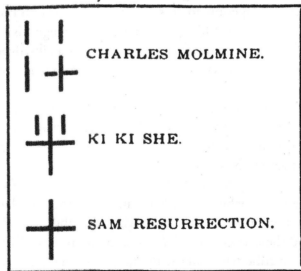

These are the signatures that are appended to a couple of remarkable letters that are to be sent eastward soon by chiefs of the Flathead tribe who are opposed to the opening of the reservation and who have other grievances that they wish to have adjusted right away.

Sam Resurrection is in town from the reservation and he is on the warpath. Sam is one of the Flathead chiefs and he has a long list of wrongs that he proposes to redress if it takes all summer. In the first place, Sam is dissatisfied with almost everything and he realizes that he is the man who must make conditions right. His principal grievance is that Charlot, hereditary chieftain, is no longer fitted to govern the tribe. "Charlot is old and blind. He does not know. The white man says we do this and we give you hundred dollars. Charlot says 'Give me the money' and he don't know what it is the white man will do. We cannot have him for chief. Sam Ressurrection is a smart man. He is the man for chief."

If he can get the reins of government and the tribal war bonnet to wear, Sam will take care of all the other matters the minute he gets the authority; he has the signatures of a lot of the tribe — he says — to his declaration of rights, but in order that no time may be lost, he is getting the work started along other lines.

He is planning to stop the opening of the reservation right away and he is going to make the Northern Pacific restore the old free-ride contract with the Flatheads. He came to town yesterday with a gripsack, eight inches long, stuffed with documents. He consulted several lawyers and then came with his interpreter to The Missoulian office, where he made an extended speech and submitted two letters which he is going to send, one to President Roosevelt and the other to General Superintendent Gilbert of the Northern Pacific.

When he had concluded his speech, he asked through his interpreter: "Is that good talk?" Upon receiving assurance that it was a gilt-edged stemwinder of a talk, the interpreter remarked: "You bet. He smart man. He ought to be chief, that man."

Sam has two propositions to make to the Northern Pacific. One is that the Flatheads be restored their right to free rides between Umatilla and Billings and the other is that, in lieu of this restoration, the Northern Pacific pay the tribe $3,000,000. Either will be satisfactory.

The letter to Presi[d]ent Roosevelt gives a history of the relations between the Flatheads and the white men. Sam, in his address, declared that "Mr. Columbus was a good man. I never see Mr. Columbus, but Flatheads don't fight him." And then he goes on with an accurate review of the treaties and contracts that his tribe has made with the government. It is an interesting communication and is given herewith:

The First Letter.
Theoder Rosevelt, Washington, D.C.

I am writing you a few lines, dear friend Roosevelt. I want to let you know how long we see the first white man, we see Columbus its 416 years, that's the first time we see whites and the flatheads never fights white mans, and thats why we always say that is our friends and our hundred years ago we see 7 white men Louis Clark at Larsses Hole, and now when we see them we were very glad we put all our blankets on the ground and they walk on it and come and see us we were very glad and talk them good and talk to us good one of them. Mr. Stevens fifty-three years ago and he see the three chiefs name was Victor Martin Flathead and Alexander Michel and they make the treaty here Stevens told the three chiefs this would be our reservation as long as there were any Indians here these two people did not tell the Indians that the president would sell the reservation. After that they send three men here Garfield was the head man when he got here he asked the three chiefs what kind of treaty they made with Stevens the chiefs told Garfield this would be a reservation as long as there was any Indians Garfield told them that was right he thought it ought to be that way. Certainly two years ago you send a man here that came here and did not ask no permission and went ahead and surveyed you must recalect Stevens and Garfield made a treaty with the indians out signed a contract and we have got that contract yet. They don't like to make a treaty and then have the whites to come here and give us a piece of land and sell the rest. There three people Joe Dixon Major Blue Totain they are working hard to throw the reservation open. The appraicors are fooling the land away Johnny Matt and Angus McDonald they put $1 50 cents one acre they don't want the appraicors they want some one else that don't want to give away the land. I want to know what kind of a law you got when my mail comes here the major opens them and read them Those men come here and made a treaty and we would like to stay by the contract make arrangements with you this spring there are three tribes here the flathead ponderay and Cootnay the three tribes will sign a contract. They have been working for two years ago to open the reservation and then it would of the tribes satisfied the three tribes don't know what they are doing the whites are trying to fool them those three men that name that made the treaty with us and we have got the writing here to show for it and we believe that these three people told us right. this is from yours truly signed bye chief

Shall Moolmine,
Patie Ka Ka She,
Sam Resurrection.

The letter to Mr. Gilbert is more peremptory and is as follows:
F. W. Gilbert, General Superintendent, St. Paul, Minn.

Sir, My Friend — It has been 27 years since we made a treaty with you to put you road our country you were to give us so much money and a free ride over the road from Umatilla to Billings. The Chieves that made this treaty and also the agent, Major Ronan, are dead. Us that are living still remember this treaty. When Ronan, died we have had three agents since, Carter, Smead and Samuel Bellew. Ronan took the right away from us without our knowledge. These last three agents, we have never spoke to them about the treaty. If this right is not given back to us we figure you out in debt to us to the amount of $3,000,000. Please ans by return mail. Yours truly.

Chas Molmin,
Ki Ki Chee,
Sam Resurrection.

This petition is by the prominent chieves of Flathead.

* * * * * * *

Sam Resurrection in Jail
Flathead Chief Gets Full and Loses Tribal Documents and Heraldry.

Sam Resurrection, lord of the Flatheads, is in jail. Worse than that, the tribal records, important documents, Sam's coat of arms, and all sorts of valuables are lost, along with a valise that was the pride of Sam's young life. Sam was arrested yesterday morning by Officer Therriault on the request of an attorney, in whose office Sam had created a scene. The Flathead chief, full of indignation over the prospective opening of the reservation and loaded to the guards with a vitriolic brand of firewater, entered the lawyer's office and began to accuse the legal light of having appropriated his satchel with its priceless records and heraldry. Sam continued his tirade and a cell in the county jail was the only recourse of the lawyer, who did not care to sit all day in the surf beat of broken English and Indian profanity.

Sam Resurrection is of the opinion that nobody loves him. He thinks he is the victim of a conspiracy and that President Roosevelt is the instigator of all his troubles. He thinks that a minion of the government stole his valise, for he is now of the belief that the Missoula lawyer didn't get it. Sam recently addressed a letter to the president, along with other chiefs of his tribe, and he firmly believes that the loss of his documents came as a direct result of that epistle, which, although it has not yet been given official attention, he is sure has aroused official wrath. Sam can see his lands and the lands of the Indians who call him chief, or would like to call him chief, or whom he would like to have call him chief — according to how the reservation folk arrange their affairs of government — snatched rudely away and usurped by whites. Sam can see nothing but dark clouds on the sky of his future, and he is sore. Nobody loves Sam, he is sure of that. Today Sam will be sobered up and, if he manages to get out of jail, the sun may shine again for him, but now — last night, at least — Sam Resurrection was moodily morose.

* * * * * * * *

Sam Resurrection Is Released from Jail

Sam Resurrection was yesterday morning released from the county jail, where he had been locked up for several days on a charge of having been drunk and disorderly. Sam didn't know what to do with his liberty at first. He left the jail and, within a few minutes, returned and stood around the place until the janitor, not recognizing the chief, locked him up again. Several hours later Sam Resurrection was again released and this time he did not stand upon the order of his going. Sam has not yet fully decided as to whether or not he will go to Washington to lay his grievance before President Roosevelt. First of all, Sam will institute search for his famous grip, which he lost early in the spree that landed him behind the bars.

Source: "Chief Sam Pines for Washington D.C.," *The Daily Missoulian*, October 15, 1908, page 2, col. 2; "Flathead Chief Makes Good Rock Pile Man," *The Daily Missoulian*, October 23, 1908, page 2, col. 2.

Chief Sam Pines for Washington D.C.
Resurrection Tries to Get Out of Jail to Continue Trip to Capital.

While Sam Resurrection is languishing in the county jail the Flathead reservation and everything connected with it is going to the demnition bow-wows — so Sam thinks. Sam is again in jail, as was stated several days ago when he was arrested, his second attempt to start for Washington having resulted as disastrously as did the first. The first time Sam got too drunk and was pinched. He served his term and returned to the reservation, where he accumulated the means for another trip, and again Missoula was the limit of his journey. This time booze and the carrying of poorly concealed weapons caused the incarceration of the chief. With him he had again his precious grip and its priceless papers, which concerned the welfare of Sam's people and the redress he intends to ask of his "friend," President Roosevelt. After a few days Sam began to yearn for liberty and a chance to continue his trip to "D.C.," as he calls his destination. Sam is now using all his influence to get out of hock, and he may make the hill.

Yesterday he had a long conference with Chief Ki-Ki-Che and two of his braves. To Ki-Ki-Che, who says he is 80 years old, and who looks as if he were 800, Sam gave papers he had intended to show his "friend" himself, with the understanding that the old chief should make the trip in case Sam fails to get out. "Ki-Ki-Che no good," said Sam yesterday. "Him too old. President he my friend. Mister Bryan, he my friend. Ki-Ki-Che no good; too old."

Sam said that everybody connected with the agency was a robber, and then made this statement include the entire government, excepting President Roosevelt. Sam contends that the lands of his tribe are being frittered away on Crees and other kinds of Indians, and that a few white people are also getting in on the melon. He thinks that it is absolutely necessary for him to get to Washington, and he says he will walk 'way around Missoula and its pitfalls for unwary Indians if he gets another chance. Sam has no particular desire to be good, but he wants to get to Washington.

* * * * * * * * *

Flathead Chief Makes Good Rock Pile Man

If Sam Resurrection ever wants a letter of recommendation he can apply to Patrick Hale, the presiding genius of the rock pile. For a week now Sam, the titled lord of the Flathead tribe, has been doing manual labor at the penal institution on Main street and, according to the deputy in charge, has been working hard. Sam accomplishes the impossible in that he preserves his dignity while converting large rocks into little ones. In blanket and moccasions Sam sits and works and it is probable that he is composing an address to President Roosevelt while he pecks away, for the chief is only awaiting the expiration of his sentence to go to Washington to present the wrongs of his people to the executive.

Source: "Sam Resurrection Is State House Caller," *The Kalispell Bee*, January 29, 1909, page 5, col. 6.

Sam Resurrection Is State House Caller
Flathead Indians Object to Throwing Reservation Open to Settlement.

Governor Edwin L. Norris had an unusual caller today in the person of Sam Resurrection, a splendid specimen of the red race, and who is chieftain in the Flathead tribe of Indians in northwestern Montana. Sam announced his arrival by informing Private Secretary Aiken that he wished to see "the great white father," meaning the executive of the state.

In fairly intelligent English the red man presented a petition to the governor, signed by numerous members of his tribe, protesting against the throwing open of the Flathead reservation on the general ground that it was not too large for the tribe as it now stands, and intimating that they were firm believers in the Roosevelt anti-race suicide theory, and that as a consequence, more were to be expected as the years roll on.

Governor Norris read the petition with much interest and in turn gave Sam a letter, instructing him how to proceed in the premises, he being powerless to act in the matter, of course. In essence, the letter instructed the Flatheads to take the matter up with the Indian bureau at Washington.

"Too many whites there already," said Sam to a representative of The Record. Sam was gorgeously attired in a white hat and red blanket and wore pearl earrings.

— Helena Record.

Source: Jno. L. Sloane to Commissioner of Indian Affairs, February 26, 1909, from file 16,991/1909 Flathead 313, Central Classified Files, RG 75, National Archives, Washington, D.C.

United States Department of the Interior
United States Indian Service
In the field, Ronan, Montana,
February 26, 1909

Relinquishments for
reservoir sites.

The Hon. Commissioner of Indian Affairs,
Washington, D.C.
Sirs:—

In am experiencing a great deal of trouble in obtaining relinquishments of allotments on the purposed reservoir sites for the Reclamation service.

In one instance of Samuel Inclaywhensu, #1352 — he positively refuses to sign the relinquishment, giving as his reason that he did not want any allotment given him, but as long as it was seen fit to allot him he intends to keep what was given him. He is a full blood Indian, 51 years of age, and one of the agitators who have been opposed to the opening of the reservation, being the chief instigator and solicitor of funds for the visits of the malcontents to Washington in the past three years; the only reason he has not accompanied them being, that when they would stop at Missoula to purchase their tickets, he would become intoxicated and land in the city jail for 30 or 60 days.

Another case is Charles Kickinghorse, #859, who refuses to sign the relinquishment to his allotment and that of his son, or to permit his wife to relinquish her land and that of her children, until he is paid for his improvements, consisting of a comfortable log house, shingle roof, a log stable and some fencing; I estimate the value of his house at $125.

I have talked with Mr. Tabor, Project Engineer of the Reclamation service, in regard to the payment for improvements and he has taken the matter up with Mr. Savage, Engineer in charge.

Kickinghorse is also a full blood, 37 years old, and exerts a considerable amount of influence among the full bloods of his generation, so much so that his neighbors, also upon or adjoining the reservoir sites, viz: Andrew Woodcock and his wife, William, Philomene, Antoine and Alex Finley, all full bloods, allege as their reason for declining to sign relinquishments, that they want to see what I am going to do for Kickinghorse.

If the third reservoir site — the plan of which I understand is now in Washington for approval — is approved, it will affect eighty-one (81) allottees, some of whom have extensive improvements upon their lands, one family alone having nearly four hundred acres under cultivation, one hundred and forty acres of which is now sown to winter wheat; and other improvements such as buildings, etc., of a value, roughly estimated, of $2000.

If these people are to be disposed [sic] of their lands and it is purposed to pay them for their improvements, I would respectfully suggest that a commission be appointed to appraise the value of such improvements, which should include the cost of preparing the land for cultivation.

In the cases I have cited of refusal to relinquish and in any other that may arise, I desire that I be given definite instructions as to procedure in vacating the allotments; I might state here that the trust deeds are still at the Agency office, not having yet been distributed.

I have been greatly hampered in my negotiations with these full bloods, by not having the assistance of an efficient interpreter, although I have made repeated request to employ one — and have had to rely on such volunteer assistance as I could obtain.

Very respectfully,
Jno. L. Sloane
Special Allotting Agent.

Source: Sam Reslection to William H. Taft, March 9, 1909, from file 76,667/1907 Flathead 054, Central Classified Files, RG 75, National Archives, Washington, D.C.

William H. Taft
Cincinati
Ohio
Mar. 9, 1909
Arlee,
Mont.

My Firend.

Did you received my letter. today I am droping you a few lines. It was nearly two years ago when Johnie Mat and Angus McDonald. to work for our Reservation. It wasnt us that want them, because It was our Magor that caught our Chiefs. When they had a treaty for our Reservation. And all our chiefs said it was all right. When they started to surveyed our Reserection. They told our Chiefs that if they would have a Indian Reservation it would be theres for ever. From Washington the man that came to make a treaty with them was Mr. Stevens. And all our Chiefs made a petition, because they made a Indian Reservation. It is what we are thinking of. Since 54 years ago, that's what we are all taking. And I am telling you that we never spoke to Dixon. Three men that are trying hard to throw the reservation open Our Magor, and Father and Dixon. today we find out you law and we are following the laws. And our Chiefs, I have asked them when did they talked to Dixon and they say they never talked with him no place. It shows plenty that when they have a treaty for any thing. You see that time when our Chiefs had a treaty with Mr. Stevens. We remember it yet. And there was another man which was Garfield, he said that our Reservation was to be ours for ever. There are 217 people in my petition. You saw it already. There are eight Chiefs in the petition. Well I want to know how you are thinking of my letter.

Please return by mail right away.

Your sincerly Your
Good bye,
Sam Reslection,
Arlee P. O.
Mont

Source: "Sam Was on Deck," *The Daily Missoulian*, March 24, 1909, page 10, col. 2.

Sam Was on Deck.

There were a good many people waiting to talk to Senator Dixon yesterday when it became known that he was at home, and in the head set were Sam Resurrection and a couple of his cronies. Sam had on his warpaint as usual; he was against the government and he didn't care who knew it. He was especially anxious, in fact, that his attitude should be clearly understood. And when he encountered Senator Dixon he proceeded to unburden himself. He said that the Indians were getting the worst of it and that there were none of the chiefs who had agreed to the opening; he was going to Washington to stop the thing before it got any further. Mr. Dixon listened to the old chief for a while and then said: "Sam, I saw the president before I came home and he said he had heard from you. He said you has started for Washington before but you had got drunk and had got into jail. He said he couldn't see any Indian that did these things." Then Sam was mad. He said it was true he had got into jail but it was a base falsehood that he was drunk. He had been jobbed and that was the way it was with the poor Indian. He intimated that the police force and the sheriff's office are combined against him and that there is really no show for the poor Indian any more. Then he went away shaking his head and determined to get another drink if he could, all the while wondering how it was that the president found out that he been drunk in that mad carouse that consumed all of his money that was to take him to Washington and left him stranded for 60 days on the city rock pile. It was a mystery that he couldn't solve.

Source: "Sam Goes to Bill," *The Daily Missoulian*, June 3, 1909, page 10, col. 2.

Sam Goes to Bill

Sam Resurrection — our old friend of the insatiable appetite and the unquenchable thirst — has made another start for Washington to head off the opening of the reservation. "Me go see Willie Taft," was his declaration to his particular friend in the business office of The Missoulian, the friend who stakes him to a ticket to Arlee every time the chief gets out of jail after a sentence for intoxication. With Sam is his nephew as interpreter and Chief Great Bear as associate terrible example. Sam is armed with a letter of introduction from Judge Hiram Knowles to Senator Carter, and thinks he will have no trouble in getting to see "Willie Taft." Sam is shy of Senator Dixon since the latter learned so much about Sam's bibulous habits, and he hopes to get his business transacted without coming in contact with the junior senator. Sam was reasonably sober yesterday morning, and declared that he had the demon rum by the throat and would not let go his hold until he gets back from Washington. He has made the trip many times before and knows the way all right. If he keeps sober he will be able to get to the capital, and then he may gain an audience with the president, but it is doubtful if he succeeds in changing the plans relative to the opening of the reservation. He will have to see Judge Witten about that; the matter is in the hands of the judge with power to act, and he will be in Missoula by the time Sam gets to Washington. But Sam has made a new start, and he will get there — maybe and maybe not. He has started so many times before and has always got tangled up with John Barleycorn that it is doubtful if he keeps out of trouble all the way to the Atlantic coast.

Source: "An Indian Chief Seriously Injured," *The Daily Missoulian*, August 26, 1909, page 1, col. 1-2, and page 12, col. 4; "Tells of Drinking with White Men," *The Daily Missoulian*, August 28, 1909, page 2, col. 2; "Big Chief Sam Goes to Helena," *The Daily Missoulian*, September 2, 1909, page 6, col. 1.

An Indian Chief Seriously Injured
Sam Resurrection Found by Railroad Track with His Skull Fractured.
Says He Was Assaulted
Noted Sub-Chief of the Flatheads Sustains What May Prove to Be Fatal Injuries in Mysterious Manner Near Bonner —
Lies in St. Patrick's Hospital in Precarious Condition.

Sam Resurrection, sub-chief of the Flatheads, noted Indian orator and one of the best known Indian characters in Montana, lies at St. Patrick's hospital in a critical condition, suffering from a fractured skull and a broken wrist. His injuries are such that they may cost him his life.

The stalwart chief declares that white men got him drunk and attempted to murder him. But whether this is true or whether the red man fell from a train while trying to join a portion of his tribe near Bonner, or was injured in some other accidental manner, is a mystery Sheriff Graham and his deputies are trying to solve.

Early yesterday morning some section men on the Northern Pacific found the Indian chieftain lying near the tracks of the company a short distance west of the Missoula river crossing. The Indian was unconscious and his head was covered with blood. The section men flagged the first train going toward

Missoula and Sam was brought to this city and turned over to the police. He was taken to the office of the sheriff and there it was discovered that his injuries were so serious as to necessitate an operation upon his head. The stolid red man refused to talk after he had regained consciousness and submitted to the setting of his broken wrist without a murmur.

Chieftain Talks.

After being removed to the hospital Sam recovered himself sufficiently to talk to an Indian interpreter in the presence of the county physician and several other witnesses who were present. He told the interpreter that two white men had gotten him drunk and taken him from Missoula toward Bonner in a rig, then had attempted to murder him. He protested that he did not know the identity of the white men and could give no details of the alleged assault upon himself.

His condition was such that Dr. G. F. Turman, the county physician, decided to operate early yesterday afternoon upon the fractured skull. When this operation was performed it was discovered that the skull had been badly fractured above one eye, the injury being of a nature that might easily prove fatal. The fracture was reduced as much as possible and an examination for other injuries was made. Aside from some scratches on the hand and the broken wrist, no other injuries could be discovered. In the opinion of Dr. Turman the fracture of the skull was caused by a blow from some heavy, blunt instrument, and the fracture of the wrist was the result of Sam's falling upon it, and not from a blow, as there were no bruises on the arm to indicate that he had been struck there.

Sheriff Investigates.

As soon as the facts in the case were made known to the sheriff he went to Bonner and made an investigation. He learned that a portion of Sam's tribe were encamped on the river near Bonner, also that Sam had not been seen in the vicinity until his unconscious form was found. No strange or suspicious characters had been observed about the town, and so far as the officers could learn no rig left Missoula Tuesday night for Bonner.

The sheriff's opinion is that the Indian sought to reach his fellows by stealing a ride on a train, and either fell from it or was thrown off, but he proposes to make a thorough investigation of the case.

Recently Sam was one of the principal witnesses in a case against "Foxy" Cyr, a Missoula saloon man accused of selling liquor to Indians. Sam testified that the stuff sold him by Cyr was not beer. Later Sam made a sworn statement that he received money to testify falsely in Cyr's behalf, and Cyr was held to the federal grand jury to answer a charge of subornation of perjury. Sam is the principal witness in this case and is under subpoena to appear in Helena on

September 2 to give his testimony. But his injuries may preclude the possibility of his being there at the time set.

Sam Resurrection, while he is not the head chief of the Flathead tribe, is one of the most prominent Indians among them, and wields a wonderful influence over the tribe. He is an orator of note among his tribesmen and on one or two occasions had made trips to Washington, D.C., to plead in behalf of his tribe with the government officials.

Late last night a report from the hospital was to the effect that the chief was in a very critical condition.

* * * * * * * *

Tells of Drinking with White Men
Sam Resurrection Says He Was Riding in Box Car and Drinking Whisky.

That Chief Sam Resurrection had been to Helena and Butte on a trip and was riding back to Missoula in a boxcar and drinking whisky with two white men on the night he received the injuries that may cost him his life, was learned yesterday by Major Fred C. Morgan, Indian agent for the Flatheads. But whether the chief sustained his injuries through a fall from the cars, was thrown from the train or was struck and then fell, or was thrown off the car, is still a mystery. Sam admits that he was too drunk to remember just what happened after he left Bonita.

When Major Morgan learned of the condition of the noted chief he came to Missoula and secured an interpreter by the name of Joe Blodgett, an Indian who was very friendly with the chief. With the interpreter Mr. Morgan went to the hospital yesterday and talked to the patient. At first Sam told conflicting stories, but the interpreter finally succeeded in getting him to tell the same story twice without any variation. This story is that he first went to Helena and then to Butte on a trip. He started back to Missoula on a freight train, riding in a boxcar. The Indian declares that at Garrison he met two white men, who got into the car with him. He says he had $6 in his pocket and gave the men money at Garrison to buy whisky. This they drank between Garrison and Drummond, and at the latter place he gave them money to buy more whisky. This they consumed before they got to Bonita. Sam asserts that at Bonita he again supplied the finances to secure some more liquor. He remembers helping drink this, but says he got very drunk and cannot recall what happened later.

The chief declares, however, that when he recovered consciousness all his money was gone, and all his "valuable" papers had disappeared from his pockets.

Major Morgan believes that this much of Sam's story is correct, and is inclined to believe that he fell from the train, though it is possible that he may have been thrown from the train by tramps.

Whether or not they are responsible for the Indian's injuries the men are amenable to the law for supplying liquor to an Indian, and if a description of them can be secured an effort will be made to bring them to justice.

Sam's condition yesterday was very serious. One lung has become affected, and as an injury to an Indian's lungs seems to be particularly fatal, his chances for recovery are said to be very slim.

* * * * * * * *

Big Chief Sam Goes to Helena
Sam Resurrection to Be Witness in Federal Court Against "Foxy" Cyr.

Sam Resurrection, the well-known Indian chieftain who was so nearly fatally injured near Bonner a couple of weeks ago, left last night for Helena, where he had been subpoenaed as a witness in the United States court in the case of Levite Cyr, charged with subordination of perjury. The case is a long one and grew out of the arrest several weeks ago of Levite ("Foxy") Cyr for selling liquor to Indians. "Foxy" was a bartender in the Board of Trade saloon on West Front street, of which his brother, George Cyr, was proprietor, and it was claimed by Sam Cone, United States secret service operative, that he sold Sam Resurrection and Gray Bear, two well-known Indians, some beer. At the hearing, held before United States Commissioner Wallace P. Smith, the testimony as given by Sam Resurrection, through an interpreter, was such as to secure the dismissal of the charge against "Foxy." Sam Cone was not satisfied with the showing made by the prosecution and unearthed damaging testimony against Cyr, in which the latter was accused of having bribed Sam and the interpreter to give testimony in his favor at the hearing. At the second hearing Sam Resurrection went back completely on his former testimony, repudiating that of his former appearance in court. Cyr was bound over for trial in the federal court. The case is scheduled for today.

Alas, poor Lo! And alas for human frailties. Sam Resurrection was permitted to leave the hospital only last Monday morning, after having been so nearly killed by a train near Bonner, and yesterday the lure of the white man's firewater proved too much for him and he fell by the wayside. Under Sheriff Miller found the man, fallen from grace, behind a bill board yesterday and took him to the county jail for safe-keeping. But he was in condition to leave last night for Helena.

Source: Louie Vanderburg, et. al., to William H. Taft, March 1, 1910, from file 20,251/1910 Flathead 154, RG 75, Central Classified Files, National Archives, Washington, D.C.

Arlee Mont.
March 1, 1910.

Mr William H. Taft.
White House
Washington D. C.
Dear sir,

Last summer when I went to Washington I talked about the cattle and I told you that the Agent sold half of them and we did not get nothing from that and we would like to know where is going to be our money for that. the Agent Kept all for himself. it is more than 30 years we were to get the money, and another thing I am going to tell you about the money made up last summer for the dich. it is from our money being paid it was the commissioners who told me. it is $250,000 and we find out that every thing they work and make they pay it with our money, and all our chiefs dont like it at all. We dont want it the way your crazy children do to us. And another thing we found out last summer from the commissioners that $100,000 is also our money, and will you please make them stop for us because we dont want it and they did it any how.

The commissioners told me that there $10,000 left in the treasury. I am going to tell you to make them stop doing every thing and using our money without us knowing it because we all know that you are the head and chief of all the white people. Last year our Agent told us we were to have 9 men and the Indians did not want them because we think we are Indians and not White people. Your children that are staying here are the ones who bread our land making ditches. they always us red flags and we think it is a sign for our blood to spill and we dont like it very well. You know there are 2 kinds of chiefs the Indian chief and the white man chief and we want is always that way. We 1350 people that dont want our Reservation opend. We also find out that the ditches they are making are paid with our money and still when they are finished we are to pay it again with our money. we would like to find out you laws for that. they are making ditches all over and we dont want it and now you see they are just making us mad.

All we Indians living in Ameria are now thinking very hard. all of all of us Indians will never forget our dear lovely place we will never forget it becaus we all love it very much. ever since we seen you white people you are just telling us lies and stealing from us. ever since the good George Washington was the President you are 25 President and How you all treat us.

Columbus was the first who crossed the ocean and we never fought with him. at least we get from Warm Spring and Ronan back on this side we will feel good and you can have the other side for you may be you want it too bad it leat we can gain that much. Ans as soon as you get this letter.

Louie Vanderburg
Louson Red Owl
Peter Joe Hi Hi to
Antee
Martin Charlo Chief
Sam Reslection.

Our Agent wants us to have a license for fishing and hunting here in our little place here now and we havent enough of money to be paying it all the time. it is 3 days since he started this affair. all our chiefs dont want is at all and they want you to please make the Agent stop it at once. even last year our Indians had a license last year when those white people Killed them all. you white people just want to make it smokey all over and that is all.

All those Indians that were Killed last yeare had a license we would like to know what you mean to do to us. tell us please.

Our Agents never helps us at us they just want us to be poor.

<hr>

Source: Sam Cone, Special Agent, to Commissioner of Indian Affairs, April 12, 1910, and enclosure, Robert Leach, Jr., to Sam Tooskahkutskuts, April 7, 1910; and Sam Cone to Commissioner of Indian Affairs, April 19, 1910, from file 23,780/1910 Flathead 150, Central Classified Files, RG 75, National Archives, Washington, D.C.

Department of the Interior,
United States Indian Service,
Flathead Agency, Jocko, Montana,
April 12, 1910.

Defrauding
Flathead Indians.

The Honorable,
Commissioner of Indian Affairs,
Washington, D.C.

Sir:

In regard to some person trying to defraud the Flathead Indians of $5000, I have the honor to report as follows:

Upon my arrival at the agency this A.M., I received a letter from Robert F. Leach, jr., copy of which is herewith transmitted. I am also writing Leach today and getting a more definite statement as to what he proposes to do. What I am after is for him to tell me positively that he can stop the opening of the reservation for the sum of $5000, which he speaks of in his letter. I wired Chief Finch yesterday for his description, for the reason that I want to be able to tell Sam Resurrection the description of the man, for I am sure that Sam Resurrection has seen him personally and talked the situation over with him.

I leave the agency today for Dayton, Montana, and will return about Saturday, and I expect to have Superintendent Morgan send out after Sam. I feel sure that he has not destroyed all the letters he has received from this man Leach for he carries them on his person and at times hides them away, so the Indians tell me. Leach has requested the Indians to burn the letters, so they inform me.

Leach seems to scorch the Officials in his letter, but he does not set forth anything definite that he will do.

Postmaster Harris of Baltimore is assisting me very much and I received two letters from him today. I will be glad if we can bring this man to justice, because it is simply a scheme to defraud. If you have any suggestions I would be glad to have you make them.

Very respectfully,
Sam Cone
Special Officer.

P.S. As time is short I am sending you this direct. I have written Chief Johnson and sent him a copy of this Leach letter.

Cone.

[Enclosure:]

Robert F. Leach, Jr.
Attorney at Law,
213 Courtland Street,
Baltimore Md.,
April 7, 1910.

Mr. Sam Tooskahkutskuts,
Jocko, Mont.
Dear Friend: —

Your letter came to me to-day by registered mail. I am glad to hear from you. I have waited a long time expecting the money — $5000 to be sent to me.

That is what Sam Resselection said would be done. $5000 is what you must send before I go to work again for the Indians. Send it right away. You ask me to tell you what can be done? I can't do any better than to repeat what I have already said: —

"There are 2 ways to go ahead about your Reservation. One way it to go into Court, if I find I can establish what is called in Law a property right. With this end in view, I have already done a great deal of work and intend to do a great deal more before I decide which course to take. The other way of the 2 I have referred to, is to make a fight before Congress. Both of these are hard and mean a lot of time and a lot of work. The Government is trying to break up all **Indian Tribes** and force all indians to live on a small farm instead of having their Reservation. In trying to do this, the Government officials have not hesitated to violate the common sense understanding of Sacred Treaties made with Indian Tribes. If I can ever get the case of your people before Court on the question of property rights, I can win. This will be hard to do. If I do not take that course, then I shall appeal to Congress for relief. There are some men in Congress who are honest and who will vote to see that the Indian is treated square. In order to get this matter to the attention of these men in Congress, it will be necessary that a great deal of traveling, a great deal of time and a great deal of money will have to be spent. It is for that reason that I have asked you for the money. If your people do not try to do something then your tribes will be broken up surely. The only thing for you to do is to raise the money and make a fight. Write and let me know what you think after you get this letter. I can't go ahead until you send the money."

Your people must do something and do it quick. Write to me right away as soon as you get this letter and tell me what your people are going to do. And also tell me when you are going to send the money. Tell me if you have the money on hand now.

I beg to remain,
Your Friend,
Signed: — Robert F. Leach, Jr.

[Editors' note: Sam Tooskahkutskuts was the identity Sam Cone assumed in writing to Leach hoping to entrap Leach into saying something so that Leach could be charged with fraud.]

* * * * * * *

Department of the Interior,
United States Indian Service
Flathead Agency, Jocko, Montana,
April 19, 1910.

Opening of
Flathead
Reservation.

The Honorable,
Commissioner of Indian Affairs,
Washington, D.C.
Sir:

I am enclosing for your information in the Robert F. Leach, jr., case, two letters written by him to Sam Resurrection at Arlee, Montana. One of these letters is practically the same as one written to me by Leach. As I wrote you last week that I had been told that Leach was instructing Resurrection to destroy the letters written by him, but I understood Resurrection had some of the letters that had not been destroyed, it was up to me to get these from Resurrection, and Superintendent Morgan and myself decided that, owing to some dissention among the Indians owing to the opening of the reservation, and to the building of irrigation ditches, it was thought advisable for me to hold a council with the Indians and talk matters over.

I saw Sam Resurrection, made arrangements with him to hold the council, set the date and place of meeting. The council was to be held at 10 o'clock April 19th. Upon my arrival at the place of meeting I found 22 Indians. At one o'clock I proceeded with the council meeting. I was the only white man present. The Indians were of the opinion that I could assist them a great deal in stopping the opening of the reservation. One of them would make a speech and the interpreter would interpret to me what he said. Then they would ask that I give suggestions. I told them I had no suggestions to make, but was simply listening to them. They were all opposed to the opening, and at the proper time I asked them how they expected to stop the opening unless they had friends outside the reservation to assist them, and if they had friends if they had had any communication with them. Sam Resurrection said he was the only one who had been in communication with a friend on the outside, and that he had received a number of letters from him but had destroyed most of them, but still had some in his grip. I told him I would like to see the letters and see how much influence and power there was behind them. Sam got the letters and I read them to the council and they were interpreted by the interpreter. I then told Sam that I would like to borrow these letters from him, and would return them at the proper time. He agreed that I should have them.

I also enclose an envelope that contained a registered letter to Sam Resurrection from Leach, but the contents were destroyed. You will note that the letter to Sam was in a plain envelope, without Leach's name being on the left-hand corner. I am expecting to receive another letter from Mr. Leach today or tomorrow, and will forward it to you upon receipt.

Sam Resurrection says that Leach told him personally while he was in Washington that he would absolutely stop the opening of the reservation for $5000.00.

I think this is practically the case, or, in other words, all the case except the letters that Sam destroyed at Leach's request.

I would be glad if, upon receipt of these letters, your Office would write me and state your opinion of the status of the case, or make any suggestions that you see fit, for they will be appreciated.

Very respectfully,
Sam Cone
Special Officer.

Source: Sam Resselection to Wm. H. Taft, June 22, 1910, from file 47,604/1909 Flathead 056, Central Classified Files, RG 75, National Archives, Washington, D.C.

Arlee Montana
June 22 1910

Mr. Wm. H. Taft
White house
Washington D.C.

Well this is another one of my words. little over one month ago we went to our agent to Fred Morgan. It was thirty of us and they all listen to me talking to Fred Morgan and they all here what Fred Morgan said to us. I say to Fred Morgan if the white people have a law could they change it again, and Fred Morgan said no the law never change. And we all were glad what he said. we three tribes Flathead, Pondry, and Cuitney Indians.

Of course we remember when our three chiefs meet together with Mr Isaac Stephens fifty five (55) years ago. And now we find out our resevation cannot be broke open to the white people because the law never brakes because this resevation have been finished. Already they finished this resevation 55 years ago with the law. And we are thinking about half-breads (half Indians). The half Breads wants to go under the white law and not under the Indian law and that is something I don't like because the white law and Indian law is different altogether. The Half-bread Indian is half your blood and half my blood, and if the halfbread Indian goes on your law he belong to you and if the halfbread Indian goes on my law he belong to me. And another thing if they are on your law they have no buisnes in this reservation because they are just the same as the white people. Your people. Lots of the half breads already wants to be on the white Citizens law and something I don't like. three tribes of people in this reservation, Blackfoot Candinian [Canadian] Indians and Scotch people of course those three tribes have no business in this reservation.

And now President I wish you would send those people where they belong. And one thing we find out our agent Mr. Fred Morgan don't help us one bit. Our Agent should be our assistance, for this reservation and for our selves too but he is not. The Servel [surveyors or severalty?] Came around the last two years ago cuting up this reservation and our agent did'nt help us one bit. And one thing our Agent is doing he have been renting the white people our land and we did'nt know it. some of the people don't know it. And lots of the Indians go and ask Fred Morgan for the money for renting their land and he says its gone to Washington. And we all three tribes already say they are stealing our money and trying to steal our resevation too. And thats why I think our law will be two lines all the time. You have your law and I have my law and our law is different, the time the Servele came around cuting up this land giving the people land I did'nt take any because this reservation already belong to me because I rember 55 years ago it was finished already for me. thats the time I'm believing from that time until now.

And one thing I don't like the half-breds are all ready wanting to take a piece out of the Indians land. One thing we'd be glad to get half our Resevation land back from Ronan Montana and on the West side of Hot Springs Montana. I would like to have all on the South side of this resevation back.

But I'm not saying I'm going to lose the rest of the reservation for nothing but I want something out of it.

And here is another one of my lines to You Mr. President to Congress of law, Sectiary, and all you United States Government people. I want you to go back to Europe across the Atlantic Ocean where all you White people belong and take this N. America and join it together, and maybe I'll take your law and you'll take my law. Or may be we might join together with our law. And if you United State Government people can't join this North America and Europe together, I'll keep my law and you'll keep your law too. Or we'll have to have two laws. Because you white people when you are going to make a new law you never let us know. We would like to know every time you are going to change your law so we could know what to do or what to say.

But you never let us know anything about it until its too late, and too many of our people have lost their lives because they did'nt know about your law. And we North American Indians are the one to know all about the United States law. But if you go to Europe and make so many different laws we can'nt say anything because thats your own. But this North America belong to all Indian tribes and you Government people should let them know every time you are going to have a new law.

And now we all just find out you are just robbing this place.

And now I want to let you people know about how many agents thats been on this resevation, its been five thats been started trouble and I'll let you know their names, first one Pete Rononan, second Joe Carter, third H. Smead, Forth Sam Belew, and Fifth Fred Morgan. All the Government people go on the agents side, the Secetary, Doctor, Intepteor, Carpenters, and Blacksmith, they don't help the Indians one bit and they are getting paid just for nothing. We don't think they are doing us right one bit and we don't like it. We like for you to change everything and send us a good agent who will help us Indians one right from your hands from Washington. And we find out this agent is not helping us Indians he is helping the White people. And I say that agent belong to the White people not for us Indians. And our Agent now, Mr. Fred Morgan wants to turn us to the white law and we all don't like it one bit. The first start of the Servele Cuting up this land not one of us three tribes told them to do it. the fathers on this resevation made them do it. And I think the fathers have lost their positions. they are just staying here for the resevation. And I think our law will always be two laws all the time because this North America belongs to all tribes of Indians and I think it should be our power. And here is another thing. I've been to Washington D.C. twice and I never got to see you Mr. President and I've been sorry every since! I've been writing to the President since last 4 yrs. ago and I never had an answer yet. I wish you would see my letter this time and I'll be very glad. And here is another one of my words for half-breads or half Indians. We just find out that they don't help us Indians either. they want to go on the white law and we don't like it. Not only on this resevation but all over the U.S. all halfbreads wants to take the white law and not the Indian law. And I think now that'll be all right if they want to take the white law because they have half my blood and half yours, but if they want to they can go on my side. the halfbread Commissioners don't help us Indians one bit. they don't tell us any thing and they don't tell our Chiefs anything either. Our halfbread Commissioners names are Johny Matt, and Angus McDowel [McDonald]. these two Commissioners we know have not got any business in this reservation. they haven't got one drop of blood from any of us three tribes. All the halfbread Indians in this resevation haven't any prospects at all. they just want to get money out from this resevation. And here is another thing we don't like our agent here he put another man for judge a Canadian Indian. we don't think its right one bit, and that Canadian Indian have got his citzense already his name is Duncan McDowel [McDonald]. And Mr. President I think you should see that all these different tribes that don't belong in this resevation should be sent where they belong. And we find out that the halfbreads have not got any power to talk about this Place.

I'm one of the Indians to do what I please because its our power. And here is another thing I want to let you Know we heard from Washington before and they wanted seven fullblooded Indians from this place. And the time our Chiefs heard from that he was thinking which seven good men he could send to Washington D.C. The time our Chiefs had their seven men he wanted to go to Washington D.C. our Agent put them aside and picked out seven he wanted to go. These ones our Agent picked out himself was Duncan McDowel, Cha Charle, Pelea, Moes Jocawea, Anteais, Auth Mechele, and himself Mr. Fred Morgan. And thats why our Chief Mr. Martine Charlo didn't go with them because he say those people are not on his side. And we don't know what those seven people did or said because they have'nt let us Know yet what they did. And this is another thing I did'nt take the eighty acres of land which was given to the Indians, because I already Know that this resevation belong to me. its my land. And here's another thing two old people want to say a few words to you. Mr. Antuine Chew mim Clea Cheawa and Matlea Shica Saie think Husband and Wife who is going to speak to you.

Mr. President Wm. H. Taft. We — me and my wife seen Joe Dixson 3 years ago July 4, 1907. the time he gets to us he wanted to take a picture of us, and he got three men to make us take our pictures with him the first man we refuesed and also the second and the third made us to take it anyway, those three men were his Intepters. The first mans name was Henry Matt, tribe Blackfoot, Second Alick Matt tribe Black Foot, Third Duncan McDowel, Tribe Canadian. Now me and my wife find out that time they were taking our Picture those three men were Intepter for Joe Dixson and me. Those Intepters made lies for us and Joe Dixson to me and my wife did'nt say one word about this reservation because we don't like for this resevation to be open one bit. Joe Dixson and the Intepeters made the lies for us. me and my wife they made out that we said to him we'll open this reservation together. I can go in any big Court house and raise my wright hand up and say I did'nt say that. and my wife too she can say the same and do the same as I do she said. I have lots of witnese all of my tribe now and I'm saying I'll say this way of course we were sent for me and my wife by the chief for this what I'm speaking about Now Mr. President. I wish you would stop Joe Dixson's mouth about us, he's just telling lies about me and my wife because they say I join with him to open this resevation. I follow this Chief way Mr. Sam Reselection way this is all for me and my wife. Antoine Chew Mim Clea Cheawea and Matlea Shica Saie.

Well I guess you understand me allready and I guess you understand those two people too.

Flathead Indian Chief
Mr. Sam Resselection.

[P.S] It is 55 years since it was made it was July 16. The Chiefs were Victor Alexander, and Mechell. they talked with Isaac Stephen and Garfield. They both told us we were to have our land till we all Indians die. The tribes will settle it ourselves. Flathead, Pondery and Kootany.

Irs our Power. We'll never forget what the five Cheifs told us Indians. Victor, Alexander, Michel Isaac Stephens and Garfield.

There is 1,353 Flathead that don't want to be open.

Mr. Sam Resselection.

[Postscript includes hand drawn map of Flathead Reservation.]

Source: Fred C. Morgan to Commissioner of Indian Affairs, August 17, 1911, from file 47,604/1909 Flathead 056, Central Classified Files, RG 75, National Archives, Washington, D.C.

Department of the Interior
United States Indian Service
Flathead Agency, Jocko, Montana,
August 17, 1911.

Request for
report.

The Honorable,
Commissioner of Indian Affairs,
Washington, D.C.
Sir:

I have the honor to return herewith letter from Samuel Reselection, transmitted by your Office under date of August 11, 1911, for report. Regarding same I would state that prior to receipt of this letter we wrote, and sent word, to this Indian several times that we would like to have him come to the office and furnish information regarding certain matters that have been brought to our attention. He, however, has so far failed to pay any attention to our requests.

As I have advised your Office heretofore, this Indian is one of the most dissolute, shiftless, worthless that we have, and his influence is far from beneficial to the other Indians. He keeps himself from starving by living off Indians who pay no attention to his advice or teachings, but who endeavor to make a living by honest work.

As doubtless your Office knows, not alone from my reports, but from letters from, and interviews with, Sam Reselection (he has already made two trips at the expense of the tribe to your Office) he is a chronic kicker, but never seems to take up matters of real interest to his people. His pet delusion seems to be that if he can get to Washington he can prevent the opening of the reservation; or, failing to restore it to its original status, he can at least have adopted a plan of separating the mixed and full blood Indians, that part of the reservation given to the mixed-bloods to be opened, but no white men at all to be allowed on that part given to the full-bloods. By playing upon the feelings of the old-time, full-blood Indian (who naturally disliked the coming of the white man) with these plans, Sam Reselection has not only turned their passive resistance in many cases to open antagonism, but has retarded, or prevented, their adoption of progressive methods.

It is my opinion that Sam Reselection is less interested in "preventing" the opening of the reservation than he is in the prospect of a good time he will have should he be allowed to visit Washington.

Respectfully,
Fred C. Morgan
Superintendent

Source: Samuel Ressurrection, et. al., to President, May 28, 1914, from file 62,010/1914 Flathead 056, Central Classified Files, RG 75, National Archives, Washington, D.C.

Arlee, Montana, May 28, 1914.

Memorial to Our President,
at Washington, D.C.

We, your wards, most respectfully submit for your determination certain grievances which have been considered at out [our] Indian meetings both at Flathead, Pondera, Kootenai and Selish (tribes) Indians, wards, and members of the respective reservations above mentioned — have concluded with your permission and executive help, to be enabled to send twelve selected representative members (Indians) to confer with you as to the adjustment of matters and things connected with our tribes, which they will lay before your excellency to be determined in good faith to your wards (the Indians).

We, your wards, most earnestly invoke your aid to enable our chosen tribesmen to reach Washington, D.C., that transportation be furnished them from here, to see you at Washington, and that cost of this transportation be checked against our Indian monies belonging to your wards.

And, Mr. President, in conclusion, we hope to hear from you in answer to this communication especially the transportation (car fare).

We, as a committee chosen by the tribes to write you this letter, Father, allow us to sign in good will to you.

I am blaming all of you white people because you never do help us red men. You are renting with us. We all tribes of Indians are Americans. We do not know how many centuries we have been on this continent. When you landed on our continent you never done a favor for we Indians.

Samuel Ressurrection,
Paul Looking,
Alex Parker,
Eneas Adams,
Frank McClure,
Michel Dominick,
Peter Greybear,
John Delaware,
Michel Parker,
Peter Madies,
Eneas Badroad,
Louie Dominick.

Address
Selish Indians,
Samuel Ressurrection,
Arlee, Montana..

Source: Samuel Resurrection to E. B. Merritt, July 31, 1914, from file
62,010/1914 Flathead 056, Central Classified Files, RG 75, National Archives,
Washington, D.C.

Arlee, Mont.
July 31, 1914.

E. B. Merritt.
Dear Sir,

It is twice that I have wrote to you and have not as yet received an answer.
Now you are fully acquainted with what we want. Prehaps [sic] you may not
understand so I will write again. I wish that you would please send us the
money you owe us. It is (59) years that you owe us for. You say it is not in your
power to give us money enough to send (12) twelve delegates to Washington
D.C. to look after our affair. Now we Indians are in a bad condition out here
and we need *money*. Yes money for our support. So I wish you would please be
so kind as to answer & pay us. Thats all we ask of the whites.

Yours respect.
Samuel Resurrection
Arlee Montana.

We wish to Including the following wishes of these said Indians

Samuel Resurrection, Eneas Adams, Frank McClure, Michel Dominick,
Peter Greybear, Michel Parker, Lornie Dominick, Louie Saxa, John Delaware,
Sam Batist, Antoine Sten, Felix Barnaby.

Source: Fred C. Morgan to Commissioner of Indian Affairs, August 27,
1914, and enclosure, statement of Frank McClure, August 26, 1914, from file
62,010/1914 Flathead 056, Central Classified Files, RG 75, National Archives,
Washington, D.C.

Department of the Interior,
United States Indian Service
Flathead Agency, Jocko, Montana,
August 27, 1914.

The Honorable,
Commissioner of Indian Affairs,
Washington, D.C.
Sir:

Referring to office letter of August 21, 1914, forwarding copy of letter dated July 31, 1914, from Sam Resurrection and also copy of Office reply thereto, I have the honor to state that I have made an investigation of the matter and learn that last fall or winter some person whose name they state they do not remember (but which I shall try to ascertain), made a short visit with some of the Indians. One of the Indians informs me that this person informed them that he was for a long time employed by the "Government in Washington" and knew all about how things should be handled. It was he who advised Sam Resurrection that if he would select a delegation of twelve Indians and simply go to Washington they would surely get their money, as that plan never failed; and that besides the Government would pay their expenses.

Sam is very much put out that one of the replies to his letters of May 28, 1914, was sent to me for delivery. This letter *was* delivered to him. He states that there is something wrong with the post office, as that letter should have come to him direct, and that he is going to "investigate."

The money he refers to is for the lands the "whites" have taken from the Flathead Indians since Columbus discovered America, and which it was agreed by treaty 59 years ago was to be given to the Indians.

Sam Resurrection has made two visits to Washington. The records of your Office will show that his expenses while there, and also his return transportation, had to be paid by the Government on at least one of these trips. The files of your Office will also show, I think, something of the character of this Indian. Whenever he can get enough money he gets drunk. At Missoula, Montana, on August 3, 1914, he had to be arrested by the city police and confined in jail for drunkenness and creating a disturbance. He will not work, but spends his time in agitation, causing trouble among the other Indians, and is supported by the money he can borrow or secure from Indians who do work.

He is a bad influence among the Indians, especially those who are trying to get a start in life, and I believe if your Office would write him a letter telling him he will have to go to work that it would help the other Indians. If Sam will try to cultivate his land, or will work, I will assist him in whatever way I can.

Frank McClure, one of the Indians whose name is attached to the letter received by your Office, was quite indignant when I asked him about the matter, and from him I got a statement, which is enclosed, which tells what he knows about the matter.

Respectfully,
Fred C. Morgan by H. S. Allen, Actg. Supt.
Superintendent.

[Enclosure:]

State of Montana) SS
County of Missoula)

Frank McClure, first being duly sworn, deposes and says:

That he has read the letter from the Indian Office dated August 21, 1914, also copy of Indian Office letter of same date to Samuel Resurrection, of Arlee, Montana, and copy of the letter dated July 31, 1914, to the Indian Office, signed by Samuel Resurrection, and to which his, Frank McClure's, name, is also attached; that he did not know any such letter had been written; that he did not sign the same, or authorize Sam Resurrection or any one else; that he is not desirous of making a visit to Washington; that he has steady work, and is trying to make a living and support his family, and has no time to spend in senseless agitation; that he was working at day labor until about July, when he was given a steady job; that Sam Resurrection is a schemer who will not work himself, but tries to obtain money all the time from those who do work; that just after he was given steady work Sam Resurrection came to him and told him he had decided to take him to Washington with him; that he told Sam he had no business in Washington, but that Sam stated he would have to go any how, as he had been selected by him; that Sam then asked him for $5.00; that he told him he would not give it to him, as $5.00 meant a great deal to his family; that the money Sam Resurrection refers to is for the land which Sam Resurrection claims has been taken from the Indians since Columbus discovered America; that he, Sam, also claims that the Treaties with the Indians give them this money; that when Sam can collect money from any of the Indians who work he goes to Missoula to see his "lawyer," and gets on a drunk and spends the money; that he, Frank McClure, heard Chief Martin Charlo tell Sam Resurrection to stop writing those letters to the Indian Office, as they were doing the Indians more harm than good because they were not true; that last fall some person, whose name he does not know, was visiting on this reservation, and he is the person who told Sam to get twelve Indians and go to Washington and get their money; that Sam Resurrection told him this; that these twelve signed to the letters were selections by Sam Resurrection, without their knowledge or consent.

Frank McClure

Subscribed and sworn to before me this 26th day of August, 1914.

H. S. Allen

Notary Public for State of Montana, Residing at Jocko.

My commission expires May 6, 1915.

Source: Samuel Reserrection to unnamed, November 14, 1914, from file 62,010/1914 Flathead 056, Central Classified Files, RG 75, National Archives, Washington, D.C.

Arlee, Mont. Nov. 14th, 1914.

Dear Sir:—

Am making you think of the treaty of July 16th, the year 1855, in Hell Gate.

All the wild game was reserved by the three tribes of twelve (12) chiefs, and the hunting trails were supposed to be open to go after these game.

The lakes, rivers and springs were reserved by the twelve chiefs. Everywhere I wanted to go hunting and fishing outside the Reservation, it was supposed to be free.

It was reserved by the twelve chief's Bitter Root, Camas and wild carrots, and also indian fruits.

The twelve chiefs told the white people not to be stingy with the cherries, etc., berries of all kinds.

Isaac Stevens asked the twelve chiefs where they wanted their agency, and they said at Jocko, Montana. Isaac Stevens told the twelve chiefs that they should have a clerk, doctor, blacksmith, carpenter and school house, grist mill, saw mill and a gun shop, and tin shop. Isaac Stevens told them all what he mention should come true.

Isaac Stevens told these twelve chiefs that they have chosen their Agency and it shall not be moved till all three tribes are dead and gone.

He told them not to let any white people's stock come in the reservation, horses and cattle, without paying, then you can let them in. He told them that the agent wasn't their boss, it was their workman. He told them [if] anything goes wrong, take it in hand and if you twelve chiefs can't fix it, that's the time for you to look back at your agent and tell him to fix it for you. If he can't fix it, go to the Government Post and get your help. These twelve men told Isaac Stevens all the agreements we made has to be done that way.

Isaac Stevens said soldiers help indians. White man steal horses from indians. Never help indians to find out who steal horses. We want soldiers to help indians.

Our land line passes at Big Hole, Butte, Helena, Little Rock. The government bought from the indians, their hunting grounds at two and a half cents (2½¢) per acre. The three tribes would like to have that money while they are living.

Isaac Stevens told them to write the correct names of the head chiefs: Selish head chief, Victor, Tondray head chief, Alexander, Kootnay head chief, Michell.

Thirty-four years ago there was two women and two men killed by you white people for hunting and five years ago there were four indians killed for hunting. We three tribes feel sorry for these four men killed.

The law that Isaac Stevens had made, we three tribes cannot forget. That was the treaty the (12) twelve chiefs and Stevens had made in July 16, 1855.

Yours truly,
Samuel Reserrection
Arlee, Montana.

Source: "Sam Resurrection Again Agitates Freedom," *The Daily Missoulian*, June 21, 1915, page 8, col. 2.

Sam Resurrection Again Agitates Freedom
Flathead Indian Goes to Helena to Plead With Stewart for Redmen.

Sam Resurrection left yesterday afternoon for Helena to present a plea for his red-skinned brothers to Governor S. V. Stewart. Abuses in regard to money and land are criticized by the Indian chief, who feels that the aborigines should be allowed to govern themselves as they see fit. Sam has sent several pleas to the government at Washington and even made one trip to the capital to spread his brief before the secretary of the interior.

The request which he will present to Governor Stewart is as follows:

"Us North American Indians were first known to be natives and inhabitants of North America. Then Christopher Columbus was the first white man who came into our country. He sailed from Spain on his last voyage on the 3rd day of August and landed on October 12 in 1492, 423 years ago. Since then we have had 27 presidents and they were all failures to us. They were supposed to look after us by the government law or their words and we have sent a number of delegates to Washington asking for help and they have never done us any good. We Indians are supposed to be free in our country or on our reservation we are supposed to look after our own land or our own country.

"And I am blaming you white people because you never do help us Red Men. You are renting with us as far as I see is we never had the chance to look after our country. I am getting tighter and tighter by your laws and rules towards us Indians. You've made rules but you've broke it yourselves and still you haven't helped us. We don't know how many thousand years we have been on this continent and you rich people are the ones who are treating us Indians the worse way, and not only us poor Indians. There is lots of poor white people who are treated just the same as we are and another point there is sure sign that we Indians have got money in the treasury at Washington, D.C., and you couldn't send enough money for the expenses for the twelve (12) delegates to go to Washington, D.C. I've tried to get the money out from what we've got coming from the white people for our reservation and now I wish you people at Washington, D.C., would let us Indians do as we please and have our own laws. If you can help us to give us our money and now I wish you would let us have our money and let us make use of it for it is not doing us any good where it is now.

"We all believe in these few words and we are to make a petition for this said few words.

"Mr. Samuel Resurrection."

This statement follows a rather unintelligible letter sent to Washington last month. The first letter was as follows:

"To the Secretary of the Interior:

"I have now found out that all you congressmen are not a friend of mine, for you haven't helped us. And also the commissioner is not a friend of mine and now I am going to look for a friend that will help me. You may find this work done some time this summer and it will be in the newspapers some day. This is made by all Indians of the United States, not only by us Indians of the Flathead Indians. All of the Indians in the United States are 375,000.

"Samuel Resurrection."

Sam says that he has six other Indians who are ready to appear and plead for a change of laws. Whiskey should be harder to get, says Sam, and he will try to have the "men in Washington" fix them for him.

Source: "San Resurrection Completely Proves Indians' Patience," *The Daily Missoulian*, September 13, 1919, page 1, col. 4, and page 5, col. 6-7.

Sam Resurrection Completely Proves Indians' Patience
After Many Years of Effort He Gets Petition to President.

Helena, Sept. 12. — Special. — When we were children and studied in school or heard stories about Indians, we always were informed of the exceeding great patience of the redman — that same patience which, by the way, has so many times been called a virtue.

The great crowd here when President Wilson spoke in Helena on Thursday had plenty of ocular proof of that fact. And Sam Resurrection of Arlee, the ancient warrior of the Selish, furnished the proof. Perhaps, however, many of those who witnessed did not know that they were learning a lesson.

For many moons, Chief Sam has diligently sought to obtain a hearing with the Great White Fathers at Washington. He has sought recognition from the chief executives for a score of years past for his appeal for help for the Flathead tribe. Never has he been successful, but never did he give up his effort. He never grew weary in well doing. To him, being an Indian, time meant nothing.

And at last his patience was rewarded. Chief Sam in person handed his petition to President Wilson at the Marlowe theater here Thursday night while the photographers' flashlights recorded the event in pictures.

Asks U.S. to Uphold Treaty.

The petition asks that the United States abide by the treaty negotiated with the Selish in 1855. The treaty in question, according to the aged Indian, was signed by his mother [sic]. To get the precious document into the president's hands, Sam had to make his way past the secret service men who guarded the executive.

His bent form proceeded slowly across the stage. President Wilson, noting him, arose, accepted the document, solemnly shook hands with the old warrior, who strode in dignified fashion from the stage.

Chief Resurrection's petition follows:

"Many years ago God put the earth here and gave this country to the true natives, born Americans, the red men. In 1492 Christopher Columbus discovered this country.

"Our first president, George Washington, and after him 27 presidents, none of whom tried to help the Indians of the tribes in Montana. We are the Selish.

"One hundred and thirteen years ago Lewis and Clark came to this country. Our chief was Three Eagle. When we first saw them we Indians thought that they were God, and they spread the buffalo robe and gave them to these white men, and now the whites do not try and help us.

"In 1852 there was a battle at Spokane Falls, about 67 years ago, the white settlers and the Indians. Our chief, Victor, sent Adolph to help the whites, which he did.

"Later on in 1867 [1877], when the Nez Perces had trouble, Charlo sent help to the whites.

"When the war broke with Germany we sent many young men across to help win the war.

"We want you to know we are loyal. We always have helped the whites. I wish all you men in high rank in the White House would help me.

"In the treaty in Grass Valley, state of Montana, July 16, 1855, the war chiefs which were in at that time, made the treaty with Governor J. J. Stevens.

"It is 65 years since that treaty was made. Now in that treaty is what we want, not only me, but all of my tribe, and we would like to get the benefit of this said treaty.

"The law readings of this treaty say that same was to expire (99) ninety-nine years from date of its issue. Same was drawn up between Governor J. J. Stevens and four war chiefs of the Flathead, and when (99) ninety-nine years have elapsed we were to have another treaty.

"Yours Truly,
"Chief Sam Resurrection."

Being without sufficien funds to get home, the chief this morning sought United State Marshal Joseph K. Ashbridge, who usually advanced money to the Indians. The marshal, however, was out of the city.

Chapter 2

Pablo Buffalo Roundup

1907-1910

Pablo Buffalo Roundup
1907-1910

Editors' note: One of the biggest events on the Flathead Reservation between 1907 and 1910 was the roundup of the Pablo buffalo herd for shipment to Canada. The opening of the reservation to white homesteaders meant the end of open range grazing, and Michel Pablo was forced to sell the herd. Apparently, Pablo negotiated with the United States government to purchase the herd, but he was unable to reach a deal. The Canadian government made an offer and the buffalo were sold and moved to Canadian national parks. By 1910, just a few of the wildest animals were left to round up and, after a last attempt, the final shipment was sent off for Canada. Pablo wanted to offer buffalo hunts to kill the remnant, but had to fight a claim by the State of Montana that the remaining animals were wild animals controlled by state hunting laws.

The roundup attracted wide publicity across Canada and the United States and much was written about the events surrounding the move of the buffalo. The editors have chosen a sample of the articles from *The Daily Missoulian, The Missoula Herald,* and *The Anaconda Standard* to describe the event. The full literature produced by the roundup would easily take a book by itself.

Most of the cowboys rounding up the herd for shipment were tribal members, but few were named in the newspaper coverage except for Michel Pablo who directed the roundup. Several accounts covered the daring riding of Johnny Decker, one article described the riding of Mrs. Billy Irvine, and another article told of Duncan McDonald butchering a dead buffalo cow to serve diners at his Ravalli hotel. See Bon I. Whealdon and others, *"I Will Be Meat for My Salish": The Buffalo and the Montana Writers Project Interviews on the Flathead Indian Reservation,* ed. by Robert Bigart (Pablo and Helena, Mont.: Salish Kootenai College Press and Montana Historical Society Press, 2001) for interviews with tribal elders about the reservation buffalo herd and the 1907-1910 roundup. The Séliš-Ql'ispé Culture Committee at St. Ignatius is currently working on another book of elder memoirs of the importance of the buffalo in tribal culture and the Flathead Reservation buffalo herd.

Source: "Loading the Allard Buffalo for Shipment to the North," *The Daily Missoulian*, May 29, 1907, page 2, col. 1-3.

**Loading the Allard Buffalo for Shipment to the North
Interesting Scenes at Ravalli Station, Where the Huge Beasts Are Being
Entrained for the Journey to Their New Range
Across the Canadian Boundary.**

Ravalli, the sleepy little village that skirts the foot of the bluffs that rise along the narrow canyon through which the Jocko river finds its way westward to the Pend d'Oreille, is stirred this week from its accustomed quiet. It is thoroughly busy. The scenes that transpire there never been duplicated in the world; in all probability they will never be repeated. Five hundred head of buffalo are being loaded into heavy stock cars for transportation to Canada, where they are to be placed by the Dominion government upon a special reservation, there to be carefully protected that their species, if possible, may be saved from utter extermination.

Historic Ground

Many historic scenes have been enacted along the Jocko river and in the shadow of the gray bluffs that now look down upon the stirring scenes of this week. Indian councils were wont to gather there long years ago, before the white man had set foot upon this mountain region. Along its banks and through its fords journeyed slowly the black-robed Jesuit missionaries who brought to the Selish Indians the Gospel of Peace. Later, over this same trail, trod the gold-seeker and the trapper. Along this stream, in succeeding years, moved the vanguard of the railway engineers seeking a route for the line of steel whose slender web should bind the balmy shores of the Pacific to the bustling coast of the Atlantic, and here were enacted some of their most hazardous exploits. And here, again, in more recent years, did travelers leave the train for their journey northward to the fabulously fertile plains and valleys beyond.

Behind the Bluffs.

For many years missionary and trapper and gold-seeker journeyed along this stream, little realizing the great extent of the wonderful region that lay back of the gray, forbidding bluffs, until one day an Indian told the priests of the Mission valley and led them through the clay-banked coulee that opens back of what is now Ravalli station, named in memory of one of those same holy men. Down that coulee yesterday, out of that peaceful valley, rumbled the largest herd of bison in the world; down the narrow draw to the outward side of the cliffs they came at their awkward pace, their hoofs treading for the last time upon American soil, for when they leave the cars into which they are being loaded they will be under the union jack. They are lost forever to America, in whose possession they should have remained at any price.

Vale Buffalo.

But these creatures have been sold and there's no use crying over spilt milk. Yesterday the work of loading them was continued and last night it was announced that the train will leave Ravalli tomorrow forenoon. It will go to Helena over the Northern Pacific and then over the Great Northern and the Canada Northern. The famous herd which was collected with so much pains and at so great expense by the late Charles Allard will be lost to America and will become the property of our northern neighbor, whose enterprise and progress have out-Yankeed the Yankees more than once in recent years. The herd is known the world over as the largest collection of bison extant. It was estimated that the Canadian government would receive about 400 of the animals, but now that they have been rounded up it is found that there will be nearer 500 in the trainload that will be sent north tomorrow.

A Famous Herd.

The history of the herd is too well known to call for repetition here. From a small beginning in the 80's, Mr. Allard developed it, by breeding and purchase, to upward of 100 head in 1893, when he bought the famous Buffalo Jones herd from Kansas and brought the animals full bloods and half breeds, to the reservation in the early autumn of that year. The cross breeding of cattle and buffalo was soon abandoned as impracticable as the "catalo" was neither one nor the other and seemed to possess all of the poor qualities and few of the good qualities of either. The cross-breeds were accordingly separated from the bison and the latter were placed on a range near the Big Butte, near where Mud creek empties into the Pend d'Oreille river. On this broad plain the animals multiplied and they seldom left their range. Very little herding was required.

Early Sales.

When Mr. Allard died his partner, Michel Pablo, began to sell the herd, a few at a time, and most of the best specimens of bison in eastern zoological gardens and private preserves in the East come from this herd. Probably 150 head have been sold in this way. Howard Eaton, the well-known hunter and expert of Wolf, Wyo., acted as sales agent in most of these instances. When the prospective opening of the Flathead reservation foretold the destruction of the free range that the animals had enjoyed and made it evidently impossible to preserve the herd intact, Mr. Pablo naturally turned to Mr. Eaton for assistance in disposing of his valuable band. Mr. Eaton made earnest attempts to bring about the sale of the herd to the United States government, but for some reason that is not clear to anybody his efforts were unsuccessful. Nor could he interest the American Bison association in the matter to the extent of raising the funds necessary to purchase the herd. So, when all attempts had failed in this line, the offer of the Dominion government was accepted and for a smaller sum than $150,000 Canada becomes the owner of the largest herd of bison in the world.

Too Late.

But it is useless to grieve over the matter. It is settled and settled finally, and while it is regrettable that the settlement is as it is, there is none the less interest in the scenes attendant upon the loading of the unwieldy animals at Ravalli and the work is being watched with deep interest by many visitors who have been attracted to the spot. In addition to the contract price of the herd, Mr. Pablo made a deal for loading the animals. For this work he receives $5,000; but there will be little profit in the job, for it is tedious and expensive. Thirty-five men are engaged in the work and it keeps them all busy.

Driving In.

The animals have been herded enough on their reservation to become familiar with mounted men and the drive down the Mission valley to the railway is accomplished without much difficulty. They shy a little at the coulee after the climb up the hill from the valley, but the herders press them on and before they know it they are plunging down the narrow draw to the Jocko. The Indian riders handle the animals with wonderful skill and it is not until the corrals are reached that any serious trouble is experienced.

At the Corrals.

But at the sight of these loading pens the big beasts attempt to back away. Their speed, however, has been checked and they can not run over the line of horsemen that is drawn close around them. Gradually they are worked into the big pens as they are wanted for loading, and when they are once in these corrals the real trouble of loading begins. The pens are built as strong as they can be made. Previous experience with these creatures has taught the necessity of this. The first buffalo that were driven to Ravalli for loading, a few years ago, walked through the high inclosing fence as if it had been made of straws; yet it was built for rough cattle.

In the Pens.

Once in the main pen the animals are cut out, one by one, and run into the loading pen. They are wild and by this time angry. A few pawings at the earth, a toss of the mighty bead and the imprisoned bull looks around him. A narrow gate is open and it seems to him to lead to liberty. Through the opening he dashes, the gate swings shut behind him and he is in the chute that leads to the car.

Perched on a running board along the chute is a big Indian with his lariat loop swung wide open. As the buffalo lunges forward below him, he drops the noose over the angry head. A turn around a snubbing post and the noose is tightened and the animal is held fast, bars are thrust across the chute behind him so he can not back out; then he is under control and is eased into the car.

Loaded.

Once in the car he is given hay and water and made to feel as much at home as possible, but the temper of a buffalo bull is sullen and his imagination is not keen enough to make dry hay in a stockcar resemble in any way the sweet grass on the Mud creek prairie.

The cows, as a rule, are more easily handled than the bulls, unless they have calves at their sides. In that case they will fight for their babies. But the cows are handled by themselves and are generally loaded without much trouble. There have been a few vixens among them, however, that have fought as stubbornly as the worst bull in the band and have kept the herders on the jump.

Not So Easy.

All this sounds easy when you read about it. But it is slow and vexatious work in reality. When the first day of loading was finished there were 16 buffalo in the cars and the herders wondered if they had struck a summer's job. However, the next day the work was easier and since then the loading has progressed more rapidly. To get a good idea of the difficulties that attend this work, take the most "ornery" range steer that ever stood on hoof, multiply his meanness by 10, his stubbornness by 15, his strength by 40, his endurance by 50 and then add the products; you will then have some conception of the patience and skill than are required to load a buffalo into a stockcar.

One Accident.

The loading has been accomplished with but one serious accident. One bull so injured himself that it was necessary to kill him. In an incredibly short time the carcass was skinned, the meat distributed among the Indians and the head and robe packed away for presentation. That taste of buffalo meat whetted the Indians' appetite, and after that their look at each buffalo that passed through the chute was like the longing gaze of a colored watermelon tosser as he sees a particularly fine piece of fruit come down the line and is tempted to drop and break it. But a buffalo costs more than a watermelon and the Indian is less emotional than the negro, so no more buffalo legs were broken.

There have been some amusing incidents in connection with the loading. One morning a new car had been pushed in front of the chute and a number of spectators, among them some Missoula people, seized upon the roof of that car as a good vantage point. They climbed up and watched with interest the preliminaries of loading. Then the first bull came up the chute. In some way, perhaps intentionally, the lariat slipped around the snubbing post and the bull entered the car under pretty good headway. He hit the back side of the car with an impact that shook the very rails and rattled the spectators on the roof

Michel Pablo
Source: Photograph Archives, Montana Historical Society, Helena, Montana,
photo 944-242

Michel Pablo and a few of his buffalo wagons.
Source: Photographer N. A. Forsyth
Photograph Archives, Montana Historical Society, Helena, Montana,
photo ST 001.043

Scenes from the buffalo roundup.
Source: Toole Archives, Mansfield Library, University of Montana,
Missoula, Montana, top photo 83-0108, bottom photo 84-0239

in more ways than one. Some of them didn't wait to climb down the ladders, they just jumped.

The train with its strange load will probably pass through Missoula tomorrow afternoon. It will be the quaintest trainload that ever passed this way and it will no doubt attract much attention.

Mr. Pablo will retain a few of the herd, probably a couple of bulls and a dozen cows, but the great herd will be gone and Americans, who should have retained possession of the bunch, will witness the passing of the most characteristically American animal of all our western fauna. It is too bad, but it can not be helped now.

Representing the dominion government at the loading are: Superintendent Douglas of the Canadian National park at Banff; M. Ayotte, who negotiated the purchase of the herd; Dr. David Warnock, dominion veterinarian, and General Freight Agent McMullen of the Canadian Pacific railway.

Scene from the buffalo roundup.
Source: Toole Archives, Mansfield Library, University of Montana,
Missoula, Montana, photo 82-0251

Source: "Unwilling to Leave Their Home," *The Daily Missoulian*, September 14, 1907, page 4, col. 5-7.

Unwilling to Leave Their Home
Pablo Buffalo Make Trouble for the Cowboys Who Are
Shipping Them Away.

N. K. Luxton, representative of a newspaper in Banf, Alberta, with Superintendent Douglas of the Banf National bank, and Alex Ayotte, the local representative of the dominion government, came down yesterday from the reservation, where they had been to see about the buffalo, which it was expected would be ready yesterday for the loading. The gentlemen came back without having seen any loading, but they saw the buffalo under splendid conditions and witnessed some of the finest riding that they ever saw anywhere.

"It was magnificent," said Mr. Luxton yesterday in Missoula. "Out on the big flat beyond the Pablo ranch there were two bands of the buffalo. In one of these there were 60 head; these were easily handled and were in the corral when we left. In the other band there were more than 200 and they were bad ones; they had in their number a lot of the renegades and they refused to be corralled.

"The Pablo cowboys are splendid riders and their mounts were all as fine horses as could be found anywhere; they were the best horses that I ever saw; but the buffalo were too much for both men and horses. They were not corralled when we left and there will be a hot chase before they are penned.

"There was a race that must have taken each one of the horses 35 miles before they got the buffalo to the corral. I never saw such horses; they were splendid. They ran with the buffalo and when the corral was reached they were reeking with sweat and they were all in — every bit in. They had pluck left, however, and they were ready for the fray when the chute was reached.

"But they had run themselves out; they really had hardly strength enough to stand; yet they tried their best. The men were about as tired as the horses and it was a great sight to see the desperate effort that was made to check the buffalo when they broke away at the sight of the chute and scattered.

"The horses were too weak to hold the maddened brutes and though the effort was a good one the big beasts broke away and there was no such thing as rounding them up again that night. But I never saw such fine work with horses as we saw there. It was a show worth seeing.

"Mr. Pablo will make another trial Saturday. He has added to the size of his group of riders and there will be 50 picked men with the best mounts on the reserve when this trial is made. It is believed that this time the effort will be successful and that the buffalo will be corralled at the Pablo ranch by Sunday.

"The band will be cut in two for the drive to Ravalli and the loading will begin as soon as the beasts can be brought down to the railway. This will be next week sometime. What day nobody can tell.

"The buffalo are certainly loyal to their native soil; they are not willing to leave the United States and it is hard work to get them loaded for Canada. But they will be loaded soon and and [sic] the herd will be sent across the line; though I should not be surprised if Uncle Sam bought some of them yet."

Mr. Luxton and Mr. Douglas went to Butte last night to see the big mining camp, and they will spend a day or two there looking over the sights of the greatest of its kind on earth. Then they will go back to the reservation, getting there in time to see the buffalo placed on the cars.

Source: "Woman Herds Bison with Success," *The Daily Missoulian*, September 20, 1907, page 8, col. 3.

Woman Herds Bison with Success
What Thirty-Five Skilled Horsemen Fail to Do She Accomplishes Alone.

Again the loading of the buffalo has been postponed and there is no telling when it will be done. The cars have been ready for some time and one lot that was set out at Ravalli for the bison has been used for other more urgent purposes and another one collected for the big brutes that are causing so much trouble.

Word from the reservation yesterday was that the round-up has been very slow and unsatisfactory, as the buffalo are wild and hard to handle. There are 70 of 300 in the Pablo corral at Mud creek and there have been three unsuccessful efforts made to add to this number.

There are 35 of the best riders on the reservation engaged in the attempt to drive the rest into the corral, but each time that they get the buffalo close to the chute the big animals fly the track and get away.

There has been a lot of hard riding and those who have watched it say that the horsemen are splendid; they have the best mounts that can be had and they ride as hard as men can ride; but they have not been successful in getting the buffalo into the corral.

After the third unsuccessful attempt to get the buffalo into the corral, Mrs. Billy Irwin [Irvine] from the Warm Springs country, just to show the riders what could be done, drove in one of the biggest and toughest of the bulls and put him into the corral as if he were an old milch cow.

With this example before them, the riders have started out to get the herd together; they have been unmercifully chaffed on account of the achievement of Mrs. Irwin and they are determined to do something now.

There are many Missoula people who want to see the buffalo come down to Ravalli and to watch the loading; they will have to wait a while according to the present indications, as it is not likely that there will be any loading this week. It may be that it will be started by Sunday.

Source: "Montana Has Many Bison," *The Daily Missoulian*, July 21, 1908, page 9, col. 5.

Montana Has Many Bison
Indian Agent Says Canadian Government Has But Half
of the Allard Herd.

In the opinion of Major Samuel Bellew, agent in charge of the Flathead Indian reservation in Northwestern Montana, where the remainder of the noted Allard herd of buffalo ranges, it will be fully 50 years before the last of the untamed bison are exterminated, and if some of the societies take steps to look after them, they may be propagated and the species saved from extinction, says the Helena Record.

The Canadian government last year contracted with Michael Pablo, the owner of the Allard herd, to buy the animals at so much per head, they to be delivered at the stockyards at Ravalli. As the animals had free range on the Flathead reservation and were seldom disturbed, they became wild and their number could only be approximated, but it has been conservatively estimated that the herd numbered about 550 animals, including the calves.

After the sale to the Canadian government, Pablo secured the best range riders in the west and the fleetest horses he could find to round up the herd. The roundup continued several months, but only about one-half of the entire herd was corraled. The bulls, especially were intractable and declined to be driven. Any number of times they were driven off their accustomed range and were within 10 miles of the shipping point, where they bolted and the most daring efforts of the cowboys were futile to turn them back or even to hold them. Back they went to the mountains, and in the mountains they remain today.

"According to the best figures obtainable there are around 300 buffalo remaining on the Flathead reservation," said Major Bellew today. "These animals are the pick of the herd, the hardiest and most obstinate. It was learned last summer, after repeated trials, that it was a hopeless task to attempt to corral them. Of course, it will be comparatively easy to round up this year's calf crop and take these animals to Ravalli for shipment, and the cows will follow their offsprings. But at the outside not more than 100 animals will be rounded up this year, and this is a very liberal estimate. The remainder will stick to the mountains in the Flathead reservation.

"The Indians never molest the buffalo, but cherish them as the only reminder which is left them of their own free life years ago. The country is ideally suited to the animals and until the range is fenced up I see no reason why the remnant of the largest herd of buffalo in the United States, or in the world for that matter, should not thrive and multiply."

Source: "Montana Buffalo Shipment," *The Daily Missoulian*, October 25, 1908, page 3, col. 5-6.

Montana Buffalo Shipment
Final Consignment of Bison for Canadian Government Being Made.

Calgary, B.C., Oct. 24. — "The buffalo will be on their way to Canada by October 25," said Howard Douglas Saturday, when interviewed with reference to the last shipment of these animals from Ravalli, Mont. The Canadian government is about to fulfill its part of the contract made last year with reference to these roamers of the plains. This year the buffalo will be corralled in the mountains and for the purpose a 500-acre enclosure, some 32 miles from the railway, has been constructed at a cost of $3,700. The trap into which these animals are to be driven is in a valley on the banks of the river. Long wing fences have been constructed and the buffalo, when rounded up, will be guided along their old trail to a point where a suitable crossing of the stream can be made. It is here that a high timber fence has been built across their trail so that there is nothing for them to do but take to the water. The river at the point of crossing is 520 feet wide and an average depth of 19 feet. Long booms have been swung across the river, so that there is no possibility of the animals escaping either up or down stream.

Riders Must Tame Animals.

When once in the corral that has been constructed they will be tamed by means of riders, whose duty it will be to ride among them quietly for about a week. This will in a measure accustom them to the sight and smell of man, which allows of their loading with greater ease.

Eighty of the best riders of the state have been secured for the purpose of the roundup and at least a week will be required to gather the many little bands that are scattered throughout the foothills and plains. Skilled as these cowboys are, it will not be possible to bring more than 75 head at a time from the corral to the point of shipment. The buffalo travel fast, however, and it is expected that the 32 miles will be made in about four and one-half hours, including in that time the fording of the river. Arriving at the station, the large and strong enclosure will be used until they are ready to load into the cars.

The loading of itself is an interesting feature, each beast being taken separately into the car and there tied with a rope around its neck, the rope being later attached to the floor of what will be its home for a few days. At times it is necessary to spend as much as an hour on one particular animal, but others, again, are forced into the cars with little or no effort. Once in the car and securely tied, a partition is built so that each individual is placed in a stall-like enclosure. In many cases it is found impossible to put more than eight buffalo into a car, but those in charge of the undertaking expect that a train of about 20 cars will carry the herd.

A Buffalo Special.

As soon as loaded a rush will be made for the border, and later the destination. Orders will be issued to give clear right of way to the buffalo special, which, by the way, will probably be the last special of this nature the world will ever see. The journey to Wainwright will this year be made by way of Regina and Saskatoon, instead of coming via Calgary, this being the more convenient route from the fact that the Grand Trunk Pacific is now constructed to within three-quarters of a mile of the buffalo park.

Artists and journalists are already on the ground witnessing the roundup, but next week large numbers are expected to arrive at Ravalli, hotel accommodations having been booked so far ahead that the tardy ones now find that it will be necessary to sleep in tents. Among those already there are Charles Russel of Great Falls, Collier's representative. Those from Calgary, who will leave next week are Colonel Walker, Livestock Agent McMullen of the Canadian Pacific railroad, Dr. Riddel and a newspaper representative.

— Spokesman-Review.

Source: "Chased by Buffalo Has Narrow Escape." *The Anaconda Standard*, November 14, 1908, page 7, col. 3.

Chased by Buffalo Has Narrow Escape
Thrilling Experience of a Butte Photographer.
Saved by a Handy Tree
Leader of Herd Tosses Man, But the Latter Gets Away —
Camera Reduced to Souvenirs
— Failure of the Pablo Buffalo Roundup.

N. A. Forsythe, a Butte photographer, had a thrilling experience and a narrow escape from being killed by a herd of mad, charging buffaloes on the Flathead reservation last Sunday. With Charles M. Russell, the cowboy artist, and several other men, Mr. Forsythe had been invited to the reservation to witness the roundup of the remainder of the Pablo herd of buffaloes, which the owner, M. Pablo, has sold to the Canadian government. The roundup, however, proved a failure, and will be attempted again next spring. A big trap, covering about 1,000 acres, had been built on the Pend d'Oreile river, high, precipitous cliffs on one side of the river being employed for one side of the trap and on the other a strong and high fence being built. From the end of the trap two wings were spread out a distance of about three miles.

Only six men were employed in the drive, and on the first day 350 head of the 400 buffaloes on the range were rounded up and started toward the trap, but all except 117 escaped.

Mr. Forsythe was stationed on the side of the river to which the buffaloes had to cross. He had with him two large cameras, and with one of them he took several good pictures of the big herd of buffaloes as they were swimming toward him. They were turned some distance away from him and he anticipated no danger, yet he had had experience before and had taken the precaution to pick out a tree and cut away a few branches so he could get into the tall timber quickly in case of the appearance of danger.

Herd Headed for Him.

He had just reached for his second camera when he looked up and saw that the head buffalo had made a landing and was coming toward him head down and full tilt. Mr. Forsythe grabbed one of his cameras and made a spring for the tree. He had thrown one arm, with the camera, over a limb, grabbed a higher branch with his right hand and stepped up on the lowest limb within reach, when the buffalo struck him. Fortunately the mad animal passed between Forsythe's legs and raised him up. For an instant the photographer rested on the hump of the buffalo, but he never let go his hold on the limb of the tree, and as the buffalo rushed on Forsythe swung himself up into the tree, safe out of the way of the remainder of the herd, which came rushing on after the leader. When the herd had passed the tree, it turned and recrossed the river, and as the buffaloes got into the water Forsythe got down out of the tree and co[o]lly took several more pictures of the retreating herd.

Unique Picture.

When Mr. Forsythe developed his plates, he found that he had taken a picture of the onrushing herd just the moment before he sprang into the tree, but he declares he never knew that he took the picture until it was developed.

Charles M. Russell and the Canadian government agent, with the Pablo cowboys, were witnesses of Forsythe's thrilling experience, and they picked up the fragments of one of his cameras, tripod, hat, etc., which the buffaloes trampled, and retained them as souvenirs.

During the night following the 117 buffaloes escaped from the trap, climbing the almost perpendicular cliffs. The next day the men went out again for a roundup, but did not get a single buffalo. It was then decided to give up the attempt until next spring. In the meantime the trap will be strengthened and the wings extended. In the trap will be built a stockade and 50 crates will be constructed on 50 wagons. It is proposed to put one buffalo in each crate and haul them a distance of 25 miles to the railroad, from which point they will be shipped to Edmonton, Alberta. Pablo has already delivered 400 head under the contract with the Canadian government, receiving $250 each, and he reserves only 12 head out of the whole herd.

Their Small Start.

Twelve head was the number with which Pablo and Charles Allard started into the buffalo-raising business many years ago. After the death of Allard his interest in the herd, amounting to 800 head was sold, and the Allard buffaloes now comprise the Conrad and Yellowstone park herds.

Mr. Forsythe, who returned to Butte last evening, says that, aside from his own experience, there were a number of interesting incidents connected with the attempted roundup. In the herd were a number of calves. As the animals were swimming the river one of the calves became tired and placed its forefeet on its mother's hips and the old one carried it safely across the river.

C. M. Russell, the cowboy artist, was there to study the buffaloes for the purpose of getting material for pictures, and it is probable that the experience of the Butte photographer will form the subject of one of Russell's thrilling comics.

"I am probably the only man living who can say he sat on the hump of a wild buffalo," said Mr. Forsythe last night.

Source: "Charges by Canadian Commissioner Are Ridiculed," *The Daily Missoulian*, November 26, 1908, page 5, col. 5; "Canadian Official Says He Never Said It," *The Daily Missoulian*, December 6, 1908, page 1, col. 4.

Charges by Canadian Commissioner Are Ridiculed

Winnipeg, Man., Nov. 24. — The Canadian government has decided to make a protest to the authorities of Montana against the action of certain persons at Missoula who are opposed to allowing the buffalo in the Pablo herd, in the Flathead reservation, to be shipped to Canada. Howard Douglass, Canada's commissioner, claims that some one opened the rear end of the corrall and allowed 250 buffalo purchased by Canada to escape after it took weeks to round them up. There is much resentment in the states, it is believed, against allowing this herd to be removed across the border.

* * * * * * * * *

The above allegation by Superintendent Douglass of the Banff National park that Missoula men had been instrumental in frustrating the attempt to load buffalo at Ravalli for shipment to Canada was vigorously denied yesterday by Dr. M. J. Elrod, who is a member of the board of managers of the American Bison society. "The charge is absurd on its face," said Dr. Elrod. "I never heard of such a thing and I know of no one with a desire to do any such thing. It seems to me that, outside of the American Bison society, there is no one who would be tempted to take such a step to keep the buffalo in this country, and I am the only one in Missoula who has been active in the society's interest. I was not near Ravalli during the corralling of the bison and I do not even know the men in charge at that time.

"There could be no object in going to such extremes as Mr. Douglass charges," Dr. Elrod continued, "for the society has no money with which to buy so many animals and, beside, we have had as many buffaloes offered us already as we have money to buy. There is no resentment here against Canada. What sentiment the removal of the bison has prompted has been simply a profound regret at the tardiness of the United States government in taking action after it was too late."

* * * * * * * * *

Canadian Official Says He Never Said It
Howard Douglas, Park Commissioner, Denies Interview as to Buffalo.
"Editor Missoulian:

"In your paper of the 26th inst. you have an article in regard to the rounding up of the Pablo herd of buffalo, and in which you state that I had reported that the buffalo were intentionally let out of the corral on the Pend d'Oreille river. I wish to state most emphatically that I never even thought of or made any such statement (although one of the Canadian papers had an article to that effect several days before I returned from Montana). I have only the best to say of the treatment we have received from all with whom we came in contact while engaged in a most difficult undertaking, and have so expressed myself at all times.

"I am sending you copies of my first interview with newspapers here on the first day I returned from Montana, which will show that I had no thought of the matter contained in your article, or the article that was printed in one of the Canadian papers, which latter I regret very much, as there was no foundation for it.

"I trust that you will kindly publish this and place me right with my friends in Missoula, whom I hope to meet again in a few months.

"Yours truly,
"Howard Douglas.
"Commissioner.

"November 30, 1908."

Source: "Canadians Assured of Bison," *The Daily Missoulian*, December 21, 1908, page 4, col. 3-5.

Canadians Assured of Bison
A. Ayotte Tells Manitoba Paper of Buffalo Roundup and Escape.

The Manitoba Free Press, in a recent issue, gives a comprehensive account of the roundup of buffalo on the reservation last summer and tells in detail of the negotiations between the Canadian government and Michael Pablo. The article is based on an interview with A. Ayotte, immigration agent in this city. It begins as follows:

"Notwithstanding the fact that the recent attempt to round up the balance of the great Pablo buffalo herd, which was purchased by the Canadian government, ended in discouraging failure, every hoof of bison on the Flathead range will eventually be corralled and safely delivered in Canada is the assuring news which A. Ayotte, immigration officer at Missoula, Mont., brings almost direct from the exciting scenes in the roundup. Mr. Ayotte is the gentleman who has been largely instrumental in carrying this remarkable enterprise to practically an assured and successful conclusion from the very inception of the negotiations; and none but he and those associated with him in the undertaking have any conception of the difficulties which had to be overcome.

"Michael Pablo, who is the soul of honor, is determined to fulfil his contract with the Canadian government, no matter what it may cost him to do so. He has already expended thousands of dollars in his efforts to do so, and is prepared to spend forty thousand more if necessary. Piqued by the treatment accorded him by the government of the United States in their negotiations to buy the herd prior to the time when the Canadian officials sprung their little coup, and the subsequent determination of the congress to throw open the Flathead reserve wherein his range was located, he vowed that every buffalo, except those he desired to retain for his personal ownership should cross the line, and now that vow he is going to respect. Reverses seem but to increase his determination in this respect, and all that money and ingenuity can do to corral the animals will be done.

"The buffalo have been chased so much that they are now extremely wild and scatter to the timber on the mountain sides at even the sight of a horseman. Then, too, they have escaped so repeatedly from cordons thrown around them that they gained confidence in their ability to defy the cowboys, while they are fierce and dangerous when forced to close quarters."

Continuing, the article tells of the preparations for the corralling of the bison, of the great amount of labor expended — for nothing, as it proved — and finally described the breaking away of the angry herd. A long paragraph is devoted to the escape of Photographer Forsyth of Butte from being trampled to death by the herd in its rush for freedom. The Free Press concludes as follows:

A Correction

"Such is the correct explanation of the escape and the report that the corral fence had been broken by some parties maliciously disposed is absolutely without foundation of any kind. Both Mr. Ayotte and Mr. Douglas are unanimous in an emphatic contradiction of this charge, which was based on an article published in a Calgary paper and sent out by the Associated Press from Winnipeg. The mischievous part of this report, which has antagonized the residents of that section of Montana, and has even attracted the attention of the governor of the state, lies in the fact that it was credited to Mr. Douglas, who was recognized as the representative of the Canadian government. It has created a great deal of resentment and newspaper comment throughout the state, and demands are being made to compel Mr. Douglas to give an official retraction. The Free Press has assurances that Mr. Douglas never made such a charge and never thought of such a thing as the actual facts of the case were familiar to him.

"After the escape of the herd another attempt was made to corral them, but they escaped into the mountains, and as the winter season was opening, it was decided to abandon the roundup for this year.

Extending Fences.

"Already preparations for this have begun, and everything possible will be done to make certain the capture of the animals. The wings of the corral, which were found to be too short, will be extended back 12 and 14 miles into the mountains, thus making an escape of sections of the herd almost impossible once the drive has begun. Inside the corrals the weak spots will be strengthened, sections will be built wherein the animals after being driven in can be handled and fed, thus taming them down slightly. This will require the erection of 12 miles of new fence within the corral proper.

Will Haul Animals to Railway.

"The idea of driving the animals to the loading corrals on the railway at Ravalli had also to be abandoned, and the animals will be loaded into crated vans out on the range and driven to the town 35 miles away, where they will be unloaded directly into the cars. Eighty teams have been engaged for this great contract alone. A more difficult or dangerous task it would be hard to imagine — in fact it will be as dangerous as it will be unique. The shipment will be made early in June, the majority of the buffalo still on the range are cows and young animals, the very class of stock the Canadian government wants for breeding purposes.

Cost $40,000.

"This vast amount of work will necessitate an expenditure of about $40,000, all of which is borne by Mr. Pablo, as the terms of the contract require him to deliver the buffalo at Strathcona, Alta. The only thing he asks is that the Canadian government pay him for the natural increase of the herd since the sale was first concluded. In view of the vast expenditure and the trouble he has incurred this looks like a reasonable request indeed, one which could not very well be denied since Mr. Pablo has been obliged to pasture the animals ever since. It will no doubt be agreed to at least in part.

May Be Old-Time Hunt.

"So determined is Pablo to clear the range that he says he will invite some of his friends to a real old-time buffalo hunt on the range when any outlaw animal which cannot be corralled will be shot. The Flathead reservation is being thrown open to settlement next spring, consequently Pablo's range will pass out of existence. The same is true of the Blackfoot reservation where he has vast ranching interests, and now his attention is turned toward Canada. When he comes up with the shipment of buffalo next summer he will look over the land with a view to securing ranges for his great herds of cattle and horses, and it is not improbable that shortly the remarkable old half-breed millionaire will be a citizen of the Canadian west, bringing with him his immense capital.

"Mr. Ayotte will spend Christmas with his family at St. Jean. He was called hime [home] suddenly by the serious illness of his mother, now almost eighty years of age, but as she is now considerably improved in health he will likely return to Missoula early in the new year."

Source: "Roundup Task Progresses Nicely," *The Daily Missoulian*, June 1, 1909, page 1, col. 2, and page 8, col. 4.

Roundup Task Progresses Nicely
Canadians Tell of Herding Buffalo Together to Ship to Parks.
A New Method Employed
Those in Charge of the Task of Segregating and Shipping the Animals to Be Sent From the Pablo Herd to Canada Are Taking No Chances on Losing the Herd as They Did Before.

Howard Douglas, superintendent of the western Canadian parks, and Alex Ayott, immigration agent for the Canadian government, arrived in the city from the reservation late Sunday night. They had been at Ravalli, where they were attending to the roundup of the buffalo bought from the Pablo herd, the animals to be taken to Canada, where they will be placed in national parks.

Mr. Douglas, in speaking of the methods used in this year's roundup, said to a Missoulian reporter: "We are using a somewhat different method this spring in the roundup, such having been made necessary when we learned that the animals could not be loaded by the system we attempted last fall. All that time we tried to load the beasts into the cars by herding them into long V-shaped chute leading to a large corral, or loading pen; but they escaped, much to our surprise, by climbing what we had thought to be an unsurmountable hill. That is why we have changed the system. This year the cowboys are busy at the present time in rounding up the buffalo in small herds, taking them to small corrals in various places in the region. There are about 25 cowboys engaged in this work, and for their use about 100 horses are made necessary on account of the superior hardihood of the wild beasts. Just now we have about half of the animals in these corrals, or say 150. As yet there is a large drove of them, consisting of from 140 to 175, which have not been molested, and will not be until the last. Then they will be rounded up.

"After the animals have been corralled we will try the scheme of hauling them by wagon to Ravalli, where they will be placed in loading pens, supplied with chutes, from which they can be easily driven into the railroad cars.

Nearing End.

"The work of corralling is expected to be completed about the end of this week, and then the teaming will be started. To haul the animals to Ravalli there will be 30 four-horse teams, and we think it will be advisable to handle only one bull or two cows at each load. This will take some time, and when that is done, which should be in about two weeks, the loading will commence. This, in itself, is no small task, and will keep us busy for a while.

"The work of rounding up the animals is very strenuous and hard on both horses and men. It is often the case that a man will catch sight of one of the animals about one-half mile away. The beast, for the buffalo are very shy and far-sighted, will at once choose a direction in which he intends to go, and the cowboy might just as well make up his mind to follow along. The animal simply cannot be headed, and will run almost blindly ahead in a direct line.

"One of the incidents of the roundup happened a few days ago. One of the cows was being chased by a cowboy, and had headed straight toward a perpendicular bluff, and when the bluff was reached instead of stopping and giving in to the inevitable, she started vertically us the precipitous sides. It looked to be almost impossible for a fly, much less a buffalo, to scale the heights, but she made a brave effort. She had attained a height of about 40 feet when she started to fall, tumbling head over heels, around and around, until she struck the ground. Here is where the difference between cattle and buffalo is made apparent, for instead of being seriously injured, or killed outright, she alighted on her feet and was off like a flash, this time shooting off at a tangent to her former course. It took much riding before she was finally caught.

Wear Out Horses.

"The cowboys will often wear out four horses in a day while rounding up the wild and wiry animals. I know that one time one of the boys started after a tough and shaggy bull, who put up such a hard and strenuous run that it was two days before he was brought in, tired out, but still defiant."

The animals will be shipped to what is known as Buffalo park, which is on the new Grand Trunk Pacific railroad, 120 miles east of Edmonton, the capital of Alberta. It had been the original intention of the Canadian government to place the animals in the park at Banff, but this was changed. A part of the herd, which will consist altogether of about 300 animals, will be placed in Elk Island park.

Mr. Douglas is superintendent of the western parks of Canada, which number six, and are located west of the lakes in Alberta and British Columbia.

Buffalo park consists of 800 square miles and about 110,000 acres have been fenced. This park, together with Elk Island park, in Alberta, will be used as the principal game preserves in Canada. They are splendidly adapted to that purpose, as they are rough in some places and smooth in others, with an abundant supply of feed for all varieties of game and animals.

Fine Parks.

Among the well-known parks of Canada are the Banff, the Yoho, the Glacier and the Jasper, besides the two mentioned before. The Banff park is about twice the size of the Yellowstone national park, and is somewhat of the same character; it contains about 7,000 square miles. The Yoho, in British Columbia, has about 2,300 square miles, and the Glacier, of which so much has been heard of late, has about 900 square miles. The Jasper park, in Alberta, contains 5,000 square miles, Elk Island park has 560 square miles.

In Buffalo park there is already a herd of over 400 buffalo, these having been purchased from the Pablo herd some time ago. There are about 100 head of the animals in Banff park also, so that the Canadian government will have, as a grand total, more than 800 head.

Mr. Douglas left yesterday morning for Banff, but will return in about two weeks to the reservation to watch the loading of the animals. Mr. Ayott left yesterday afternoon for the reservation.

Source: "Bison Herd Ready for Shipment," *The Daily Missoulian*, June 17, 1909, page 12, col. 4.

Bison Herd Ready for Shipment
Allard Buffaloes Are Soon to Start on Long Trip to Canadian Park.

Yesterday for the second time in its history the Flathead buffalo herd was rounded up and started on its last journey over its native soil. For weeks Canadian cowboys have been busy collecting the giant herd, 225 in all, at Ronan preperatory to shipment and yesterday the bison were started on their way in crates on wagons to Ravalli, where the special train which is to carry them to Canada is waiting.

Last fall an attempt was made to get the herd off but the buffalo proved too wild and made their escape from the carefully constructed corrals, which was thought escape proof, climbing up an almost perpendicular cliff. This time, however, every possible method of escape has been barred and so far things are running smoothly.

The herd, which is the largest in the world, is to be sent, for the most part, to Canada, where it is to be put in the Banff National park, while a few of them will go to parks in the eastern part of the United States. The Canadian cowboys, who have been sent here by the colonial government for the purpose, have been hard at work for some months collecting the buffaloes and have at last gotten them together at Ronan. There they are being loaded onto wagons in crates one or two being taken at a time and put on the cars, which are waiting for them at Ravalli. The Northern Pacific, has gotten together a special train for the animals, all of them fixed so that they cannot injure themselves or make their escape in any way and the shipment will be made just as soon as possible.

Henry Avare, state game warden, and W. W. McCormick, deputy game warden, left his morning for Ronan to be present at the finals of the roundup.

Source: "Buffalo Roundup Progresses," *The Daily Missoulian,* June 26, 1909, page 12, col. 4.

Buffalo Roundup Progresses
About 200 of the Bison Will Be Shipped Next Monday or Tuesday.

Howard Douglas, superintendent of the western parks of Canada, who went to the reservation a couple of days ago to watch the loading of the buffaloes, which will be shipped to Canada, arrived in the city yesterday from Ravalli. Mr. Douglas says that about 110 of the animals have so far been loaded into the cars, and by Monday or Tuesday of next week it is expected that enough to make the total 200 will be loaded, after which the shipment will be started to Buffalo park in Alberta. The shipment will be accompanied by Mr. Douglas.

During the process of roundup and loading the animals about 15 or 16 have been killed, some by exhaustion, one or two by suicide, and some even by what might be termed a broken heart at being compelled to leave the range which has been theirs for so long. Most of the dead animals, however, were calves.

The shipment which will be made in the early part of next week will include all the buffaloes which have been rounded up, and during the trip to the park in Canada, the work of the roundup will be continued, under the supervision of Mr. Pablo, the former owner of the herd. As soon as the roundup is concluded the final shipment will be made.

Mr. Douglas says that since he was in the city several weeks ago he has been busy in transferring a large herd of about 340 head from the Elk Island park to the Buffalo park, both in Alberta. To make this move the same methods now being used at Ravalli were used, and the animals were taken over about 500 miles of railroad to their final destination. With the addition of the Pablo herd, together with what animals have already been in the place, Buffalo park will have considerable over 700 of the once numerous roamers of the prairies.

Mr. Douglas will remain in the city until Sunday morning, when he will return to assist in the loading.

Source: "Rides Against Death on Horns of Buffalo," *The Daily Missoulian*, June 28, 1909, page 1, col. 1-2, and page 4, col. 7.

Rides Against Death on Horns of Buffalo
Bison Goaded to Madness Charges Roundup Rider's Horse and Gores It to Death
John Decker Is Hero of Thrilling Experience
Infuriated Beast Lifts Steed Upon Its Horns and Half Carries, Half Pushes Animal and Rider for a Distance of Three Hundred Yards or More Across Corral at Ronan.

With his horse impaled upon the horns of a maddened buffalo, Johnnie Decker, expert roundup rider, had a ride against death Saturday on the Flathead reservation such as few men experience and live to tell the story. The horse was gored to death by the infuriated beast and it is little short of a miracle that its rider escaped without a scratch save a few minor bruises, sustained when he and his horse were thrown from the horns of the beast.

Decker's thrilling ride to what seemed certain death occurred at Ronan, where the famous Pablo herd of buffalo is being rounded up for transportation to Ravalli and shipment to the Banf national park in Canada. Decker and his brother, who were employed as expert riders to corral the bison and aid in leading them into the cages, in which they are being hauled from Ronan to the railroad cars at Ravalli, were endeavoring to drive the unruly bison from the corral at Ronan into the waiting cages when the herd, goaded to madness by the efforts of the drivers to force them into the wagons, rebelled and stampeded. One shaggy monarch of the herd, which Decker had been trying to force through the loading chute, wheeled suddenly, lowered his massive head and, in blind fury charged toward the rider. Traveling with speed of the wind, almost, the beast bore down on Decker's horse. The rider was unable to swing his steed clear of the beast's path and in an instant the horse was impaled upon the buffalo's horns. With an exhibition of strength almost beyond belief the buffalo raised horse and rider from the ground and half carrying, half pushing them, bore them across the corral for a distance of 300 yards or more.

Tries to Shoot.

With almost certain death staring him in the face, Decker attempted to draw his revolver from the holster and kill the beast. But the weapon caught and his efforts to release it were futile. While the five other riders, unable to lend their comrade any assistance, watched to see him go beneath the hoofs of the buffalo, Decker clung firmly to his saddle and struggled with his revolver. Just then the buffalo stumbled and the gored horse and his rider were hurled from the horns of the beast into the dust. The horse never moved from where he fell, but Decker, fortunately, was thrown beyond the animal, and aside from a few bruises and a severe shaking up, escaped unhurt. Undaunted by his narrow escape, Decker mounted another horse and assisted his bother and the other drivers to force the unruly beast into a wagon cage in which he was safely transported from Ronan to the cars at Ravalli.

Decker's horse, which was the property of Michel Pablo, former owner of the buffalo herd, and one of his finest animals, was the second horse to fall a victim to the horns of a buffalo since the roundup commenced. Only two days before Decker's experience, another animal belonging to Pablo was charged by a buffalo and so badly injured that it died, but in this case there was no rider.

Exciting Experiences.

These are but two of the thrilling incidents that have marked each day's work since the Canadian government undertook to move 200 animals of the Pablo herd from their boundless and untrammeled native heath into captivity within the confines of a Canadian park in Alberta. Incidents almost equally exciting but without the same menace to human life as Decker's ride occur every time the animals are loaded into the hauling wagons at Ronan and their [sic] is considerable excitement at Ravalli occasionally, when the loaders force an unruly animal into the railway cars. Since the hauling and loading commenced about 20 buffalo have been killed through the frantic efforts of the beasts to pit their brawn in a winning contest against man's ingenuity.

Killed in Corral.

All but one of this number were killed at the roundup corral at Ronan. Here the untamed animals, fresh from the wild free range, first discover that they have been trapped into limited confines and the last remnants of those proud monarchs of the plains rebel most violently against man's encroachment upon their freedom. Captivity is to them something before unknown and every instinct of the animal rises against it. Sullenly and defiantly the beasts which have been unwittingly trapped in a pen, whence there is no outlet save a chute leading into narrow cages on wheels, fight against being driven through this exit. Goaded by the drivers, portions of the herd have several times rushed blindly into the Pend O'Reille river and swum two miles down the stream to escape from the corral. At other times they have rushed madly against the corral fences, the result being death to some and escape for others. One cow recently exhibited astonishing agility by clearing the 10-foot fence of the corral in a jump. Another surly bull, after being forced into the cage, tore the heavy timber stall to pieces in his fury and, when bound in with wire, snapped the metal as though it were but a thread. This animal was landed at Ravalli only after he had been chained in a cage by means of a log chain. Still another jumped through the top of his cage and is still at large. The only animal to be killed at Ravalli thus far was a young cow, which succeeded in slipping the noose from her neck after being gotten into the freight car, and rushed against the side of the loading chute with such blind fury and force that she broke her neck and fell dead in her tracks. This animal furnished toothsome buffalo steaks for the hundreds of visitors who have been daily flocking to Ravalli to witness the loading of the animals.

Unique Methods.

As for the methods that have been adopted for handling the buffalo since the escape of the herd last year, they are unique in many respects but have proved fairly successful. It was deemed useless to attempt to drive the herd from the bison range to Ravalli and it was decided to construct a corral at Ronan in which to collect the animals and then to haul them in wagons from Ronan to Ravalli, a distance of about 36 miles over rough mountain roads. To accomplish this, crates or, stalls just large enough to accommodate one buffalo, and constructed of heavy timbers, were built upon wheels and provided with removable endgates. These wagons were backed up against the end of the loading chute in lines of five to 10 or so as to form a continuous passageway to the front cage. The buffalo are then driven through the chute and through the crates until there is an animal in each crate, when the endgates are shut and the animals are safely enclosed and ready for hauling. Three crates crates [sic], or wagons, are then attached together and a 20-horse team then pulls the wagons from Ronan to Ravalli. Here the animals are unloaded into a series of corrals, the large bulls and cows and small bulls and cows being segregated. All of these corrals connect by means of lanes with a central corral, from which the loading chute leads to the freight car that is to be loaded. A force of Indians and cowboys numbering some 20 or 25 men, by dint of much maneuvering, force the animals into the loading corral one at a time. Being partially tamed by their experience in the corral at Ronan, their close captivity during the long ride from Ronan to Ravallia [sic] and protracted incarceration in the pens at Ravalli, the animals are driven into the loading chute with comparative ease, but when they are driven into the cars, the excitement commences. A one-inch hemp rope lopped about a post firmly planted in the ground, and manned by a dozen strong men is the instrument which induces the animals to enter the car and holds them there until they can be crated in. This rope is provided with a running noose, which is prevented from drawing too tight by a carefully placed knot. Two men hold this open loop over the mouth of the loading chute and as the animal is driven up into the car, his head runs through the noose. A shout, a tug by the muscular men manning the line, a terrific struggle on the part of the beast, and the kicking, snorting, frantically fighting monarch of the prairie lies raging in ignominious captivity. Then he is released and left to vent his fury in vain kicks at the car sides and snorts of rage. His exertions cause the massive cars to tremble as through about the collapse, and timid spectators beat a hasty retreat to safer distance. Ten buffalo thus loaded into a single car fill the space; the loaded car is moved out of the way and another is shunted into place. Three or four cars is a big day's work when there are no accidents and in event of the latter perhaps one car loaded is a strenuous task.

The Record.

When the loading force quit work yesterday afternoon 178 buffalo had been placed in the cars ready for shipment. But 18 more remain to be hauled from Ronan to the loading corral. These are due to arrive about 4 o'clock this afternoon and Howard Douglas, superintendent of the western Canada national parks, who is supervising the work of shipping the buffalo, expects to have the remaining animals in their cars and to have the entire shipment of 196 started on its way to Alberta by Tuesday night or Wednesday morning.

The 18 animals yet to be loaded are the largest and wildest of the entire herd and were left until the last in anticipation of trouble in handling them. They were in the corral at Ronan yesterday morning and were scheduled to be loaded into the wagon crates during the day. Whether or not this work was successful will not be known until word is received from Ronan today.

"These animals will complete our shipments for the present," said Mr. Douglas to a Missoulian reporter at Ravalli yesterday afternoon, "but there are about 150 more animals to be rounded up during the coming fall. These are all renegade animals and will undoubtedly prove very difficult to handle. However, we will attempt to corral and ship them this year."

Source: "Fighting Spirit of Buffalo Causes Thrilling Incidents," *The Daily Missoulian*, June 29, 1909, page 1, col. 6-7, and page 10, col. 2-3.

Fighting Spirit of Buffalo Causes Thrilling Incidents

Stubborness and a fighting spirit on the part of a bunch of particularly unruly buffalo made the work of loading the Pablo herd at Ravalli yesterday unusually spirited and difficult. Excitement in plenty was furnished by a fight between two monster bulls, the destruction of a portion of a fence by another infuriated animal and the stubborness of all the animals, which necessitated their being dragged into the cars by main force.

With the delivery of nine monster bulls yesterday afternoon at the loading corral, the work of transferring all but eight of the famous herd from the native range to the railroad cars was completed. The remaining eight buffalo will be delivered Wednesday afternoon about 4 o'clock, will be loaded the following morning and the shipment of 200 will start toward Canada over the Northern Pacific Thursday night.

Securely held in wooden cages, mounted upon wheels and pulled by four and six-horse teams, the rebellious monarchs of the plains were hauled over the rough mountain road for a distance of about 35 miles. Eight cage-wagons were required to handle the bison, and as these circus-like wagons wound around the hill from the canyon leading into Ravalli they afforded a sight that few are likely to witness again. Stringing along in single file, the heavy vehicles moved slowly down the hillside through the center of the little town and lined up in the wings of the corral. Many curious eyes gazed through the bars of the wire and chain-bound crates at the massive shaggy beasts which strove furiously but vainly again[st] the restraint imposed upon them. Notwithstanding the long, tiring ride, some of the buffalo were still kicking, pawing and butting viciously against the sides of their prison, when the remarkable caravan arrived at the loading corral. So vicious had been the attacks of some of the animals upon the cages that the later had been bound with heavy wire to save them from being torn to pieces.

Crates Unloaded.

One by one the wagons were backed up against the chute leading into the pens, the sliding endgates were raised and the imprisoned buffalo were allowed to spring from their cages into comparative freedom. During the operation of opening the endgates the shaggy animals would roll their big eyes in wonder and shake their shaggy heads in sullen defiance. Prodded by the attendant, they would lift their heads and, with a snort, bound from the wagons into the corral runway and speed down the lane with their stubby tails flying in the air. Some of them manifested a disposition to fight and with lowered heads charged back and forth against the sides of the chute, pawing the earth and snorting in rage when the stinging end of a long rope in the hands of a loader descended across their noses. The loaders have learned from experience that patience and persistence only will win in handling a herd of wild buffalo and after many and repeated efforts the nine bulls were finally driven into one of the pens.

Bulls Fight.

When an attempt was made to load two of the largest bulls the excitement of the day was furnished in the form of a fight between the animals. They were no sooner in than each began to eye the other savagely. Their heads lowered until their short, stubby horns pointed defiantly at each other. Viciously pawing the earth and snorting a challenge, both charged. The impact was terrific. The force was so great that the huge bulk of each fighter was carried almost to the ground. The honors were even and the fight was brief, ending after a few exciting clashes.

Another infuriated bull rushed against the side of the corral, hooked his horns under a long 2x6 board that was firmly nailed to the posts and, without any apparent effort, tore the board from its fastenings and hurled it over his head. The crowd of sightseers scurried back in fright, thinking the beast was going to tear his way through the fence, but the shaggy monarch, seemed satisfied with this exhibition of his wonderful strength and went sulking into a corner.

Very Unruly.

The animals loaded yesterday afternoon proved the most unruly and sulky that the loaders have yet had to deal with. Nearly all of them showed fight and there were numerous spirited exhibitions of buffalo anger. Heretofore it has been a comparatively easy matter to run the animals up the loading chute into the cars but yesterday a streak of stubbornness developed and every one had to be roped and dragged through the chute before they were finally landed in the cars. Every ruse employed by the loaders to frighten the bison into running through the chute failed. The only alternative was to rope the beasts and pull them by main strength.

The sulky, muscular animals would brace themselves and the task immediately became similar to that of tipping over a mountain by means of a rope around the peak. By teasing the stubborn brutes with dangling tin cans and sacks, some of them were induced to kick and in this would lie their defeat, for the moment their hoofs were raised there was a "heave-ho" and the buffalo would start on an unwilling and ungraceful slide into the car. Some of the animals were too stubborn to even kick and these had to be dragged abroad by a force of twenty or twenty-five men pulling on ropes attached to the neck, horns and feet of the resalritrant [recalcitrant] brutes. In this manner the struggling, snorting beasts were landed in ignominious captivity.

Outwits Them.

But when the loaders undertook to put the patriarch of the herd into a car defeat was theirs. They failed completely and last night the old bull, said to be about 25 years of age and the oldest of the herd, lay in the entrance to the loading chute a victor over the ingenuity of man. The animal fought desperately against going into the loading pen and when he had once been forced within the inclosure he refused to be driven up the chute. When the ropes were resorted to he calmly laid down in the entrance to the chute and refused to budge. Every effort to make him move was without effect save to cause him to raise his shaggy head, roll his round eyes until the white showed menachingly [menacingly] through the matted hair, then he would lay his head back upon the floor of the chute. There he was still lying at a late hour last night and unless he chooses to move or some means is is [sic] discovered of forcing him to rise, that loading chute is indefinitely blocked.

Shipment Delayed.

It was expected that all of the animals at Ronan would be delivered at Ravalli last night, but the freighter found it impossible to do so and because of this the starting of the herd toward Canada has necessarily been delayed. Howard Douglas, superintenden[t] of the western Canada national parks, stated to a Missoulian reporter last night that he would get the shipmen[t] under way as soon as possible, that the animals may not be forced to stand in their small stalls in the railroad cars any longer than is necessary. Many of them have now been in the cars for eight days and the close confinement is beginning to tell. None of the animals have shown any signs of sickness and Mr. Douglas is anxious to avoid any trouble from this source.

Source: "Patriarch of Herd Expires in Corral," *The Daily Missoulian*, June 30, 1909, page 1, col. 5.

Patriarch of Herd Expires in Corral
Oldest and One of Largest Buffalo Dies in Pens at Ravalli.

The oldest and one of the largest bulls of the Pablo herd died in the loading pens at Ravalli yesterday afternoon. The animal refused to be loaded into a car Monday afternoon and successfully defeated the efforts of the loaders to get him aboard by lying down in the entrance to the loading chute and refusing to move. There the animal lay until he died.

The patriarch of the herd manifested a spirit of fight when the first attempt to load him was made, then his fighting inclinations gave place to stubborness, after he had had a fierce encounter with another bull of about his size. So far as could be learned by the loaders there was no physical ailment to cause the buffalo's death and he had not been injured in any way. He lay for almost 24 hours, however, refusing to eat or drink water, and death soon claimed him. This animal was estimated to be at least 25 years of age and, despite his years, was one of the finest specimens of the herd. His death means a big loss.

This morning the freighters started from Ravalli back to Ronan with the hauling crates and were scheduled to arrive at the roundup corral during the afternoon. The remaining eight buffalo will be loaded and hauled to Ravalli today. These will be loaded on the cars as soon as possible and the shipment will be started on its way toward Canada, probably Thursday afternoon.

Source: "Roundup Rider Is Injured and His Horse Is Gored," *The Daily Missoulian*, July 1, 1909, page 1, col. 1-2.

Roundup Rider Is Injured and His Horse Is Gored
Johnnie Decker Is Hero of Another Thrilling Escape From Death in a Buffalo Pen.
Roundup Men Ride for Lives Before Bulls
Angry Beasts Charge in Blind Fury Upon Horsemen and Decker's Steed Is Borne to Earth With Rider Underneath — Saved From Death by Bullets Fired Into the Bison.

Charged by an infuriated buffalo, his horse gored under him, injured himself and pinned to the ground beneath buffalo and horse, Johnnie Decker had another narrow escape from death at the Ronan buffalo corral Tuesday afternoon. The horse was ripped and torn by the maddened beast's horns and Decker sustained severe though not serious lacerations and bruises. But for the fact that Michel Pablo and Fred Decker saw the precarious position of the injured man and drove the fighting buffalo from his victims by firing revolver bullets into his neck, both horse and rider would undoubtedly have been gored to death by the beast. With a dozen bullets in his neck, the bull sprang over his victims, charged through the corral and made his escape to the range. Another bull demolished a cage after being loaded and succeeded in making his escape.

Decker's thrilling experience occurred just before sundown Tuesday afternoon. Six of the eight bulls that remained to be loaded into the crates for transportation to the loading corral at Ravalli had been successfully caged, and but two — the most unruly and wildest of the herd — remained in the corral. Six riders, headed by Michel Pablo, the owner of the herd, mounted upon the finest of Pablo's horses, strove in vain for an hour or more to drive the stubborn animals into the chute leading to the crates. The wily beasts refused to enter the chute and, as the riders redoubled their efforts to force them in, began to manifest a disposition to fight. As darkness was coming on and delay in loading meant delay in shipment at Ravalli, the riders became more reckless and pressed the buffalo closely.

Charge Riders.

Goaded to madness by the continued teasing of the riders, both beasts turned upon the horsemen and charged. The riders took refuge in flight and for the next few minutes the race between the buffalo and horses was thrilling. With lowered heads, dilated nostrils and rolling eyes, the beasts rushed in blind fury toward the horsemen. Around and around the corral rode the men in their race for life. Watching their opportunity, the riders wheeled suddenly and eluded the buffalo, which continued in their blind rush until they brought up against the side of the corral.

Decker, who is known as a fearless rider, renewed his efforts to drive the beasts into the loading chute. One of the animals charged Decker's horse. The rider was unable to get his steed out of the way in time and the bull caught him full in the side. Horse and rider went to the ground, the rider being pinned under his mount. With his sharp stubby horns the bull was ripping the horse when Pablo and Fred Decker, a brother of the bull's victim, drew their revolvers and began firing bullets into the buffalo's neck. The sting of the leaden missiles forced the beast to jump over his victims and burst out of the corral. He made his escape to the outside range and soon disappeared. Decker though lacerated and bruised, mounted a horse and returned to the work of caging the other buffalo.

Wrecks Cage.

This, the last animal in the corral, was finally driven into the hauling cage and securely bound there with ropes. But when the drivers rolled from their blankets yesterday morning they found the cage in splinters and the buffalo out in the corral. He was roped but snapped the lariat as though it were a thread, and showed such a spirit of fight that it was finally decided to make no further attempt to load him.

The six animals loaded were hauled to Ravalli, where they were delivered in the loading corral at 3:30 p.m. These and a few others were then loaded into the railway cars.

At 6:45 the buffalo extra, in charge of Conductor Leek and Engineer McCann, pulled out of Ravalli over the Northern Pacific tracks on the trip to the Banf national park in Alberta. There were 15 cars, carrying 190 buffalo. A

Duncan McDonald skinning buffalo killed while loading
at Ravalli, Montana.
Source: *The Daily Missoulian*, July 4, 1909, part 2, page 4, col. 5-7.
Thanks to Frank Tyro, SKC Media.

trip of about 1,200 miles must be made by this train before the bison are finally unloaded at the Canadian park.

End of Roundup.

This marks the end of the roundup and shipment of buffalo from the reservation for the present. The work will be resumed in September, when riders will endeavor to corral about 150 outlaws that yet remain to be shipped to completely fill the order of the Canadian government. These animals are the wildest of the entire herd and considerable trouble is anticipated when the riders undertake to corral them. Since the work of rounding-up has been in progress these outlaws have strayed far from the regular range, but it is reported now that they are beginning to move back toward their old feeding grounds.

Source: "Many Enjoy Choice Steaks Cut From a Young Buffalo," *The Daily Missoulian*, July 4, 1909, part 2, page 4, col. 5-7.

Many Enjoy Choice Steaks Cut from a Young Buffalo

The accompanying cut shows Chief Duncan McDonald of the Flathead reservation in the act of skinning a buffalo cow, which was killed during the loading of the Pablo herd at Ravalli a few days ago.

The animal, about 4 years of age, was so unruly that the loaders could do nothing with her. She fought desperately against being driven through the loading chute into a freight car and in a mad rush across the corral butted blindly into the side of the pen, breaking her neck. She was immediately bled and the carcas was removed to the back yard of the Ravalli hotel, where it was skinned, dressed and butchered for use as a part of the menu for the Sunday dinner a week ago.

A large crowd of visitors, attracted to Ravalli by the buffalo loading, was unexpectedly offered buffalo steak when the dinner hour was announced. Almost everyone took advantage of the opportunity to taste the meat — just that they might say they had eaten buffalo. And almost everyone who tried the novelty expressed himself as delighted with the flavor. The popularity of the meat is attested by the fact that the supply was exhausted before the day was over, several persons securing large cuts of it to carry home with them.

Source" "Outlaw Bison Start Upon Long Journey," *The Daily Missoulian*, October 11, 1909, page 1, col. 5.

Outlaw Bison Start Upon Long Journey
Twenty-Eight Buffaloes Are Rounded Up at Ravalli and Shipped.

Staff Correspondence.

Ravalli, Oct. 10. — By dint of patience and perseverance 28 head of buffalo were loaded here today and will start on their long journey to the Canadian national park in Alberta tomorrow morning.

The work of loading the buffalo was not so exciting as it was a few months ago, when nearly 200 of the animals were loaded upon one train and sent from the Flathead reservation across the border, but there was plenty of interest in the sight to a large crowd from Missoula and the country surrounding Ravalli. The animals, all cows and calves, fought stubbornly against being loaded into freight cars like so many common cattle, and it was with no little difficulty that the shaggy beasts were pulled into the cars and crated into the narrow stalls that will be their home until they are delivered at the park.

Outlaws.

The animals, a portion of an outlaw herd that was purchased by the Canadian government and not to be rounded up when the former shipment was made, were corralled in a big pen at Ronan and hauled and driven from there across the mountains and through the beautiful Mission valley to Ravalli several days ago. Since that time they had been kept in the corrals at Ravalli.

Bright and early this morning Alex Ayotte, the Canadian government representative, Michel Pablo, from whom the herd was purchased, and a force of buffalo punchers commenced the task of driving the animals from the pen through a loading chute into the cars. As each animal reached the end of the chute a noose was dropped about his shoulders and a score of husky men would pull him into the car by half-hitching the rope around a post firmly planted in the ground, and literally dragging the stubborn, fighting, snorting beast from the chute into his stall in the car. Some of the animals fought desperately against being imprisoned and at times there was considerable excitement when a particularly unruly beast would almost overcome the strength of the men and appear to be on the verge of making his escape into the crowd. No such accident happened, however, though one cow resisted so strenuously that she sank to the floor of the car from sheer exhaustion. It is feared that she will die before she reaches the Canadian park. Another animal broke its leg and had to be turned out to wander upon three feet back to its native heath.

Though there are still some 50 or more of the animals upon which the Canadian government has a claim, they have not been rounded up and it is stated by representatives of the government that no further attempt will be made to secure these beasts before next spring and it is possible that no effort will be made then.

Michel Pablo, former owner of the herd, will accompany the present shipment to Canada and assist in unloading the animals at the park. Mr. Ayotte will also accompany the shipment.

―――――――――――

Source: "Buffalo Shipment from Flathead," *The Daily Missoulian*, October 8, 1910, page 10, col. 3.

Buffalo Shipment from Flathead
Howard Douglas Here to Superintend Details — Outlaws to Be Shot.

Howard Douglas, commissioner of Canadian dominion parks, reached Missoula from Edmonton, Alta., to make final arrangements for the transportation of another portion of the Michael Pablo buffalo herd to the Canadian government. This consignment is now on the wagons en route to Ravalli, where the animals will be loaded on Northern Pacific cars, to be moved immediately to Sandpoint, where the cars will be transferred for transportation to the north country.

Speaking of the present shipment, Mr. Douglas last night said he had been advised that 31 buffaloes had been rounded up and would be loaded in two cars for transportation as soon as he reached Ravalli, the shipping point. The last shipment was in June, when it was expected that after a month's time had elapsed the scattered herd would have collected and the rounding-up process could again be attempted. The men in charge figured well, but their plans were frustrated when the forest fires attacked the ranges, again driving the animals out of the territory where they could be readily handled. Besides the 31 bison now on wagons there are about 100 animals at large. These will be rounded up in December and forwarded to the Canadian government to close the contract entered into between the dominion representatives and Michael Pablo in 1908, which involved all the buffaloes forming the Pablo herd.

"The cowboys have experienced a lot of difficulty in rounding up this last lot," said Mr. Douglas while discussing the closing shipment of Pablo buffaloes. "There are about 25 old outlaw bulls, which have not only charged the ponies ridden by the men engaged in gathering the scattered herd together but have even driven the men themselves to seek cover. These animals will be shot and then the remaining buffaloes will be rounded up to make a shipment in December."

Last June, after a long fight with the herd, 46 animals were finally loaded on the cars and sent north. The original shipment, made in 1908, consisted of about 200 buffaloes and since that time consignments have been made from the original herd until there are now about 700 of the Pablo stock sheltered in Canadian parks. The present bunch will go direct to Lamont park, some 40 miles east of Edmonton. The big bunch is located in the new buffalo park, about 127 miles east of Edmonton. In this park there are about 110,000 acres of fenced land.

Source: "To Kill Buffalo at Ravalli," *The Missoula Herald*, October 11, 1910, page 2, col. 2-3.

To Kill Buffalo at Ravalli
Outlaws Will Be Hunted Down to Save Rest of Herd for Canadians.
Chance for Sportsmen
Pablo Bison Will Soon Be Gone to Happy Grazing Ground
or National Park Across Line in British Territory.

That the native buffalo of Montana is rapidly being sold and shipped away is evidenced by the fact of the Canadian government representatives being at Ravalli this week arranging for the shipment of 29 head to the Canadian national park near Wainwright, Alberta. Early this morning two cars were loaded with the buffalo at Ravalli and shipped west by way of Spokane and Kalispell.

Alex Ayotte, who has camped on the reservation since April, with his wife and family, was in Missoula yesterday to meet Howard Douglas, the commissioner of the national parks in Canada, who has been in Missoula for the past week. In talking to a Herald reporter regarding the summer months' roundup of the buffalo herd, Mr. Ayotte related the following interesting story:

Ayotte Talks.

"I have been spending the summer months with my wife and family camping on the reservation west of the new town of Camas, known more generally by the name of Camas Hot Springs, and assisting in roundup the herds of buffalo still on the reservation. During the early spring we shipped 30 head away, and since then we have been busy getting together another bunch, and recently succeeded in rounding up 33 more, which we intend to ship Tuesday to Wainwright, Alberta, where they will be placed in the park to roam with the others that the government has corraled in the park during the last 10 years.

"Early Saturday morning eight wagons arrived in Ravalli with 16 head, and 15 more will be brought in this morning. In rounding up this herd we lost three of the largest bulls. One was drowned in the Pend d'Oreille river while crossing from one corral to another. Another one was killed in the wagon, while being brought into Ravalli. He was a fine specimen, about 5 years of age. While skirmishing around in the wagon he fell in such a position that his back was broken, and we had to shoot him in order to save the hide and mount. The mount is fine and Mr. Pablo will likely be able to realize $1,000 for it alone, to say nothing of what he will realize out of the hide when properly tanned.

"All of the buffalo still on the reservation are found between the Pend d'Oreille river and Camas Hot Springs. The country where they roam is very mountainous and rough. In some parts of the timbered country a man on horseback would be helpless, as no horse was ever known to penetrate certain mountains where the buffalo constantly hide themselves. During the forest fires large herds were seen traveling north, and it was believed at one time that the entire herd belonging to Mr. Pablo would be lost forever in the wilds of the dominion government, but such was not the case. As soon as the fire and smoke cleared they came back to their old grounds.

Settlers

"When the Flathead reservation was first opened to settlers four years ago Michael Pablo believed that he would have to dispose of the buffalo, as he thought that settlers would begin to arrive at once and homestead the entire reservation. Such was not the case, however, but when he realized his mistake it was too late to do anything, as a contract had already been entered into by him with the Canadian government for the sale of the herd. Two hundred and fifty dollars is paid for every animal taken from the reserve, both old and young. This price does not seem very high when you take in comparison the price that is realized from the sale of a mount or the hide. I have known buffalo mounts to be sold for $1,000, and the hides equally as well. At the present time a person would experience extreme difficulty in obtaining either at any price, as they are very scarce, especially the hides.

"Along the west bank of the Pend d'Oreille river Mr. Pablo has erected a corral that the buffalo are first driven into and then made to jump a steep embankment into the river. On the opposite side another corral is built, extending out into the river, and the animals are driven into it by men on horses and in boats, who are stationed at the end of the fence in the river. Sometimes the buffalo, while in the water, get away by either swimming down or up the creek in defiance of the men who have lighted torches and firearms that they shoot repeatedly in order to scare them as much as possible. After a buffalo gets away from the corral once the men are never able to get him in the enclosure again, as he is very smart and alert when the horsemen try to surround him. Since we commenced to round up the herd, four years ago, a large number of valuable saddle horses have been killed, but luckily no human lives have been lost. A big bull will charge at a horse and stick his sharp horns into his flanks and carry him 50 yards. The rider is able to dismount and make his get away before the bull is able to turn on him.

Outlaws.

"When the buffalo get away from the corral they are considered outlaws, and nothing but a gun will ever subdue them. There are left on the reservation about 100 head of buffalo, and of this 35 are outlaws. Mr. Pablo is going to start killing these off between now and the middle of December.

"Any sportsman or hunter who would like to have one of these outlaw buffalo may go up to the ranch of Mr. Pablo's, west of Ronan, and he will be furnished with a saddle horse and two guides to go along and show him where the buffalo stay. If one is not a good shot and fails to down his bison, the guides, who are expert riflemen, will kill the buffalo themselves, but the man after the buffalo may have the glory. Mr. Pablo has 75 saddle horse and a number of men that he can send along as guides through the timber. I do not believe that Mr. Pablo is going to ask an exorbitant price for these outlaw buffalo, as he is anxious to get them killed off. As long as they roam with the others that are not outlaws the capture of the rest will mean several more years, and we are very anxious to get them all shipped away before spring.

"After we secure the remaining herd we expect to enter the forest in northern Canada, where a herd of about 100 are located. At the present time the dominion government has stationed some mounted policemen through the reserve to guard and watch them until we begin our roundup.

"Although the dominion government has 1,000 head in the national park, 750 we secured at Ravalli. The herd near Kalispell, belonging to the Conrad brothers, is the only one left in this country that is now for sale."

Source: "That Buffalo Hunt Due at Early Day," *The Missoula Herald*, October 25, 1910, page 6, col. 5.

That Buffalo Hunt Due at Early Day
Canadian Government Will Invade Flathead Country and Kill Outlaws.

The last great buffalo hunt in the history of the world, in all probability, will take place next month on the Flathead reservation, says the Anaconda Standard of today.

There is a part of a herd there, and it is now the property of the Canadian government. The herd is so unruly that it has been decided that the only way to move it to Canada is to kill off most of the ugly bulls.

When the Flathead reservation was opened the Pablo herd was sold to the Dominion of Canada, it being considered that with the opening of the reservation to settlement the buffalo could no longer roam over the lands of that section. The Pablo herd numbered close to 800 head. Since the opening of the reservation the process of moving the buffaloes over the line to Canada has been going on, but each time there seems to have been more difficulty, and the parties who had in hand the matter of taking the buffalos found some so unruly that they had to leave them and narrowly escaped injury.

The last detachment of buffaloes was moved to Canada the first of the present month, there being 31 in this body. That made 706, all told, which have been moved over, and there are still about 75 left. These are the cream of the herd so far as ugly temper is concerned, and it has been decided by the Canadian officers to kill off this remnant, or at least the ugly bulls, and those which seem tractable will then be taken over the line and placed with the herd already there.

N. A. Forsyth of this city received the following letter yesterday from Howard Dayton [Douglas], commission[er] of Dominion parks, who has charge of the buffalo enterprise, the letter being dated from Edmonton, October 20:

"I expect to take over 15 or 20 men from here on November 3 to shoot buffalo in Montana. Will reach Ravalli about the 6th of November. Would it not be well to get this big hunt in connection with the photograph of buffaloes you already have? This will really be the most thrilling part of the business.

Mr. Forsyth is making arrangements to go over to the scene of the hunt with his cameras, and will endeavor to take some pictures of the buffaloes while charging, perhaps, at some of the hunters.

Reports from the reservation are that the remnant of the Pablo herd is doing great damage there, not being confined and having the whole reservation to roam over. They have frequently treed some of the new settlers, who have had to be rescued from the buffaloes after great danger and hardship. The band of 75 left was at last accounts west of Ronan, on the Little Bitter Root river. In making his contract with the Canadian government for the sale of his herd, Pablo reserved 12 head for his private property.

A number of Missoula marksmen are interested in the coming hunt on the Flathead reservation.

Chapter 3

Swan Valley Killings

1908

Swan Valley Killings

1908

Editors' note: The murder of four Indian hunters in the Swan Valley in 1908 was a traumatic event in twentieth century Pend d'Oreille history. The event was just one part of many decades of assault by white Montana authorities on the hunting rights of the Salish and Kootenai people of the Flathead Reservation. Montana hunting regulations were supposedly enacted to protect the wild game in the state, but they were also structured to favor the white sports hunter over white and Indian subsistence hunters.

The early years of the twentieth century were the nadir of game populations in Montana. The influx of white hunters and the extravagant killing and wasting of game by many white men led to the collapse of wild game populations in the state. Many white hunters claimed that Indian hunters were taking more than their share of the game. It would take decades for the tribes to legally establish their treaty guaranteed hunting rights.

Only a few representative sources are reproduced here. The written sources give only the white side of the story. The testimony of the eye witnesses was confused, but it seemed likely that Peyton precipitated the conflict through some combination of bigotry and miscommunication. For a more complete account and assessment of the conflict see Salish–Pend d'Oreille Culture Committee, "The Swan Massacre: A Brief History," in Upper Swan Valley Historical Society, Inc., *The Gathering Place: Swan Valley's Gordon Ranch* (Condon, Mont.: Upper Swan Valley Historical Society, Inc., 2017): 62-93.

Source: "Game Warden Killed by Flathead Indians," *The Daily Missoulian,* October 20, 1908, page 1, col. 3-5.

Game Warden Killed by Flathead Indians
Charles B. Peyton, While Attempting to Arrest Four Redskins
at Holland Prairie, Near Ovando, Is Shot to Death —
He Manages to Slay All of Assailants.
Herman Rudolph, Companion and Brother Officer of the Dead Man,
Was Witness of Shooting and Took Part in the Affray, Escaping With
Slight Injuries — S....s of Party of Illegal Hunters Escape and Posses Are
Scouring the Country in Their Pursuit — Coroner Is Notified.

Word was received in Missoula yesterday morning of the killing of Deputy Game Warden Charles B. Peyton of Ovando by Indians on Sunday afternoon. From meager reports of the affair it is understood that the deputy and his assistant, Herman Rudolph, found a band of Flathead Indians encamped on Holland prairie, about 40 miles northeast of Ovando, and attempted to arrest them for the unlawful shooting of game. In the band were four bucks and three s....s, the latter fleeing at the approach of the officers. When Peyton advised the four bucks that it would be necessary to bring them to Missoula they, with one accord, seized their rifles and fired a close range volley at the officers, who returned the fire dropping two of the bucks. Peyton was struck in the breast, and, as he staggered, called to Rudolph that he was shot, but to keep after the redskins. Peyton dropping on one knee continued to pour a hot shot at the remaining Indians, and as the last of the quartet threw up his hands, the warden fell forward on his face, and, without uttering a groan, died.

Pursue Fleeing S....s.

Rudolph, who was uninjured save for a slight scratch, ran to the assistance of his chief as soon as he was sure the last of the redskins was unable to renew the fight, but found Peyton dead as the result of rifle wounds through the breast and abdomen. Hastily carrying the deputy to a secluded place, Rudolph ran to a nearby ranch for assistance in carrying [caring] for the dead deputy and the bodies of the Indians, after which he started for Ovando, which place he reached yesterday morning. Here he advised the people of the town, who organized several posses, which started immediately in pursuit of the s....s belonging to the band.

Authorities Notified.

Coroner Marsh was notified, as was also Indian Agent Samuel Bellew of Arlee, who telephoned instructions to the Ovando authorities relative to the burying of the dead Flatheads after the coroner's inquest. The body of Charles Peyton will be brought to Missoula as soon as possible, but arrangements for the funeral are being withheld until the return of relatives who left here yesterday morning for the scene of the tragedy.

Family of Peyton.

The murdered deputy leaves a wife and three children, who left Ovando last Saturday for Grantsdale, about six miles from Hamilton, where they were to have spent a week's vacation with Mrs. Peyton's parents, Mr. and Mrs. Tip See. A sister, Mrs. Leslie Wood, lives in Missoula. Mrs. Peyton was in the city Saturday on her way to Hamilton.

Late reports of the bloody fight indicate that there were some members of the band of Indians, who were well known in Missoula, one of them being Yellowhead, who was the first to fire at the wardens and the first to fall from the effects of a bullet from the weapon in the hands of Peyton. It is also rumored that Louis Ashley, another well-known Flathead Indian, was a member of the party, but this story lacks confirmation.

Holland Prairie.

Holland prairie, where the shooting took place, is located on the Swan river, about 40 miles from Ovando, and is a most beautiful natural park and a favorite run for deer. It is about three miles from the Howland ranch, but well removed from wire or rail communication.

Fearless Officer.

Among his acquaintances and co-workers Peyton was known as a man possessing supreme nerve, being regarded as one of Game Warden Scott's most fearless subordinates, and having the reputation of being a dead shot. He was feared by the Indians, having arrested many of their number on previous occasions for offenses against the game laws.

Pays Glowing Tribute.

When word was carried to Game Warden Scott in Helena of the tragedy on Holland prairie and the killing of Deputy Peyton, he expressed deep regret and paid the officer a high tribute, according to the following dispatch:

Helena, Oct. 19. — "Pleasant and affable, quiet and unassuming, yet one of the nerviest and gamest men I have ever met," said Mr. Scott, in commenting upon the case. "He was one of the most untiring men I have ever known, his continued rides of from 60 to 75 miles a day over the mountains being remarkable, not only to me, but to all residents of that section. His vitality was perhaps unequalled, while as for bravery I doubt if the man knew what fear meant. Personally, I feel as if I had lost a brother, so intimate had our relations become, while as an officer he was one of the best I have ever known. Sympathetic to a degree, yet a terror to evil-doers, the department has suffered an irreparable loss."

Source: "Story of Peyton's Murder Told by Returning Hunters," *The Daily Missoulian*, October 21, 1908, page 1, col. 5-6, and page 10, col. 3.

Story of Peyton's Murder Told by Returning Hunters
Missoula Nimrods Give Account of Killing of Heroic Game Warden
by Indian Braves.
Wound in Breast Shows Burns from Powder
Flathead First Attacked Officer, Upon Being Informed of Arrest,
and Was Shot — Party Finds Bodies Laid Out by S....s of Dead Redskins
— Deputy Rudolph Tells of Affray.

Two local nimrods, Dr. F. W. Morris and Engineer J. W. Moon, were doubtless, the first to view the scene of the terrible slaughter of last Sunday, when Deputy Game Warden Charles B. Peyton was killed by Indian hunters. These two men left Missoula two weeks ago for Ovando with the intention of beating the woods and hills surrounding that place in search of game. The pair made their headquarters in the Holland cabin, about three-quarters of a mile from the small clearing where the tragedy occurred. Early on Sunday morning Moon and Morris prepared to leave the vicinity and were driving in the direction of Missoula when they were accosted by Herman Rudolph, the man who had been with Charles Peyton when the fight started.

Rudolph Talks.

Excitedly, Rudolph gave the local men an account of the shooting of Peyton, and asked that the pair drive with him to the place where the Indians had been in camp. He said that Peyton had been shot, but could not say that he was killed. It was learned that the deputy warden had been stopping in the vicinity several days and had been making headquarters with Joe Walbiligg, a rancher, at whose place Morris and Moon then were. From Wilbiligg [sic] it was learned that Peyton had been in conference with the Indians on Saturday afternoon, charging them with violating the game laws and threatening them with arrest. On his return to the Walbiligg ranch on Saturday night, Peyton told his host of the trouble and stated that the band was a tough bunch and were prepared to do mischief. Rudolph, who lives in the Swan river country, was deputized by Peyton to assist him in handling the rebellious redskins.

How It Happened.

Bright and early on Sunday morning the two officers left the ranch in order to reach the camp by daylight. This was the last Walbiligg saw of either of the men until Rudolph rode up with Moon and Morris. On the way to the clearing, Rudolph gave a concise account of the fray which ended so tragically. He said that when he and Peyton reached the camp stakes had been pulled and the entire outfit had been loaded on eight ponies, which stood prepared for the word to start. Two Indians were in sight, one, a buck of some 40 years of age, and a youth of about 20. The deputy approached the elder buck, saying as he did: "I shall have to take you to Missoula." The Indian, viciously seized Peyton by the throat, but was unable to hold his wiry opponent, who swung himself loose. Springing to the side of his pony, the Indian drew a rifle from the scabbard and turned on the deputy. Quickly disengaging his rifle, which he brought to his shoulder, Peyton fired point blank at this assailant, killing him instantly. Rudolph states that the young buck aimed his rifle at Peyton, and while doing so he (Rudolph) drew on the Indian, his weapon missing fire. The bullet from the Indian's rifle struck the warden in the abdomen, and, with a groan, he sank to the ground. In the meantime, Rudolph had ejected the faulty cartridge in his gun and shot the Indian through the head, following which action he ran with all speed to a place of safety. Following the trail in the direction of the Walbiligg ranch, he found Dr. Morris and Engineer Moon.

A Grewsome Sight.

With addition of Walbiligg, who mounted a pony, the party proceeded through the swamps to the clearing, where they found four dead Indians stretched in a row with a blanket rolled under the head of each. The s....s having returned in the meantime to lay them out.

Beside the body of one of the redskins lay a large dog that growled and eyed the white men with evident suspicion. Moon and Walbiligg made a casual search of the willow brush with which the clearing is surrounded for the remaining members of the party, while Rudolph and Dr. Morris examined the dead Indians. Assuring themselves that no one was lurking in the adjoining brush or that the fallen Flatheads were feigning, the party made search for the body of Peyton, which was found in the brush about 60 feet away from the bodies of his victims. Peyton lay on his back, his coat and vest unbuttoned. At his right hand, touched by the dead fingers, was his six-shot repeating rifle, with the magazine entirely empty, showing that he had used every chamber before he fell. At his left side, and also touching the fingers, was an eight-shot Automatic Colts revolver, cocked but not fired. In his belt was a single action Colt's revolver, which had not been pulled. Close examination showed a mortal wound through the abdomen. The bullet had passed through the belt near the buckle hold and lodged near the spinal column. Another bullet had pierced Peyton's breast, entering the right lung. According to the statement of the medical man who made the examination, the latter wound had been fired after Peyton had sunk into unconsciousness from internal hemorrhages, caused by the wound in the abdomen, and was nigh to death. To bear out this theory it is stated that the respiration of the victim must have been very light and death very near, as, otherwise, there would have been blood flecks evident on either the mouth or nostrils of the dead man.

That he was shot from very close quarters is evident from the fact that the woolen shirt shows unmistakable signs of powder burns around the edges of the hole made by the bullet. The theory advanced by the party is that, although Peyton undoubtedly received his death wound during the actual fight with the Indian quartet, death was hastened by the hand of some member of the band after the deputy had laid down to die. No part of the deputy's property had been disturbed by the person who fired the shot into his breast, and there was no evidence of a death struggle. The Indians had packed up all their belongings, but the ponies were still tethered in the clearing where the tents had been pitched. Everything in the vicinity pointed to a hasty retreat on the approach of the rescuing party, the pony outfit being left behind on account of the necessity of covering the trail. The party of whites covered the body of the heroic deputy with grass and hastened toward the settlement, from which place the tale of the murder was given to the outside world. The Missoula people in the party made all haste to reach Missoula, arriving here yesterday afternoon on No. 3 at 3:30 o'clock.

Scott at Ovnado [sic].

A message was received here last night from State Game Warden Scott, who was then in Ovnado with two deputies of the game department, stating that a thorough investigation of the tragedy would be made. Several of Mr. Peyton's trusted friends, including Wesley Fales of Sandpoint, Idaho; Dick Vance of Grantsdale and Frank Prince of Victor, have also gone to the Swan river country, where there are a number of Indians encamped, and no stone will be left unturned by the game department to search out the remaining members of the murderous outfit.

Mrs. Charles B. Peyton arrived in Missoula yesterday from Hamilton, in company of an uncle named Wayland, and is stopping with the family of Leslie Wood, whose wife was a sister of the murdered man.

The following Associated Press dispatch was received here last night:

Butte, Oct. 20. — Two posses of Indian police have left the Flathead agency for the purpose of rounding up the s....s who were with the four Indians who fired upon and killed Deputy Game Warden Charles B. Peyton last Sunday. There are two Indian trails leading from the agency to Swan Lake, where the tragedy occurred. The names of the four Indians who are killed are not yet known. Major Samuel Bellew, the Flathead agent, stated that one of the Indians may have been Yellow Mountain, who had a permit to hunt and who was known to have been in the Swan river country.

State Game Warden Scott arrived at Drummond late last night and started for Ovando early this morning. At that place he will meet the body of the dead deputy and will start a posse of mountaineers out to overtake the remaining Indians, who are supposed to have been in the party that murdered Peyton.

Source: "Peyton's Body Brought to Missoula by Warden Scott," *The Daily Missoulian*, October 22, 1908, page 1, col. 1-2.

Peyton's Body Brought to Missoula by Warden Scott

The body of Deputy Game Warden Charles B. Peyton, who was murdered last Sunday morning on Holland's prairie by a band of Flathead Indians, whom he was attempting to arrest for the unlawful killing of game, was brought to Missoula yesterday afternoon in charge of State Game Warden W. F. Scott and Deputy Henry Avare.

As has been told in these columns, a party left Ovando on Monday night for the scene of the tragedy to bring back the body of the murdered man. Ovando was reached late on Tuesday night. The state game officers met the party out on the trail some distance from Ovando and accompanied the body to the town.

From the best information obtainable, it appears that the quarrel, which ended so tragically, was begun on Saturday afternoon, when Deputy Peyton arrived at the Indian camp to investigate the licenses of the Indians hunting in that vicinity. In the camp were three bucks, a boy, three s....s and a girl, together with eight pack horses. The warden, unaccompanied, went up to one of the Indians and asked permission to see his hunting license. This the buck refused, and, from the information supplied from one of Peyton's friends living a few miles from the scene of the disaster, in whom he confided later in the evening, the buck attempted to draw a rifle, which the warden knocked from his hand. This phase of the tragedy has not been given publicity prior to the arrival of State Game Warden Scott yesterday. Following the act of disarming the buck, Peyton pulled his own revolver and covered his opponent. To avoid further trouble in the approaching darkness. Peyton is said to have brought the conference to a close and to have returned to the Walbiligg ranch, where he detailed an account of the fracas. On Sunday morning the warden is said to have deputized the man Rudolph to assist him in arresting the offenders.

Further than the story related above there were no new details of the tragedy brought out yesterday save that a third bullet wound was discovered when the body was brought to the undertaking office. In accounts of the tragedy which have appeared in The Missoulian it was stated that the warden received one bullet in the abdomen and another through the right breast. The additional wound was discovered in the left breast, the bullet having passed through the heart. Dr. W. B. Parsons, who viewed the remains at the morgue yesterday, declared most emphatically that the wound in the abdomen was fatal, and that the murdered man could have lived only a short time after receiving it. The hole in the stomach was, unquestionably, made by a bullet of large caliber, while those in the breast were of smaller size. Investigation proves that the breast wounds were made while Peyton was prone on the ground, and either dead or very near death. These miss[i]les went through the body.

The names of the dead Indians, as taken from a list found in Peyton's note book, which had been under date of October 16, are as follows:

Anton Stoutee, license No. 13,6334; killed two deer.

Planteway Stoutee, 13-year-old boy, no game, license No. 13,635.

Camille Paul, license No. 13,630, three deer and one elk.

Sam Eiento (blank)

Warden Scott stated last night that investigations into the death of Peyton were under way, and that as soon as they were concluded a coroner's inquest would be held. Herman Rudolph, the man deputized by Peyton to assist him in dealing with the Indians, will appear at the inquest and is expected in Missoula today.

Arrangements were made last evening to ship the remains to Hamilton this afternoon, and the services will be held at the residence of Perry Baker, the dead man's uncle, Friday afternoon. Interment will be in the Corvallis cemetery.

Mr. Scott, when asked last night for his personal opinion of the murdered man said:

"As a man he was brave, honest and true. I can say that I never knew of a braver man, or one whom I liked better. As an officer in the pursuit of his duties he was unequalled. He was absolutely fearless, and could be strictly impartial in enforcing the law. In fact, so utterly impartial was he that he made many enemies, but his friends form a host, who will say everything for his character and general worth."

Source: "Rudolph Arrives in Missoula," *The Daily Missoulian*, October 23, 1908, page 1, col. 3.

Rudolph Arrives in Missoula
Only White Eye-Witness to Killing of Game Warden Tells of Tragedy.

Early yesterday morning Herman Rudolph, the only eye-witness, excepting Indian woman, to the tragedy on Hollard prairie last Sunday, when Deputy Game Warden Charles B. Peyton killed four Indians and was himself shot to death, arrived in Missoula. Rudolph paid his respects to the body of the dead warden, lying at the establishment of Cor[o]ner Marsh, and accompanied it to the depot when, in the afternoon, it was taken to Hamilton. Last night Rudolph, who is young man of perhaps 24 years, went to Butte. He will return tomorrow in time to be present at the inquest, should it be decided that one is necessary.

Rudolph Tells Story.

Rudolph, while he talked but little, told the story of the killing in a straightforward manner. Much of what he said yesterday is not new, as The Missoulian's accounts of the tragedy and of the developments since its happening have been faithfully comprehensive. Rudolph says that when Peyton accosted one of the Indians, had beaten the redskin to his gun and had killed him, a young boy, standing on the other side of the horses, fired the shot that killed the warden. Rudolph says that he fired simultaneously with the young Indian and killed him, even as Peyton fell. It was at this time that Rudolph left. He did not see Peyton kill the other Indians. When he returned with help, says Rudolph, he found a new wound on the body of the dead man and he thinks that this was made by a .32 caliber revolver in the hands of one of the s....s. Rudolph knew nothing of the third wound until he saw the body in Missoula.

May Be No Inquest.

It may be that no inquest will be held over the body of Peyton. Coroner Marsh is at Great Falls, attending the meetings of the grand lodge of the Odd Fellows of the state, and nothing can be done until his return, which, it is expected, will be tonight. Before Mr. Marsh left Missoula he is quoted as having said that he thought an inquest would not be necessary in the Peyton case.

Yesterday a report reached the city that the bodies of the four Indians had been buried by the s....s of the hunting party, but there is no authority to substantiate this rumor. At any rate, the s....s have not yet been arrested.

Yesterday afternoon at 4 o'clock the body of Charles B. Peyton was taken to Hamilton for interment. It was accompanied by Mrs. Peyton and Mr. and Mrs. Leslie E. Wood, the latter a sister of the murdered man.

Source: "S....s Return to Headquarters," *The Daily Missoulian*, October 27, 1908, page 4, col. 3.

S....s Return to Headquarters
Indian Women Implicated in Death of Peyton Located at Ronan.

Newton Hyde, who has been spending a few days with Major Samuel Bellew on the Flathead reservation, returned yesterday, and brings word that the s....s who were with the Indian bucks who were shot and killed by Deputy Game Warden Charles B. Peyton on Holland's Prairie, a little more than a week ago, have shown up at Ronan, where Mr. Bellew has gone to hold a pow-wow in the hope that something more definite might be learned of the cause of the slaughter. During a conversation relating to the tragic death of Deputy Peyton, Major Bellew stated that the Indians who were killed had always been known as a peace-loving band of fellows, and, as far as he was aware, had never had any trouble of a serious character. Each of the dead bucks possessed government allotments on Crow creek, where they held residences and where they had their headquarters. Three of the Indians had licenses which they secured in the regular manner at Ronan, while only one was hunting without the required permit. The young buck, who it is said was shot and killed by Herman Rudolph while aiming at Deputy Peyton, the major descried as a beautiful specimen of an Indian. He said the lad's physique was a nearly perfect as could be found, and his temperament was always of the best.

It was not learned whether the s....s secured possession of the pack ponies which were tethered in the clearing where the fight occurred or whether they returned empty handed. Major Bellew will push the investigation when he reaches Ronan.

Source: "Indians Tell Graphic Story of Holland Prairie Tragedy," *The Daily Missoulian*, November 1, 1908, page 5, col. 1-7.

Indians Tell Graphic Story of Holland Prairie Tragedy

There came to The Missoulian office yesterday a letter from the reservation, which is of almost thrilling interest. Certainly it will appeal to those who sympathize with the Indians and who understand the red man's traits. That the killing of Deputy Game Warden Peyton in the Swan river mountains early this month, together with the shooting of four Indians, all over the question of the right to hunt, was not the fault of the Indians is the contention of the Flatheads. They claim that the attack came from the game warden and that his death was the result of his aggressiveness. This has been the belief of many white men who know the Indians well and who have held to the opinion that Peyton was probably the victim of his own lack of discretion. The Missoulian's correspondent does not criticize Peyton as viciously bad, but holds him responsible for the tragedy through his lack of knowledge of the Indian and his rashness in attempting to deal summarily with them. The letter follows:

Indians Defended.

"To the Editor of The Missoulian: I have followed with deep interest the events which have succeeded the unfortunate affairs in Holland prairie, in which four Indians and a white man lost their lives. I was shocked when I read the news and I formed my own conclusion as to the cause of the shooting which resulted so disastrously. It was natural that the first reports of the affair should present the Indian in the worst possible light, as the sources of the information were not friendly to the red men. This was, I say, only natural.

"But those of us who know these Indians know that they are not quarrelsome. There is, so far as I know, not an instance of authentic record where the aggressor in a fight with whites has been a Flathead Indian. From the first these Indians have held friendship for the whites; this friendly feeling is traditional with them; it is the boast of their chieftains and the source of much pride in their tribal councils.

"For ages these Indians possessed the right to hunt wherever they chose to wander; the whole country was their game preserve and they knew no open or close season. The white man came and he was permitted to hunt here without molestation. This was the condition before the Indians were penned up on reservations and before the game laws of the white man became effective.

"What wonder is it, then, that the Indian has been slow to comprehend the changed conditions? In dealing with the red men this should always be borne in mind. They should have the consideration which is due them; these Indians have never been thieves; they have never hunted the white man; there was never a time when settlers in this part of the country were not safe.

"These are the views which we hold who know these Indians. It was the remembrance of the history of these Indians that made us hold to the belief that the red victims of the shooting on Holland prairie were not dead through they own fault entirely. In substantiation of these views, and in support of this opinion, I send you the testimony of the women who were with the Indians at the time of the shooting. You may publish it or not, as you choose, but it seems to me that it is only fair to the Indians, who have the worst of it so long, that their side of the story should be given to the public.

"Yours truly,
"Z."

Following is the story told by the Indian women. They had fled from the scene of the shooting when they realized that their men were slain. The searching parties that went out to hunt for these s....s missed them in their flight, but came upon their pack horses wandering in the mountains. One of the women, the wife of old Malta, was seriously injured by the running away of her horse and is now in a critical condition. Upon their return to the reservation last Sunday, the women were examined as to the incidents of the affair and this is their sworn statement:

The First Visit.

"On Friday morning, October 16, about 10 o'clock, the white man who was afterward killed, came to our camp with another white man, Holland, they think; our men were out hunting, but while he was there, the boy, Pelasoway Stuee, came in, and, as he talked English, the man asked if we had any papers for hunting. The boy told him is he would wait a little while the men would be back and he could see the papers, as the men had them with them. The white man said all right, and went away. On Saturday, before noon, he came back again with Rudolph and went into both lodges and turned everything over. Our men were gone, but had left their licenses with us and we showed them to him. While he was looking at them the boy and Martin came back and the boy told him what game they had killed. The white man wrote on the back of the license the number of animals the men had killed and wrote something in a book of his own. The deer and elk hides were in sacks. There were three dogs with the two lodges, but the dogs stayed in camp while the men were hunting.

A Second Call.

"About sundown on Saturday the white man came back to our camp together with the man who was with him in the forenoon. Our men were in camp and it was the first time Stuee and Camille had seen the warden. The white man told Camille to stop hunting and Camille said all right. He told Stuee and the boy they could hunt. He told Martin, your paper is no good. I will be back in the morning; I have a right to kill any one, white man or Indian, who has no paper to kill deer. Martin never said a word to the white man, as he could not understand what he said. There were no angry words passed or trouble of any kind between the white man and our men while they were in the lodge.

The Fatal Morning.

"After the white man left, Camille said the white man has told me to stop hunting and we will go back over the mountains, and we all decided to go home. We got up early to start back, but we had lost three horses by straying, and it was near sun up before we found our horses and we packed right away. The sun was just up when the same two white men who had been there Saturday came to where our camp had been. Just before the white men came in sight there was a shot fired, which we think was fired by one of them. When the white men got to where we were, the man that got killed asked what we were going to do, and Camille told him we were going home, as he had told us we could kill no more deer. Stuee was standing by the white man and said, 'Good morning,' at the same time smiling and patting him on the chin. The white man said nothing, but shook his head and pushed Stuee's hand away. Stuee was not armed. The white man asked a second time, "'What are you going to do?' And Camille again told him we were going home across the mountains, as he (the white man) had told us to. After the white man had pushed Stuee's hand away. Stuee turned to one of the horses and was fixing a rope on the pack. There was 21 head of horses, including four colts. Nine of the horses were packed, the other eight head were for us to ride — three men, one boy, three women, one girl. The horses were all bunched together and the white man that was killed stood near the outside of the bunch. The other white man, 10 or 12 feet away.

Peyton Shoots.

"After the white man asked the second time where we were going, he pointed to Martin and said, 'this man is not going.' Martin at this time was helping his wife get on her horse. Camille was tying a rope on his horse before mounting and had his gun under his right arm. The other three guns were standing against a tree 10 feet or more away. The white man was on the left and opposite side of the horse from Camille. Camille again told the white man that we were going home, and the white man said, 'No, no, no!' and shaking his head, at the same time raising his gun. Camille's wife called to him to look out, the white man was going to shoot, and Camille stepped toward the head of his horse. The white man did the same, and turning around the head of the horse shot Camille in the left arm, the ball passing through and entering his side. As Camille fell he called to women to run and we all ran off.

All Killed.

"When we came back in a short time we found Stuee just breathing, and when his wife raised his head, he died. Stuee was shot in the back, the ball entering between the shoulders and coming out above the hips, tearing a hole along the backbone like a knife cut. Martin was shot through the left arm, the ball passing through the body and coming out through the right arm. Pelasoway was shot through the heart; also three bullets had passed through his hat. The men were all evidently shot with a rifle of large caliber and the boy by a revolver or small caliber rifle, from the nature of the wounds.

When the women got back to where the men were dead, Martin's and Stuee's guns were still leaning against the tree as they had been before the shooting commenced, and undischarged.

"Mary Stuee, Her x mark.
"Clara Paul, Her x mark.

Witnesses:
John L. Sloane.
A. B. Beckwith.
"Subscribed and sworn to before me this 25th day of October, 1908.
"Samuel Bellew,
"U.S. Indian Agent."

Source: C. Hart Merriam, "Indians Killed by a Game Warden," *Forest and Stream*, vol. 71, no. 21 (November 21, 1908), page 816.

Indians Killed by a Game Warden

Editor Forest and Stream:

On Oct. 22 the newspapers contained a sensational and exceedingly inaccurate account of the killing of four Indians in western Montana by Deputy Warden Charles B. Peyton and his companion, a ranch hand named Herman Rudolph. It was stated that Peyton was killed in a fight with Indians while attempting to arrest them for violating the game laws of the State.

During a recent visit to the Flathead Indian Reservation in the interests of the Montana National Bison Range, I took particular pains to secure the actual details of this most lamentable affair.

The shooting occurred in Swan River valley, directly east of the reservation, where a party of eight Indians had gone on their annual hunt. The party consisted of two hunters, Kahmel [Camille] and Tsooe [Stuee], with their wives and Tsooe's two children, a girl of five and boy between twelve and thirteen, whose name was Palasoway. They took with them, as is the custom of Indian camping parties, an old camp man — a man whose business was to remain in camp with the women. This man's name was Yellow Mountain. He was seventy-two years of age and nearly blind. His wife accompanied him. Before setting out, the old man obtained a permit from the Indian agent to leave the reservation. The three others — Kahmel, Tsooe and Tsooe's boy — each purchased a hunting license, entitling the holder to kill one sheep, one goat, one elk and three deer.

One day about the middle of October — said to have been Oct. 16 — when the men were off hunting, Peyton, a deputy game warden, accompanied by the ranch hand, Rudolph, visited the camp and asked to see the hunters' papers. He was told that the men had their papers with them, but would show them to him if he would return when they were in camp. The next day he and his companion came back a little before noon. They entered both lodges and turned everything over, examining the contents, doubtless for the purpose of ascertaining just how much game had been killed. The hunters were again absent, but had left their licenses, which were shown the warden by the women. The men went away, but returned again about sunset the same evening. This time the hunters were in camp. It was the first time they had seen the game warden. He asked to see Yellow Mountain's paper, whereupon the old man dug into his pocket and produced his permit to leave the reservation. Peyton looked at this paper and threw it back in the old man's face, telling him it was not a license and was no good, and that he had a right to kill anyone, Indian or white man, who was found on the hunting ground without a license. The old man did not understand English and made no reply. The warden told Kahmel that he had better go home, but that Tsooe and the boy could hunt more if they wanted to.

During the evening the Indians talked the matter over and made up their minds that as the warden had already visited their camp three times, he meant to make them trouble and they had better leave, so they decided to pull out at daylight in the morning. The women, therefore, made ready for an early start, and at break of day the men set out to hunt the horses. Some of the horses had strayed, so that there was delay in finding them. They were found, however, and brought into camp about sunrise.

The four guns were stacked against a tree. The riding horses were saddled and tied to bushes, then the pack horses were saddled and packed. Kahmel had taken his gun from the tree, and the members of the party were on the point of mounting to ride away when a shot was heard close by. The Indian women exclaimed that it must be the white men coming back. This proved to be the case, for the next moment Peyton stepped into camp, accompanied by the ranch hand, Rudolph, who had been with him on the previous visits. Addressing the Indians, Peyton said: "What are you doing?" Kahmel, standing by his horse, ready to mount, with the bridle rope in his left hand and his rifle in its sheath under his right arm, replied: "We are going home. You said I had better go home, and we are all going home."

Peyton, pointing his finger at old man Yellow Mountain, said: "No! no! That man is not going." He thereupon raised his rifle and Kahmel's wife seeing that he was about to shoot, called to her husband to look out, that the man was going to shoot. Kahmel, whose face was turned away from the game warden at the time, immediately stepped around to the other side of his horse. The warden instantly stepped where he could see him and without a word, fired. The bullet struck Kahmel in his left arm and passed through his chest, killing him instantly. The warden raised his gun again and shot old man Yellow Mountain, who at the time was helping his aged wife upon her horse. Like Kahmel, he fell dead at the first shot.

Tsooe's wife called out to her husband: "Let's grab his gun before he kills us all," and rushed forward. At the same time her husband, unarmed, ran toward Peyton from the opposite side. Peyton, seeing the woman almost upon him, swung his gun around and fired hastily. She ducked and the ball passed over her head. Then, seeing Tsooe rushing at him from the opposite side, he whirled and fired. Tsooe at the same time ducked his head, but the bullet struck him in the back of the neck and plowed down the full length of his back, laying the bone bare as if he had been split open with a broadax, killing him instantly.

During the few seconds in which all this was happening, no one had noticed the boy, Palasoway. He, however, on seeing the game warden murdering his people, had evidently rushed to the tree where the three guns were standing, seized his rifle and turning quickly, fired and killed the game warden. At this, the man Rudolph, who was standing near by, instantly shot the boy, two balls striking him at the base of the neck, in front. Seeing him fall, his mother ran to him and raised his head on her lap. He lifted his eyes and tried to speak, but could not, and expired, with blood and froth, as his mother told me, pouring out from two holes in his throat and chest.

The man Rudolph now disappeared and was not again seen by the Indians.

Mrs. Tsooe was so overcome with grief that at first she declared she would never leave the dead bodies of her husband and son, but the broken-hearted cries of her little girl and the entreaties of the other women finally prevailed, and after covering up the bodies, the three women and the child traveled a number of miles through the woods to the camp of another Indian. This Indian returned with them to the scene of the tragedy, but owing to the distance they were overtaken by night and did not reach the place until early in the morning. I afterward talked with this man about the details of the affair. His story agreed exactly with that of the Indian women. I asked him where he found the guns. He replied that Kahmel had fallen on his, which was still in its sheath; that two guns were still standing against the tree where the Indians had placed them when saddling their horses, and that the fourth gun lay on the ground close to the boy.

I was told by a number of white men in the region that Peyton was a surly, overbearing man, usually insulting in his attitude toward hunters whose camps he visited, and utterly unfit for a position of responsibility. Several stated openly that they expected to hear that he had been killed, but not by an Indian.

I was told by both Indians and whites that Kahmel and Tsooe, the two hunters who had been killed, were among the best men on the reservation. They never gambled, never drank, never quarreled, but were kind and industrious and set an excellent example to the other Indians. One of them, Tsooe, had a small ranch in Mission Valley which he cultivated.

The Indians were quiet, peaceable and sober and had done no wrong. They had not killed as much game as they were entitled to by their licenses. The only irregularity on their part seems to have been that the old man, Yellow Mountain, had no license to hunt. Kahmel explained to the warden that the old man was too old and feeble to hunt, and that he was so nearly blind that he could not possibly see to hunt, and consequently had not taken a license. This seems to have angered the warden, who obviously was looking for a pretext to make trouble.

C. Hart Merriam.

Source: Fred C. Morgan to Commissioner of Indian Affairs, March 24, 1909, from file 72,298/1908 Flathead 175, Central Classified Files, RG 75, National Archives, Washington, D.C.

Department of the Interior,
United States Indian Service.
Flathead Agency,
Jocko, Montana
March 24, 1909.

The Honorable,
Commissioner of Indian Affairs,
Washington, D.C.
Sir:

Replying to Office letter of February 18th, last, Land 8641 and 7464-1909, TBW, relative to killing of Indians by the State Game Warden, I have the honor to state that as the s....s have made their statements, and the same have been submitted to your Office, I feel that nothing more can be done toward getting evidence from them.

From all who knew the deceased Indians I can learn nothing but that they were very peaceful in character, and that Stuee was among the most progressive of the full-blood Indians, owning a considerable number of cattle and horses, and well fixed financially, and one of the very few who abstained from the use of intoxicating liquor.

Stuee's boy, who is supposed to have shot Peyton, was about 14 years of age, and had spent most of his life in school at St. Ignatius Mission. Like his father, he bore a very good reputation, and was always considered of excellent character. A movement is on foot among the Indians to subscribe to a fund for the purpose of purchasing a monument to erect to his memory.

Yellow Mountain, the Indian who had no hunting license, was about 50 years of age, and from statements made by those who knew him, nearly blind, and unable to hunt a great deal.

The affidavit of Joseph Waldbillig shows that Yellow Mountain showed the game warden a permit from Major Bellew, which it is generally supposed he thought was a hunting license, as I learn that when he asked for a permit he stated he was going hunting.

Camille Paul was known as a very agreeable Indian and was never known to have been in trouble with anyone. Besides leaving a wife, who has since given birth to a child, he left a blind father and mother, who depended solely on their son for their support. Broken in spirit and heart they cannot become reconciled, as they claim it is the proud boast of the Flatheads that they were always friendly to the whites, which statement is borne out by many of the old timers of Montana.

The 11th Legislative Assembly of the State of Montana appropriated $5000.00 for the benefit of Deputy Game Warden Peyton's widow and children, and I recommend that the Indian Office do something towards securing in some way some restitution for the families of the deceased Indians, who were caused an untimely bereavement.

It has been stated by one of the mixed-bloods that, in his opinion, the Indians would have revenge; that unless the matter was settled in some satisfactory manner they would get a like number of white hunters for the Indians killed.

Owing to the distance which the parties who have information in regard to the killing live from this point, and of no way to get evidence under oath, I recommend that Rudolph, the man who claims he shot the Indian boy, be arrested and brought to trial, that there may be an opportunity to get both sides of the unfortunate case in court.

Something should be done, as the Indians as a whole are very much wrought up over the affair, since they understand that the Stevens' treaty gives them a right to hunt off the reservation without securing a hunting license.

The following paragraph is copied from the above named treaty:

> Second paragraph of article 3, Treaty between the United States and the Flathead, Kootenay, and Upper Pend d'Oreilles Indians, concluded at Hell Gate, in the Bitter Root Valley, July 16, 1855; ratified by the Senate March 8, 1859;

"The exclusive right of taking fish in all the streams running through or bordering said reservation is further secured to said Indians; as also the right of taking fish in at all usual and accustomed places, in common with citizens of the Territory, and of erecting temporary buildings for curing; together with the privilege of hunting, gathering roots and berries, and pasturing their horses and cattle upon open and unclaimed land."

Respectfully submitted.
Fred C. Morgan
Supt. & S. D. Agent.

Chapter 4

Documents of
Salish, Pend d'Oreille, and Kootenai
History Between 1907-1909

Document 1

Antoine Nenemah Charged with Murder of Gabriel Nahtah January 1907

Source: "Indian Is Charged with Murder," *The Daily Missoulian*, January 3, 1907, page 2, col. 1; "Murder Case Still Being Heard," *The Daily Missoulian*, January 18, 1907, page 2, col. 1.

Editors' note: Another tribal member killed in a drunken fight on the reservation. Since they relied on the courts, the newspapers only picked up bad news.

Indian Is Charged with Murder
Caught After Pursuit of Four Months' Duration.
Shoots Twice at Police
Antoine Nenemah Brought to Missoula to Be Tried for Murder of Gabriel Nahtah, Near Ronan.

The details of a tragedy enacted on the Flathead reservation more than four months ago were made public yesterday when Indian Agent Samuel Bellew brought Antoine Nenemah, a Flathead Indian, to this city and placed him behind the bars of the county jail, there to await a hearing on the charge of murder. Nenemah is charged with the murder of another Indian named Gabriel Nahtah.

It is alleged that during the course of a quarrel which occurred August 20 last, a short distance from Ronan, the accused struck Nahtah in the head with a heavy club, inflicting injuries from which the latter died eight days afterward. A post-mortem examination was held, which disclosed the fact that Nahtah's skull had been fractured.

The nature of the quarrel which resulted in the killing has not been learned. It is believed that it was a drunken brawl. There were several eye-witnesses, who will be summoned at the preliminary examination.

Escapes Two Times.

Immediately following the fight Nenemah disappeared. He was twice arrested by the Indian police, and escaped each time. Learning of his escape, and feeling that there were persons who would shield him, the officials decided to pursue a strategical course to bring him to the bar of justice. They made no further hunt for him, believing that he would think he was not wanted and would sooner or later throw himself open to arrest.

The expected happened. A few days ago the accused Indian ventured to the settlement of St. Ignatius to visit with some relatives. The officials were notified of his presence, and on Monday three Indian police went to the house of Nenemah's relatives to place him under arrest. When Nenemah saw them coming he, in company with his wife and a brother, fled to an outhouse not far away.

Shoots at the Officers.

Nenemah was not caught easily, for although the police pursued him closely, he shot at them twice before they succeeded in capturing him. Luckily neither of the shots took effect. The prisoner was taken to the agency, and was brought to the jail here as soon as possible.

Judge J. L. Sloane swore to a complaint before United States Commissioner Wallace P. Smith early last September, charging Nenemah with murder, it being alleged that the crime was committed wilfully, feloniously and with malice aforethought. The accused will probably have a hearing before the commissioner within a few days.

* * * * * * * *

Murder Case Still Being Heard
Much Testimony in Trial of A. Ninemah.
Make Arguments Today
Witnesses for Defense Shift Responsibility of Death of Nahtah
to Indian Named Abraham.

The preliminary hearing of Antoine Ninemah, the Indian charged with the murder of Gabriel Nahtah of the Flathead reservation last August, was continued yesterday before Commissioner Wallace P. Smith in the district court room. The taking of testimony was concluded last evening and arguments in the case will be made this morning by Assistant United States Attorney J. Miller Smith for the prosecution, and S. G. Murray and Charles H. Hall, for the defense.

Considerable interest was evidenced in the case yesterday, there being quit[e] a number of Indian witnesses and spectators in attendance from reservation points. The principal witness for the government was an Indian named Abraham, who said that on the night of August 23, while he was taking Nahtah home, the latter being under the influence of liquor, the defendant came running after them, and struck Nahtah a heavy blow in the head with a fence rail. He said that Nahtah died six days after receiving the injury.

Antoine Nenemah
Source: Photograph Archives, Montana Historical Society, Helena, Montana,
photo PAc 85-91.02200

Quite a number of witnesses were placed on the stand by the attorneys for the defense, and their testimony tended to implicate Abraham in the alleged killing. Batiste Ninemah, a brother of the defendant, testified that on the night of the alleged tragedy Antoine Ninemah, Louis and Massela in one party, and Mary, Eneas and himself in a second group, were following Abraham and Nahtah, as Abraham was taking the latter home.

He said that Nahtah was so much under the influence of liquor that he was compelled to lean against Abraham. He said that suddenly Nahtah disappeared, and that Abraham got a pole from a nearby fence and came running after them. All of them, including the defendant, ran away and hid, the witness said, fearing that Abraham would do them harm, They then went back to the camp, and later learned that Nahtah had been injured.

Massela and Antoine, the defendant, corroborated this testimony. The defendant testified that he had been a good friend of Nahtah, the dead man. He denied having hit Na[h]tah, saying that he went back to the gambling camp with his companions. Batiste, Massela and Louise all testified that Antoine had no pole with which to strike Nahtah.

The Indian woman named Mary testified that on the night in question Nahtah had been drinking alcohol, and had a bottle of alcohol with him. She said she tasted it, and that it blistered her mouth.

It is difficult work taking the testimony of the Indians. An interpreter is required for most of them, and some of the witnesses find it difficult to testify to things that they themselves saw, rather than to occurrences of which they heard.

Document 2

Tribal Members Travel to Washington to Protest

January 27, 1907

Source: "Flatheads Journey to Washington," *The Daily Missoulian*, January 27, 1907, page 3, col. 1-2.

Editors' note: The bigotry of the writer was on display in this article, but it did record the frustrated efforts of tribal leaders to protest the allotment policy on the reservation.

Flatheads Journey to Washington
But They Become Financially Embarrassed and Want to Come Home.
Special to the Missoulian.

Jocko, Mont., Jan. 26. — Two weeks ago last Tuesday, Antoine Moiese, the unofficial secretary of state for the Flathead nation, and Alicot, business man of the tribe, accompanied by two interpreters, journeyed to Washington to interview the president and endeavor to have discontinued the allotment work now being done on the reservation. They were the peace plenipotentiaries personally appointed by Chief Charlo.

So skillful were their maneuvers in arranging an amnesty with Colonel Rankin, and so secret were they in departing from the reservation, that Major Bellew had no opportunity to restrain them in their hopeless task.

It might be explained that since last July Colonel Rankin has been in the central and northern parts of the reservation allotting the Indians their lands, but when he reached the vicinity of the agency, the bode of the chiefs — Indian as well as white — injunction was attempted by Charlo, with the result that he was promised to be the last one allotted.

Redskins Are Stranded.

But, lo, the story is yet to be told. Like the boy who ran away from home, they found more happiness in leaving than returning, with hardships in adverse proportion. Word has just been received from Washington by Pierre Big Hawk, who for convenience will be called secretary of the treasury, that they are stranded and want to get home. Ordinarily they would get help from this end, but at this season of the year the Indians can not sell their horses and money is as scarce as radium. It is hoped the venerable members of the

Indian Rights Commission at Washington will be able to do some of their much intended good for these Flathead Indians.

It will be remembered that Charlo made a similar trip to Washington about four years ago, but he found so many modern conveniences to overcome that when he returned he prayed devoutly that he would never be compelled to go again. He was dressed in native garb, blankets, headgear and moccasins complete, and from the stor[i]es written in Washington papers he had as much difficulty in climbing the Capital stairs as the man in his new bath-robe has to make the short flights at home.

Antoine Moise family
Source: National Anthropological Archives, Smithsonian Institution,
Washington, D.C., photo number 09939900

Document 3

Indian Held to Federal Grand Jury
on Murder Charge
February 6, 1907

Source: "Has a Hearing on Murder Case," *The Daily Missoulian*, February 6, 1907, page 2, col. 2.

Editors' note: Another death coming out of an alcohol fueled altercation. It may have been self-defense.

Has a Hearing on Murder Charge
Andrew Inhoos-tay Held to Federal Grand Jury.
For Killing Big Pierre
Witnesses Say Defendant Struck Big Pierre With Axe,
and Inhoos-tay Claims Self Defense.

Andrew Inhoos-tay, the Indian who was arrested a short time ago on the charge of murdering Big Pierre, a fellow Indian, on the Flathead reservation, had a hearing yesterday afternoon before Commissioner Wallace P. Smith, and was held without bail to await the action of the federal grand jury. There were but six witnesses for the government, and it took but a short time to hear the testimony. Assistant United States Attorney J. Miller Smith of Helena appeared on behalf of the government, and the defendant was not represented by an attorney.

Witnesses testified that during a quarrel on December 31, at the home of William Compier near St. Ignatius, the defendant struck Big Pierre a number of times with an axe, inflicting injuries which caused death three weeks afterward. Dr. Heidelman testified that he attended the injured man, and found that he had sustained a fracture of the skull, a fracture of one arm bone, and bruises on the hip and back.

Testimony was introduced to show that a number of Indians who had congregated at the place where the trouble occurred, had been drinking whisky. Indian witnesses said that Big Pierre had started the trouble by making an assault on Compier, and that he was in the act of pulling Compier from the house by the hair of the head when Inhoos-tay struck him with an axe. They said that Big Pierre retreated and that when he reached the house the defendant struck him again, causing him to fall inside the doorway.

Testifying on his own behalf the defendant said that he struck Big Pierre once on the back to cause him to liberate Compier, and that after that Big Pierre came toward him with a long knife, and that he struck him again in self defense.

Document 4

Reservation Landmark Burns

March 22, 1907

Source: "Allard House Well Known Since the Coaching Days," *The Daily Missoulian*, March 22, 1907, page 6, col. 4-6.

Editors' note: The burning of the Allard house on Mud Creek was the occasion for reminiscences of past events at the house which was also the dinner station for the Allard stage line through the reservation in the 1890s.

Allard House Well Known Since the Coaching Days

The Missoulian yesterday morning contained the news of the burning of the residence on the Allard farm on the reservation. This house was one of the best known buildings in western Montana. Situated on the Mud creek ranch which was the home of the late Charles Allard for many years. It was the dinner station for passengers across the reserve on the Allard stage line. In those days the Great Northern had not pushed its way across Montana and Missoula county extended to the Canadian line on the north, embracing the fertile and populous valleys that are now included in Flathead county's territory. All of the freight and passenger business to and from that region went across the reservation and over Flathead lake by steamboat.

Lively Days.

Those were lively days on the reservation. The travel was heavy and the trip was pleasant, not the least pleasing of its features being the dinner at the Allard ranch. There is hardly one among the older residents of Missoula who has not, at some time, taken dinner in the house that was burned Tuesday afternoon. This house was the second that had occupied the site. Charles Allard, when the Northern Pacific was completed, saw the possibilities in the way of traffic across the reservation and established his famous stage line. In 1886 he built a log house on the Mud creek ranch and made the place a stage station. That house stood until 1890, when it was destroyed by fire. In the following year the second house was built upon the foundations of the old one. This house was also built of logs but the outside was covered with clapboards.

The Buffalo.

With the completion of the Great Northern's coast extension, the traffic across the reservation became comparatively unimportant. Mr. Allard discontinued his stage line and the Mud creek ranch became the headquarters of the extensive livestock busines[s] which he subsequently carried on with Michael Pablo. Here it was that Mr. Allard assembled his famous herd of buffalo, which in 1893 was the largest herd in the world. Upon Mr. Allard's death this herd was dispersed and members of it are in nearly every zoological collection in the world. A few years ago Mrs. Allard married Andrew Stinger, who has since conducted the ranch.

A Quick Fire.

Charles Allard, Jr., who was in Missoula yesterday, said that he had come down from his ranch at the foot of the lake and Tuesday afternoon was at the

Charles Allard's ranch, 1890s
Source: Toole Archives, Mansfield Library, University of Montana, Missoula,
photo 75-6054

Pablo ranch with Andrew Stinger. They saw the smoke of the fire and rode to the Mud creek ranch as fast as possible, but the fire burned so fast that they were unable to do anything when they reached there. Mr. Allard says it was the fastest fire he ever saw. There were no men at the place when it started and it spread so fast that all the women could save was a buffalo robe and one quilt. They were driven out by the flames before anything else could be removed. The large stable, the granary and other outbuildings were not damaged. The fire started in the front room. It is not likely that the house will be rebuilt for some time.

Good Old Days.

The news of the destruction of the Allard house revived many stories in Missoula yesterday of the old staging days on the reservation. Mr. Allard did not long have a monopoly in the stage business; another line started and the rivalry between the two was intense. Every day there was a race from Ravalli to the foot of the lake and the drivers became famous all over the West for their clever handling of fours and sixes and for the speed they made over the more than 30-mile drive.

Real Racing.

From the time the stages reached the head of the draw, back of Duncan McDonald's house at Ravalli, until the reeking horses dashed on the run down the long slope to the boat landing at the foot of the lake, it was the finest horseracing ever seen. The reservation roads are, for the most part good, and the old Concord coaches rolled over them at break-neck speed. There was a change of horses at the Allard ranch and a fresh team took the stage up the hill that lies the other side of Mud creek. When the crest of the hill was reached that overlooks the lake, the horses knew by experience what was coming and, even before the whip cracked over their heads, they would jump into their collars and go down the long hill to the lake on a dead run.

True Sport.

A man who made this trip once, always wanted to make it again if he had a drop of sporting blood in his veins. It was real horseracing; there was no fixing those races; they were all run on the square and not for the pool boxes. One of the old stages is still at the Mud creek ranch, an interesting relic of the coaching days. It is too bad that the old house has gone! that, too, had many interesting associations. There was no more hospitable place in the West; guests were always welcome and were royally entertained. There are many Missoula men who have shared in the excitement of a coyote chase behind the Allard and Stinger hounds and returned to thoroughly enjoy the evening meal in the house that was burned Tuesday. There was always something doing there.

Document 5

Reservation Indian Commits Suicide

June 14, 1907

Source: "Peter Big Jim Kills Himself," *The Daily Missoulian*, June 14, 1907, page 2, col. 4.

Editors' note: According to this article suicides were very rare on the reservation in the early twentieth century.

Peter Big Jim Kills Himself
Young Indian Takes a Short Cut to the Happy Hunting Ground.

Peter Big Jim, a young Indian, killed himself last Monday near the Jocko agency, on the reservation, by shooting. The act was evidently deliberately planned, although nobody witnessed the shooting. The report of the rifle was heard and attracted other Indians, who found Peter with a wound in his abdomen and his 30-30 rifle beside him on the ground. This was at 10 o'clock in the morning and the man lived until 7 o'clock that evening. He refused, however, to tell why he had shot himself and his acquaintances are at a loss to know; no possible cause can be assigned by them for the suicide.

Peter Big Jim was a strong, healthy, young buck, 22 years old, and had had no trouble that any of his friends know anything of. Up to the time he shot himself he had appeared as usual and he had talked with his friends that morning without giving them cause to suspect that anything was wrong.

This is said to be the first instance of an Indian suicide on the Flathead reservation and it has excited the Indians more or less. The Indian usually takes his troubles as he takes everything else, stoically and without giving any evidence of flinching from them. It is his creed that it is a coward who flees from trouble and he usually glories in defying disappointment or vexation. But something went wrong with Peter Big Jim and he couldn't stand it any longer, so he sent himself to the happy hunting ground by the 30-30 route and he will not be present to receive his allotment when the reservation opens. Word of the affair was brought to town yesterday by people who came in for the circus.

Document 6

Powwow Included Visit by Secretary of the Interior July 1907

Source: "Indians Preparing for the Fourth," *The Daily Missoulian*, June 23, 1907, page 8, col. 5; "Red Men Are Visited by Secretary Garfield," *The Anaconda Standard*, July 5, 1907, page 11, col. 4; "Indian Dance Is On At the Reservation," *The Anaconda Standard*, July 8, 1907, page 10, col. 5; "Indian Dances End Saturday," *The Daily Missoulian*, July 12, 1907, page 2, col. 2.

Editors' note: The 1907 powwow was visited by Secretary of the Interior James R. Garfield, son of President James A. Garfield who negotiated with Charlot and the other Bitterroot Valley chiefs in 1872. The visit and the 1907 powwow in general must have been an especially gala affair.

Indians Preparing for the Fourth
At the Agency Secretary Garfield Will Witness a Brilliant Sight.

Judge Sloane came in from the reservation yesterday afternoon on the delayed No. 4 and spent last night in town. He will return to the agency today. During his stay here the judge busied himself with setting forth the attractions which the agency will offer on the Fourth, when a special effort will be made to have a picturesque and spectacular entertainment for the secretary of the interior when he makes his visit on the afternoon of the Fourth. It will be probably the most brilliant parade of Indian finery that was ever made on the reservation.

"The matter has been thoroughly discussed with the Indians," said Judge Sloane, "and they are very much interested in the matter. They will be at the agency in full force, and they are planning for a brave show. It will be the finest turnout that the reservation ever saw. The chiefs and head men are at work on the parade plans, and Secretary Garfield will see some real Indians when he comes to visit us.

"The special train from Missoula will not run to Arlee, but the stop will be made at the curve where the road is nearest to the agency. This will save the long drive from Arlee. The secretary and his party will be met at the train by a picked band of 50 Indians in full regalia, and these braves will act as his escort on the trip to the agency.

Chief Charlo and Secretary of the Interior James R. Garfield
and their sons at Arlee Powwow 1907
Source: Toole Archives, Mansfield Library, University of Montana, Missoula,
photo 78-226

"At the agency there will be a great turnout, and the Indians will give the best show that they know how to put up. It will be a great time. There will, in addition to the races and other entertainment, be a pow-wow with the secretary and the commissioner of the Indian bureau. It will be an interesting occasion.

"I understand that there will be accommodations on the train for any Missoula people who desire to come up to the agency. The fare will be low and there will be room enough up there for everybody to see all there is going on. But you should advise all who come to take along something to eat, as there is not any place there to get lunch. There are pleasant places for picnic parties, however, and those who bring along their lunch baskets will have a good time."

* * * * * * * * *

Red Men Are Visited by Secretary Garfield
Indians Don Their Paint and Feathers in His Honor.
And Show Him War Dance
Trip to the Flathead Reservation a Pleasant Experience
for the Cabinet Officer —
With Senator Dixon He Has Picture Taken with Braves.

Missoula, July 4. — Secretary Garfield's trip to the Flathead reservation was perhaps one of the most pleasant days on his western trip. The train bearing him to the reservation was made up of his private car, also that of General Superintendent Boyle of the Northern Pacific, and three coaches containing 400 people who wanted to see the Indian war dance as it is now being carried on at the agency. The train arrived at the agency about 4 o'clock in the afternoon and the secretary and friends were met by several hundred warriors on their horses, dressed in their war paint and feathers. It was a grand sight to see the manner in which they started for the dancing pavilion, giving the old-time war whoop, which many of the old-timers in the crowd had undoubtedly heard in years gone by. At the station the visitors were met by carriages and wagons, driven by Indians, who took the crowd to the camping ground, where the dance was held.

Meets Warriors.

Previous to the beginning of the dance Secretary Garfield was introduced to the old warriors. He will long remember the talk he had with Chief Antoine Moise, who was at the meeting many years ago when President Garfield signed the treaty with the Flathead Indians for the evacuation of the Bitter Root valley reserve. Through an interpreter Secretary Garfield heard a magnificent speech by the old warrior. The chief told the secretary that his heart was full of feeling for his tribe at the loss of their land in the Bitter Root. He said that his heart would always be in that condition, even after he had reached the happy hunting grounds above. He said he was a young man when President Garfield was in Montana and it made him feel good to meet the son of a grand man.

Secretary Garfield responded by saying that it was the intention of President Roosevelt to dispose of all the surplus land that the Indians might have plenty of money and also that it was the intention to teach them how to cultivate the lands that they might make their own livelihood.

Light Fantastic.

Chief Moise is now well along in years, but to show that he did not feel old, he stepped into the dancing pavilion and at the sound of the bass drum gave an exhibition of the latest dances as interpreted by Indians.

After the first dance Senator Dixon made a neat speech, asking for a contribution for the Indians to pay for the paint and feathers they had to buy for the occasion and $50 was realized. Just previous to the departure of the secretary's party his photograph was taken standing alongside of Chief Charlot, Chief Charlot's son, the secretary's son, Major Bellew, Senator Dixon and one or more Indians. This, Federal Judge Hunt, who was present, said was making history, and it was an impressive sight to see the old warriors and the secretary in the group together, the secretary also met Big Sam, the last of the old warriors, who is now chief warrior.

At the conclusion of the dance Secretary Garfield was taken in charge by Major Bellew and was shown over the agency. The party returned to the city at 8 o'clock this evening and will continue on west in the morning.

* * * * * * * *

Indian Dance Is On At the Reservation
Many from Missoula Spend Day Among Red Men.
An Interesting Ceremony
Hunts and Victories on the Battle Field Celebrated in Weird Manner in Accordance with an Old Custom — Feathers and Jingling Bells.

Missoula, July 7. — Two extra coaches were added to the regular equipment of passenger No. 7 this morning to accommodate the big crowd which went to the reservation to spend the day with the Flathead Indians and witness the celebration, which is now in progress. The day was perfect and the visitors, most of whom had not witnessed the dances and other features of the big powwow, had a thoroughly enjoyable time. The Indian gathering is in accordance with an old custom to meet once a year, and with feasting and dancing celebrate the many big hunts or victories on the battle field. The date for the gathering was generally later in the season, but five years ago the braves were asked by the authorities to hold the meeting on the Fourth of July, and since that time this has been the date each year. The largest gathering is at the Flathead agency, two miles from Arlee, where fully 1,000 Indians have assembled, and their camp, with the lodges placed in a circle nearly a mile around, presents a pretty sight, there being 163 tepees. There is another camp celebrating at the St. Ignatius mission, but only a small number are there assembled.

Indian Baby Christened.

The train stopped at the crossing near the agency to let the crowd alight, and from here rigs were taken to the camp. Many went to the agency, a mile away, and there witnessed the Indians attending mass, and it was a novel and pretty sight. This morning a 6-day-old Indian baby was christened, the parents naming the child after Judge John L. Sloane, chief clerk of the agency. There were no exercises at the camp until afternoon, and the visitors spent their time wandering about the shade along the Jocko river, fishing and eating their lunches.

About 2 o'clock the daily horseback parade took place, and 150 gayly-bedecked bucks and s....s, riding horses, some of which were very beautiful and in which the tribe takes a great pride, made the rounds of the camp just inside the circle of tepees a number of times. This feature over the reds dispersed, only to reappear shortly from their tents dressed for the dance, which was held in the large pavilion erected of evergreen branches directly in the center of the camp. Seven bucks seated themselves about the big, rawhide covered tom-tom and began keeping time with their low, weird cry. This soon brought the dancers to their feet.

In Fantastic Garb.

Dressed in the most fantastic colors with gaudy headgears of feathers and beaded work and having strapped to their arms and legs many strings of silver bells, which jingled with every move in time with the drum, the Indians presented a brilliant and impressive sight and called forth much applause from the crowd, which was comfortably seated about the circle in the shade of the boughs. The dance began rather slowly at first, but waxed fiercer and fiercer until fully [illegible] dancers were on the floor at one time. Each Indian's dress and style of dancing was a separate study to the onlookers, and for three hours, until the visitors were compelled to leave to take the train homeward, every moment was full of interest.

The celebration will continue for several days longer, the Indians themselves not placing any special limit to the time in camp, staying as long as the provisions provided will permit.

* * * * * * * * *

Indian Dances End Saturday
Chief Charlot Sends an Invitation to All to Be Present for a Day.

Chief Charlot has been in his glory this week. The dances of the Indians at the agency have been successful and there has been each day a large attendance of people from the city. He has had a great number of Indian guests and the pow-wow has been one of the largest and pleasantest ever held on the reserve; it has certainly been the most successful ever held at the agency. The crowds and the attention and the adulation have fairly softened the heart of the sullen old chief and he has been as suave as a dancing master. Through E. H. Boos, who came in last night from the reservation, Charlot sent word that he wished published:

"We have had a great dance. There will be good dancing on Friday, all day, and there will be dancing Saturday until noon. Then the camp will be broken and the visitors will go away. The white people who come out will see good dancing till Saturday noon and we will be glad to see them."

This is unusual for the old chief; he has seldom said anything as cordial as that since he left the Bitter Root. There will be an interesting sight for those who go to the reservation Saturday. There will be the last of the dancing and in the afternoon the visitors will have an opportunity to see the Indians move their camp. This in itself will be as interesting as the dancing to those who have never seen it.

Document 7

Indian Prisoners Escape Chain Gang

July 28, 1907

Source: "His Indians Quit Him, Strike for Reservation," *The Anaconda Standard*, July 28, 1907, page 13, col. 2.

Editors' note: Two Flathead Reservation Indian prisoners escape from the Missoula chain gang and race towards the reservation.

His Indians Quit Him, Strike for Reservation
Man in Charge of Chain Gang Has Sad Experience.
Working-on-the-Road Crew
Bill Montelious Turns His Back and Prisoners Work Their Legs
in Good Shape — Two Vacant Tin Plates at County Hotel.

Missoula, July 27. — The hot afternoon went directly against the grain of Louis Campo and Peter Vincron, two Indians, who were out with the gang from the county jail working on the streets yesterday, and they made a break for liberty when Bill Montelious, who is in charge of the gang, turned his back for a minute. The gang was working near the Rattlesnake, raking up the rocks along the road. The cool breath from trees along the creek and the roar of the tumbling water were too much for the Indians. They scented too strongly of freedom, and about two whiffs were all the duskies could stand for, and away they went down the road and up the water works hill, headed for the reservation. When Bill turned around two little streaks of dust were all he could see. His first impulse was to give chase, and he started like a shot out of Hell Gate canyon. He only started, however, when he thought of the rest of the prisoners, and going to a private house at hand, telephoned the sheriff's office. "My two Injuns have escaped me," said Bill over the phone. "You had better go and get them," was the consoling reply which came back over the wire. Bill went outside and looked again in the direction the reds had taken. Two figures met his gaze for an instant silhouetted against the sky at the top of the hill a quarter of a mile away, and then disappeared. There were two vacant tin plates last evening when the prisoners returned to the jail from their work, and two happy Indians were hot-footing it over the hills toward the reservation.

Document 8

Reservation Indian Arrested for Being Drunk in Missoula
August 29, 1907

Source: "Indians Demonstrate Their Ability to Drink Whisky," *The Daily Missoulian*, August 29, 1907, page 1, col. 6-7 and page 4, col. 5-7.

Editors' note: The arrival of the circus in Missoula in August 1907 attracted a number of Indians from the reservation and some also celebrated by getting drunk.

Indians Demonstrate Their Ability to Drink Whisky
They Come to Town in Force, and Liquor Flows in Streams for Those Who Have the Price.
Twelve Bucks and Two S....s Land Behind Bars
At the City Jail the Night Is Made Hideous With the Chants of the "Noble" Reds and the Officers Have Difficult Time Determining Whether They Are Singing a War Song or a Death Hymn.

Major Bellew, agent for the Flathead reservation, is authority for the statement that the Indians on the reserve are so well disciplined these days that they will not get drunk unless they can get whisky. There was a big crowd of the major's bards in the city yesterday, attracted by the circus, and they, conversely, proved the statement of the major by showing that they can and do get drunk when they get whisky.

There is no white man, no matter how hard he may try or how diligently he may guzzle, who can get as drunk as an Indian does. This fact was also demonstrated yesterday and there was a lot of the aborigines who devoted their time exclusively to the demonstration. They proved it so thoroughly and so cleverly that no further demonstration is necessary.

Come In Force.

It was the first big crowd of Indians that has been in town this year. When the other big circus was here these Indians were busy with their own celebration at the reservation — they had no part in Missoula's Fourth. But they came down yesterday in force; there were men, women and children, of all shades and all degree, of barbarism. There were blanket Indians and there were Indians in store clothes. There were s....s in red shawls and moccasins and there were s....s in corsets and tight shoes. There were pappooses in white raiment and there were pappooses in cradle boards.

And there were good Indians who were not dead; but there were bad Indians who should be dead and some of them did get dead drunk. The good Indians were so quiet that their presence was hardly noted; the bad Indians were so numerous and noisy that there was no overlooking the fact that they were in town.

Easy to Get Fire Water.

There was no trouble getting the red liquor. It flowed in streams for the Indian who had the price and they all had the price. If there was an Indian in town that was not drunk, it was because he didn't want to be. He had all the opportunity in the world.

Last night there were five inebriated Indians in the county jail that had been placed there by the constables. In the city dungeon there were nine of the brave boys and girls — for there were some of the copper-colored ladies who looked too frequently through the bottom of a bottle, and there was one of them who was in jail twice; there were two of them in the pit last night, and they were on one side of the bars that hemmed in the father and brother of one of them, the men being on the other side of the cage.

Up at the county jail there was quiet; the Indians were stowed away in a corner and were told to sleep it off. If they had disobeyed the kangaroo court would have cobbed them, and they knew it, so they were good. They moped and pined and yearned for the freedom of the city and plentitude of booze. But they had had theirs.

Free Speech.

Down in the dungeon under the city hall it was different. There the place was all the property of the Indians. There was no freedom and there was no booze; but there was no opposition to freedom of speech, for there was nobody there but the Indians. They had the field all to themselves and they did as they pleased.

They did it well. At midnight the air was filled in the neighborhood of the city hall with the notes of one of the chants of the Selish. It may have been a war song and it may have been a death hymn; there was nobody in the crowd who could tell. Therriault thought that it was a funeral chant and Farrell was certain that it was a war song. To the other listeners it sounded like a cross between the noise of a saw-filing machine and the sound of a Chinese orchestra.

It didn't cease; the Indians kept it up as long as they had breath left and their supply of that article was large; it was also strong and they used it to good advantage. In an endurance test those Indians would wear out an automatic siren. And when the s....s, naughty things, were thrown into the little cage they wailed with their male friends. The wailing of one of them was on the square; she cried bitterly. The other was as tough as she was plump, and the only thing that made her mad was that she had to be locked up with the girl that cried.

Amusing Incidents.

There were many amusing incidents in connection with the wholesale drunk of the noble red men. One of them disturbed the pony show and had to be locked up for that. He was so insistent that the Gentry people should present him with one of the monkeys that he wouldn't accept a refusal until an officer escorted him to the outside. Then he sputtered some more.

In the late afternoon there were two Indians who were arrayed in the habiliments of the white man. They had also a large share of the white man's burden, which they were carrying with difficulty.

On Higgins avenue they met a blanket Indian and their keen scent told them that the blanket Indian had a bottle under his gay covering. They palavered with him for a long time; it was evident that they wanted a drink from his bottle, and it was also evident that he didn't want them to have it.

A New Scheme.

Finally the blanket fellow made signs and they smiled at the motions that he made. He had found a solution of the problem of how an Indian can drink in public and not be seen. The blanket Indian took his gay blanket and deftly threw it over the head of the man who wanted a drink. Under the cover of this he handed his bottle to the thirsty one and the latter took a long swig at it. But nobody saw him do it.

This morning there will be a lot of sorry Indians in town. It may be that their sufferings will appeal to the heart of the judge, and it may be that they will have to go to jail until there is a habeas corpus suit brought on their behalf by some friend of the friendless. But they had their day at the circus.

Document 9

Indian Council Selects Land Appraisers

September 1907

Source: "Indians In Council Do Nothing," *The Daily Missoulian*, September 12, 1907, page 8, col. 4; "Indians Play Political Game," *The Daily Missoulian*, September 16, 1907, page 1, col. 6; "Charlot Dominates the Council," *The Daily Missoulian*, September 18, 1907, page 10, col. 3; excerpt from "Caught on the Run About Town," *The Daily Missoulian*, November 15, 1907, page 8, col. 2.

Editors' note: Chief Charlot insisted that one of the tribal representatives on the appraisal board for the "surplus" lands be from the south end of the reservation. John Matt and Angus McDonald were selected. The appraisal commission did not determine the value of the land. According to the Flathead Allotment Bill, they merely classified the available land as first class agricultural land, second class agricultural land, timber land, mineral land, or grazing land. The actual sale of the land was "under the general provisions" of the federal land laws which were designed to convey public land to citizens at low prices.

Indians In Council Do Nothing
It Will Take Another Pow-wow to Do the Necessary Work of Selection.

In response to the call sent out by riders and messengers to all the Indians on the Flathead reservation, there has been one pow-wow of the chiefs and the principal men. They were not quite certain whether or not they were being jobbed, and it was necessary for Major Bellew to have read to them again the treaty which provides for the opening of the reserve and then all of the correspondence that he had had with the department relative to the selection of the representatives of the Indians on the board of appraisement.

These documents were all read and interpreted and when the chiefs had heard them all, there was a long discussion. This concluded, the Indians went to their homes and took no action in the matter of selection of their members of the board of appraisement.

They did, however, agree to meet again the last of this week, and there will probably be another council Saturday, at which the matter will be talked over again and there may be a selection made. In the meantime the chiefs are talking over the matter with their tribes and there will be something definite in their minds when they assemble again.

They are very suspicious and there is no hurrying them. This is well known to those who are familiar with the tribes, and the best way to get quick results from them is to let them go their own way. If they are crowded they become more suspicious than ever and then it is all off.

* * * * * * * * *

Indians Play Political Game
Select Men to Look After Their Interests in Appraisal of Lands.
Charlot Wins the Day

There was plenty of politics in the council of Indians that met at the Jocko agency yesterday to select representatives to look after the interests of the Indians in the appraisal of lands on the reservation. The council was long and the discussion was heated and, while no definite result was reached, there was a caucus ticket selected that will go before the council at a meeting this morning for ratification.

This was the second pow-wow that the Indians have held on the subject. At the first session a week ago there was so much suspicion among the chiefs and headmen that no action was taken at all further than an agreement to go home and talk the matter over and meet again yesterday.

There are 12 in the full council, but there were times yesterday when not more than six were present; there was a lot of wrangling and the result that was reached does not, it is said, represent the real sentiment of the reservation people, but was brought about by the action of Chief Charlot in stealing the caucus and "bulling" through the nomination of his men.

It may be that the selection of the council will be formally ratified today. It also may be that it will not. There is a chance for a change overnight and there have been so many changes in this matter that another would not be surprising.

May Upset Plans.

Anyway, the election that the council makes are but recommendations to the president, who names the members of the committee. Mr. Roosevelt may upset the plans of cunning old Charlot in case he succeeds in stampeding the formal council today. Agent Bellew has notified the Indians that if they do not make a selection today he will wait no longer, but will send his own recommendations to Washington.

In the informal ballot at the council yesterday Joe Allard and Angus McDonald had six votes each. This was the highest number in the count and, according to the rules of the game, it should have settled the matter. John

Matt had five votes and Joe Pierre had five; this should have made them the alternates.

But Charlot got up when the vote was announced and said that Alex Maise was absent and if he had been there he would have voted for Johnnie Matt and therefore Johnnie Matt should have six votes. This would give Matt a place as principal; that was all Charlot wanted; there would be one principal and one alternate from the Jocko and one each from the other end of the reserve. He was willing to have it that way and that was the way he would decide the result of the caucus.

Another Session Today.

And that was the way the pow-wow broke up yesterday. There will be a formal session this morning and the vote will be taken again. There is one element that wants full-bloods on the committee for the Indians, but the more progressive of the reservation folks want some of the younger men. This is the real bone of contention. As the vote was announced by Charlot, Angus McDonald and John Matt will be the principals and Joe Allard and Joe Pierre will be the alternates. If the decision had been made according to the vote that was taken, Joe Allard and Angus McDonald would have been the principals.

* * * * * * * *

Charlot Dominates the Council
His Men Are Chosen for the Board of Appraisement of Indian Lands.

As announced in The Missoulian yesterday morning, the Indians in council on the reservation on Monday ratified the informal action of the council, taken Saturday, and chose Angus McDonald and John Matt as their representatives on the commission that will appraise the lands of the reservation. Joseph Allard and Joe Pierre were selected as the alternates, and the will of Charlot was supreme in the council; he had his way all through and the session was to his liking; it is saying much, for there are few occasions that Charlot is willing to approve.

Judge Sloane was in the city yesterday from the agency and confirmed the report that these men had been selected. The judge said that the council was notable from the fact that it was the first time that Charlot had signed any document since he was bunkoed into leaving the Bitter Root valley for the Jocko. He did place his sign manual[ly] upon the record of the council to vouch for the correctness of the record.

The members of the council were: Charlot, Antoine Moise and Pierre Big Hawk for the Flatheads; Big Cream and Louis Skulnah for the Kalispells; Antiste Dominick and Koos-Ta-Ta for the Kootenais; Sapiel Michel Incharlkom,

Martin Sinpinah and Judge Standing Bear for the Pend d'Oreilles; Peter Magpie and Pierre Pimps for the Spokanes. All of these are chiefs except Standing Bear, who is one of the tribal judges.

One of the men who watched the council is quoted as saying that it reminded him of an old-time Missoula county democratic convention with the late General Marion in the chair. Charlot, who presided at the sessions, was the embodiment of arbitrary despotism, and he ran things for the most part as he wanted them run. The men who are selected for the commission are breeds; there was a faction in the council that wanted nothing but full-bloods named, but these were in the minority. The recommendations of the council will go to the president for his ratification. There will be two Montana men on the commission and a member of the interior department for the fifth.

Speaking of conditions on the reserve, Judge Sloane said yesterday: "The cutting of the grain crop will be started in a few days; there is an unusually heavy crop; it is more than 50 per cent larger than the one of last year. The hay harvest is large, too, and will be harvested soon. The machine from the agency will start cutting next Wednesday. On the reservation this year there has been an increase of a million acres in the area under cultivation."

* * * * * * * *

Caught on the Run About Town
People You Know and Some of the Things They Say and Do.

John Matt came down from the reservation yesterday to join the Flathead commission, of which he is a member, as one of the representatives of the tribes. He will take part in the deliberations of the commission here; it is expected that the members will be ready by the first of the week to get started with their field work; they have been waiting this week for some of the maps that cover the portion of the reserve where they will start their work; this will be on the upper end of the reserve around Dayton, where the allotments have been comparatively few. There is, of course, much interest in the work of this commission; it is the last of the preliminaries of the opening of the reserve. When the work of appraisement is finished and approved, there will be nothing but the formalities of registering and drawing to be attended to. "I believe," said a well known resident of this part of the state the other day to a Missoulian man, "that the commission is as good as could have been found anywhere. I think the work will be well done and that, when it is finished, there will be nothing to find fault with. The job is a big one and it will take hard hustling to get it done in a reasonable time. But I think the commissioners will do their work with as little delay as possible."

Document 10

Indians Drinking in Missoula

September 21, 1907

Source: "Many Drunken Reds in Town," *The Daily Missoulian*, September 21, 1907, page 8, col. 3.

Editors' note: An unusually large number of reservation Indians were drinking whiskey in Missoula in September 1907. The law officers were unable to identify the white men who sold the Indians whiskey.

Many Drunken Reds in Town
Indians Get All the Booze They Want and the Jags They Acquire Are Bad.

Officer Larson had plenty of trouble yesterday with drunken Indians, and when he went home to supper last night he didn't know whether or not to wear a blanket. There were drunken Indians in the morning and at night. They were here and there and everywhere. Some of them the officer loaded into wagons and sent out of town and others he turned over to friends for safe-keeping.

There were two, however, that he couldn't get rid of, and these he locked up in the city jail. One of them was Charlie Kicking Horse, who had a wife and a baby and a jag with him. The wife followed him to the jail and tried there to get behind the bars with him, drunk as he was. But the officer told her to go home and let Mr. Kicking Horse stay where he would be better off than he would be when he was at large.

The second was a noble red who registered under the name of Jerome Wendenburg [Vanderburg], which name he pronounced with all the gusto of a graduate of Bonn. Jerome had the prize jag of the day, and when he was searched he had four quart bottles filled with whisky hidden in his raiment and a big gun that was filled with cartridges. All this was taken from him but his jag; that he took into the gloomy recesses of the city jail, and it gradually left him.

There have never been so many drunken Indians in the city as there are this week; they are as bad as they can be, and they have not the least trouble in securing all the whisky they want. They are making the officers a lot of trouble and they will do some serious harm one of these days. It is too bad that they will not do this harm to the men who give them the booze; that would be the best thing that could happen; but it will be some innocent person who will suffer.

Document 11

Indian Farmers Harvest Grain

November 1, 1907

Source: "Indians as Farmers on the Reservation," *The Anaconda Standard*, November 1, 1907, page 4, col. 1.

Editors' note: Indians harvesting grain was a positive side of reservation life that was not often noted in newspaper coverage.

Indians as Farmers on the Reservation
Some Do Well, While Others Are Indolent.
Helped by the Government
Thrashing Machine, Engineers and Feeders Are Furnished,
But the Farmers Are Required to Supply Their Own Crews.

Missoula, Oct. 31. — Charles Eaton has returned from the reservation, where he has been running a thrashing machine for the government for a couple of months. He expects to be in the city for several days and then will return to the agency, where he will be engaged in other work.

The Indians about the agency do considerable farming, and this year more than 40,000 bushels of grain were thrashed from the farms in that section. The grain ranches are mostly within three or four miles of the agency and each thrashes on an average from 1,000 to 4,000 bushels. Most of the land is irrigated, as there is a large amount of water available at all seasons, but some of the grain this year was raised without irrigation in the upland districts.

The government furnishes the thrashing machine, an engineer, and two feeders, and the farmers furnish their own crew. The machine is furnished by the government free of charge for the Indians. Most of the grain was sold and shipped as fast as it was thrashed, a large part of the yield going to the various railroad contractors in this district.

There are some real progressive farmers among the Indians, who keep their places in a farmer-like manner and seem to take an interest in their work, but others are more slovenly in their work and let their places run down badly and the yield is not so great. All of the farms now under cultivation about the agency have been selected by the Indians and will be held by them when the reservation is thrown open to settlement.

Document 12

Matt Family Looks for Inheritance from Kansas City Relatives December 1907

Source: Henry Matt to Secretary Garfield, December 21, 1907, and Acting Commissioner of Indian Affairs to Henry Matt, January 3, 1908, from file 100,053/1907, Flathead 313, Central Classified Files, RG 75, National Archives, Washington, D.C.

Editors' note: The Flathead Indian Agents' control over the personal affairs of tribal members in 1907 was limited. The Matt family was permitted to pursue their claim to land in the Kansas City area.

Arlee, Mont.
12/21/07

Secretary Garfield,
Washington, D.C.
Dear Sir:—

You will remember me as I was the interpreter who interpreted for you when you were here last July, and made you[r] speech to the Flathead Indians. Now we have matters in Kansas City which are needing attention, and we have sent a man down there to look matters up and he has found it just as we had heard that it was, but I have not time to give you details in full concerning this matter. But our Grand-father was an heir to property in Kansas City; his father boyght [bought] this land from the Government and got his final receipt, signed by the President, also got a patent from the Government which was also signed. Now some of these Indians who were brother and sisters to my grand-father signed away their right, but as he was small when his father died he was sent to a reservation in Montana and did not have knowledge of his rights, therefore they still exist. My grand-mother is still alive. This property is valuable, and we feel that it is our property, and the records show that it belongs to us. Now we want to send this man to Washington at our expense; he charges nothing for his time, nor his labor and unless he gets something, we pay him nothing, and he has already done considerable work on the matter and knows more about it than any other person here. We have asked permission of our Indian Agent here, but he will not consent for us to send this man to

Washington at this time, but gives us no reason, only says "he would not be able to do anything" while he himself knows nothing about the matter.

We are wards of the Government and this is a matter which belongs to the Government to protect us in our own property, and as we are told the law, this matter is not out-lawd [sic] from the fact that we have only discovered the real conditions, and they tell us the law does not run against matters of this kind until after it is discovered.

Also, we would like to have your opinion concerning this matter, and we want to know if this agent can hinder us from sending this man to Washington.

We would also say, that some of the heirs gave a mortgage on this property to a party who is a banker here, for $20,000.00. When they gave this mortgage, this man was then a clerk in a bank and he went to Kansas City with this mortgage and when he left here we thought we were giving him power of attorney, and yet it appears he had both power of attorney and mortgage, now he goes to Kansas City with these papers and comes back and tells us he could not do anything, but right away he started a bank of his own and is now president of the bank. This man is still here and still has the bank, and has never given us back our papers neither did he ever give us any money, and we want this matter fully investigated.

We have ordered abstracts which if this man goes to Washington he will show you, and go into the details, fully giving you all facts in the matter.

Now please tell us what we will have to do if necessary to force this agent here to give us our property rights, as it is now, he will do nothing nor he wont let us do anything, and gives his influence to keep us out of our property which is unsatisfactory, unfair and wrong to me and to my people, and we are not disposed to let the matter go without an investigation.

Please write me fully at Arlee, Flathead Indian Reservation, Missoula County and oblige.

I am very respectfully
Henry Matt

* * * * * * * *

Department of the Interior,
Office of Indian Affairs,
Washington.
January 3, 1908.

Subject: Certain land rights of
the addressee.

Henry Matt, Esq.,
Arlee, Montana.
Sir:

Your letter of December 21, 1907, addressed to the Secretary of the Interior has been referred here for answer.

It appears that you and your people have an interest in some lands in Kansas City, Kansas, acquired by inheritance, and that the title originally vested in some of your ancestors by purchase from the Government; but the Agent will not let you send some one to Washington to see about it.

From your statement of the case, it appears to be one in which the Indian Office has no interest whatever, other than to want to see all Indians obtain what belongs to them. If you have any case of the kind indicated in your letter, it will have to be established in the courts of Kansas or Missouri. It does not relate to Government affairs in any way, and therefore you may employ such attorneys as you may see fit and go where you please to attend to it.

It is probable that the Agent thinks you will be throwing away your money in attempting to establish your claim but its nature is such that he has no control over it or over your actions in regard thereto.

Very respectfully,

Acting Commissioner.

Document 13

Problems With Appraising "Surplus" Land on Reservation
January – February 1908

Source: *The Inter Lake* (Kalispell, Mont.), January 10, 1908, page 4 col. 1; John Matt to Commissioner of Indian Affairs, February 8, 1908, and Acting Commissioner to John Matt, March 4, 1908, from file 10,691/1908 Flathead 304, Central Classified Files, RG 75, National Archives, Washington, D.C.

Editors' note: The editorial in the Kalispell newspaper noted that the Indians complained about the appraisal of the surplus lands, but insisted that the Indians were being treated fairly. According to the instructions sent to John Matt by the Commissioner of Indian Affairs, the price set on the "surplus" lands was to be set for the benefit of the white homesteaders, without an effort to secure market value.

A story comes from Missoula that the Indians on the Flathead reservation are already protesting on the appraisement of the reservation lands by the commission. The report is that the commission is fixing the value of the land at $2.50 to $5.00 per acre, and the Indians claim it is worth from $35 to $50. While the report of the action of the Indians may be true, it bears earmarks of being manufactured for the occasion. The statement is made that large tracts of the lands have water rights, and are among the finest in the entire west. This is true of some of the lands on the reservation, but they have all been assigned to the Indians in the allotment, and the commission has nothing to do with appraising them. The land which the commission is working on, and the greater part of what they will have to classify, is grazing land chiefly, and the valuation placed on it is undoubtedly its full value in an unimproved state, without water, and with no means to get any. The Indians have two members of the commission and the government one, making a majority of the commission; and even though the two other commissioners should wish the appraisement made less than the actual value, which they will not, they would have no power to control the action of the commission.

* * * * * * * *

Department of the Interior,
United States Indian Service,
Flathead Agency
Jocko P.O.
Missoula Co., Mont.
Feb. 8 – 1908

Mr. F. E. Leupp Commissioner:

Only a few lines to day, asking for instruction, of this Flathead Reservation, and which I am working hard for the Indians.

First, is there any limit in classifying the Agriculture or grazing land.

Second. When the timber is appraised, shall we praise the timber land also, or not.

I am working hard for the benefit of the Indians, so that is the reason I ask for few instruction, and we'll thank you very much for return Knew's.

Yours truly,
John Matt.
Commissioner and appraiser of land on
Flathead Indian Reserve.

* * * * * * * *

Department of the Interior,
Office of Indian Affairs,
Washington.
March 4, 1908.

Subject: Appraisement of lands
Flathead Reservation.

John Matt, Commissioner to Appraise Lands,
Flathead Agency, Jocko, Montana.
Sir:

In response to your letter of February 18, 1908, in reference to the appraisal of the surplus lands of the Flathead reservation, you are informed that while the Act of April 21, 1904 (33 Stat. L. 303), does not place a limit on the price at which these lands may be appraised, in justice to intending settlers the appraised value should not be beyond the reasonable value of the lands in their virgin state, for it is clearly to the benefit of the Indians to have their country settled by progressive white people, and if the appraised value is greater than the remuneration which the settlers can reap from the lands during the time in which they have to pay for them, with a moderate recompense for their labor in improving them, defaults in payments would undoubtedly be made and the settler lose all that he had placed thereon.

In appraising the timber lands, the appraisal is for the lands and the timber growing thereon.

Very respectfully,

Acting Commissioner.

Document 14

Bazille Matt Accused of Statutory Rape

February 25, 1908

Source: "Half-Breed Is Held on Serious Charge," *The Anaconda Standard*, February 25, 1908, page 5, col. 4.

Editors' note: Family conflicts on the reservation occasionally spilled over into the courts.

Half-Breed Is Held on Serious Charge
Bazille Matt Taken to Helena by Deputy Marshal.
Represented by Attorney
Puts in But Little Evidence — Accused of Ruining Young Girl — Both Wards of Uncle Sam — Willing to Marry the Lady — Father Objects.

Missoula, Feb. 24. — Bazille Matt, a half-breed Indian who lives on the Flathead reservation, near St. Ignatius mission, and who was arrested Feb. 10 on the charge of criminally assaulting Alvina Luddington, a 15-year-old Indian girl, had his preliminary hearing before United States Commissioner W. P. Smith here today, and was bound over to await the action of the federal grand jury. The defendant was represented by Attorney Welling Napton, while J. Miller Smith of Helena represented the government.

A number of witnesses were examined among them being the girl in question. No attempt was made to deny the charge, and the principal testimony was in regard to establishing the age of the girl, and her father's evidence that she was but 15 years of age was not disputed.

Wards of Government.

Both parties to the action are wards of the government. The father of the girl was very bitter against Matt and would not listen to any settlement of the case by a marriage, although the defendant and his daughter both expressed themselves as anxious to be married at once. Matt was unable to furnish bail and was taken to Helena this evening by Deputy United States Marshal Drumm.

Document 15

Littlestone Accused of Murdering Alex Pluff

March 18, 1908

Source: "Red Man Bound Over for Murder," *The Daily Missoulian*, March 18, 1908, page 2, col. 1-2.

Editors' note: The statements conflict but the both Big Louie and Alex Pluff died. Littlestone was only accused of murdering Alex Pluff. Big Louie was a chief on the reservation.

Red Man Bound Over for Murder
Joseph Littlestone Held to Federal Court for Killing of Alex Pluff.

The preliminary trial of Joseph Littlestone, a full-blood Indian, who is charged with the murder of Alex Pluff on the Flathead reservation, some 50 or 60 miles from Plains, on February 27 last, was held yesterday morning before United States Commissioner Smith, at his office in the Allen block. Three witnesses were examined and at the conclusion of the testimony of Michel Scool-iss, Therese Pluff, wife of the murdered man, and Indian Agent Bellew, Littlestone was bound over to await the action of the federal grand jury on the charge of murder. Assistant United States Attorney J. Miller Smith of Helena conducted the investigation on behalf of the government.

The statement of Therese Pluff, wife of the murdered man, was as follows: "About noon on Wednesday, just one week before Ash Wednesday, Big Louie came to our house and told Alex that the wanted a drink of whisky. Alex told him no, that his wife, meaning me, was afraid when the men were drinking, and he would not give him any. Big Louie insisted, however, and Alex said: 'All right, but we will go out in the yard, we won't drink in the house.' I knew that they would get drunk and when they were out of the house I hid everything. I hid the axe, knives, and all of the cartridges, but in my hurry overlooked a rifle that was in the house. Alex had been to plains [sic] the day before and had a small jug of whisky with him when he returned.

Husband Was Dying.

"After they had been in the yard for some time they came back to the house, and both were pretty full. The children were badly frightened and commenced crying and went up stairs. I then went out of the house and stole up stairs, got the children and went to my Uncle Seymour's house. It was very near dark when I left. I stayed there until about 10 o'clock the next morning and then a man came to the house and said that a man had killed Big Louie; that Alex had been cut and would die before long. When I reached the house they had taken Big Louie home and only Alex was there. He said to me: 'I am very glad that you have got back. I do not think that I will live very long.' He wanted to tell me how he got cut and I told him that I did not want to hear. I felt bad because he was cut and did not want to hear about it. He was cut four times in the back and his intestines were hanging out. I tried to put them in place, but couldn't. He was also cut in several other places. There were two guns outside of the house and the stocks were both broken, but there was no blood on them. Outside of what I have stated I do not know anything more about the crime."

Statement of Littlestone.

At the hearing held at the reservation agency on March 3, Joseph Littlestone made the following statement: "I and my wife, Michel School-iss and his wife, together with a woman named Therese, heard there was going to be a dance at Timothy's and we started to go there and stopped at Charley Michel's place, and while we were there we heard that there would be no dance; right after dark we started to go back to Pierre Paul's, where we were staying, and there we heard that Big Louie had been killed. On our way to Pierre Paul's we stopped at Alexander Pluff's home. We were all in a buggy and I and my wife got out and went to the house. When we reached the door, which was open, Alex came out and said: 'I have killed your chief already and he is here dead, and I will kill some others, I will kill you.' I could not see what he had in his hand as he kept one hand behind his back. I was a policeman at Camas and I was not afraid of him. I told him that I wanted to go in and see Big Louie. I repeated to him to go away from the door, that I wanted to go in, and I then pushed him aside and entered. On the floor, right in the doorway, lay Big Louie. I knelt down and put my hand on him, all the time watching Alex. My wife had left the buggy and was directly behind me and she wanted to come in too, but Alex would not let her. As I arose I saw Alex lift his hand and strike my wife. He hit her a glancing blow and cut her blanket. When I saw him strike her, I got out my knife and lunged at him. I struck him twice and cut him in the stomach. I left at that time and started for the agency. Alex did not fall down, but just said: 'You hurt me,' and then walked from the room.

"The next morning some one took Big Louie to his home. I heard then that there were two pieces of rifle barrel on the floor and that they were bloody. I saw Big Louie and his head was all broken.

"I do not often carry a knife, but this one I had left at Michel's place a long time ago, and when I left there they told me that I had better take it along as it belonged to me. I was not drinking that day and I could not tell whether Alex had been drinking or not."

Michel School-iss was called and told what he had heard about the crime.

Makes No Difference.

When Littlestone was asked if he had anything to say in regard to the crime he said that he had not and that it would make no difference. His wife and Michel School-iss will be his principal witnesses when his case comes up for trial in the federal court at Helena, before Judge Hunt. He was taken to Helena last evening by Deputy United States Marshal J. W. Hoigler, and will remain in the Lewis and Clark county jail until his case comes up for hearing.

Document 16

Chief Charlo Makes Visit to Bitterroot Valley

May 20, 1908

Source: Excerpt from "Aged Indian Chief As Witness," *The Daily Missoulian*, May 20, 1908, page 6, col. 4.

Editors' note: According to the article this was the first time Chief Charlo had returned to the Bitterroot Valley since 1891.

Aged Indian Chief As Witness
Testimony of Member of Flathead Tribe Taken in Water Suit.

Hamilton, May 19. — An interesting witness in the water suit of Eli Downing and A. N. Mittower against Emanuel Johnson and others in the district court yesterday, to establish a water right on McKellar creek, near Victor, was Chief Charlos of the Flathead Indians. The chief and Indian Policeman Lumphrey came here from the Flathead reservation Sunday. The latter acts as an interpreter to the chief. The chief is 79 years old, and it is the first time he has seen the Bitter Root valley since the Flathead Indians were removed, 17 years ago. The old warrior is almost blind, but his memory is good and he readily answered the questions put to him. . . . .

Document 17

Reservation Baseball Games

May 1908

Source: "Mission Is Defeated by Agency," *The Daily Missoulian*, May 20, 1908, page 3, col. 4; "Reservation Teams Play Tie Game," *The Daily Missoulian*, May 26, 1908, page 5, col. 1.

Editors' note: Baseball games on the reservation involved Indian and white players. According to the second article, they must have been popular affairs. That article claimed 73 head of horses and 124 pairs of blankets were wagered on the results and 800 spectators attended the game.

Mission Is Defeated by Agency
St. Ignatius Is the Scene of Decidedly Warm Baseball Game.

St. Ignatius mission was the scene of keen baseball excitement Sunday. After suffering two defeats at the hands of the mission players the agency ball tossers put the quietus on them by a score of 8 to 9.

The mission boys started right in to "do things." Two safe ones and an error gave them their first run, but Holland's bunch were "there with the goods," and evened up the score by clean hitting.

Up to the sixth inning it was anybody's game, but in the seventh the agency team, by strong stick work and fast base running, played the team from the mission completely off its feet. Lucier went up in the air and Beckwith lost his voice.

In the ninth things looked bad for the boys from the agency, but with one gone and the bases full, Therrault struck out one and Holland, at first, gobbled up a hot liner, and the game was over.

Sterling's Cubs will play the agency team Sunday, May 24. Sterling has just signed a new player called Raffen.

Almost $300 has been wagered on the result of the game, and both teams are practicing hard. Following is the score by innings of Sunday's game:

| Mission | 1 1 0 2 0 2 0 1 1 — 8 |
| Agency | 1 0 1 2 2 0 3 0 * — 9 |

Batteries — Agency — Delaware, Therrault and Gebeau; mission — Lucier, Ashley and Belmony. Umpire — Wring. Time of game — Two hours.

* * * * * * * *

Reservation Teams Play Tie Game
Jocko and Ronan Put Up the Hottest Game the Flatheads Ever Saw.

The most hotly contested of the series of baseball games that is being played on the reservation was interrupted Sunday afternoon before it was finished, the Ronan team, which was playing at the agency, being compelled to leave before the game was decided in order to catch the train for home. The score was a tie when the game was stopped, and it will be decided June 7 by another game at Ronan, where the players of the sub-agency will try to wrest from the agency braves the laurels which were snatched from them Sunday by the steadiest and most consistent sort of play.

The Ronan team came to the agency on No. 4 Sunday morning and the game that followed was clearly the greatest game of baseball ever played in the reservation league. It was 1:30 o'clock when the game was called, and it was baseball every minute of the time that elapsed until the visitors had to leave to catch No. 3 in the later afternoon.

The Ronan players started off in the first inning at a pace that promised to land them safe winners. They touched up the Jocko pitcher for six hits, and two errors by the agency players netted Ronan five runs before the third man was sent to the bench.

Jocko came to the bat with defeat staring the home nine in the face; but they are fighters from the word go, and they didn't show that they were discouraged, if they were. They hit out one run in the first inning and went into the field again with their playing clothes on; they played an errorless game for the rest of the time of play, and blanked the visitors for seven innings.

In the second inning Jocko scored another tally, and in the third three more men were sent over the plate making the score a tie. Then it was give and take till the ninth inning; neither side scored a run till the first half of the ninth, when a wild throw gave Ronan a run. But in the second half of the ninth Jocko scored another and again the score was tied. It was necessary for the visitors to catch the train for Ravalli, so the tie remained.

The feature of the game, aside from the brace made by the Jocko team against what seemed to be insuperable odds, was the batting of John Holland at opportune times; he saved the day for Jocko.

There were 73 head of horses and 124 pairs of blankets wagered on the result of the game, beside many minor bets of blankets and other articles. All of these wagers remain in the hands of the stakeholders until the deciding game, June 7. The score by innings:

Jocko 1 1 3 0 0 0 0 0 1 — 6
Ronan 5 0 0 0 0 0 0 0 1 — 6

Batteries: Jocko — Delaware and Gebeau. Ronan — Hull and Dupreua.
Umpire — Bellew. Time of game — 1:50. Attendance — 800.

Document 18

1908 Powwow Described

July 1908

Source: Excerpt from Helen Fitzgerald Sanders, "The Opening of the Flathead Reservation," *Overland Monthly*, vol. 54, no. 2 (August 1909), pages 134-139.

Editors' note: Helen Fitzgerald Sanders was a white author who visited the July 1908 powwow on the reservation and left a long description of the events she saw. The description reflected the prejudices and bigotry of Sanders, but she did include information about the different dances.

[Selish Celebration, July 1908]

Last summer at the time when the sun reached his greatest strength, according to ancient custom the Selish gathered to dance. In this celebration is embodied the spirit of the tribe, their pride, their hates and loves. But this dance had a peculiar significance. It was, perhaps, the last that the people would hold. Another year the white man will occupy the land, and the free, roving life and its habits will be gone.

It was a scene never to be forgotten. Sharply outlined against the intense blue above and the tender green below, silent figures on horseback, gay with buckskin, beads and blankets, rode out of the filmy distance into the setting sun and took their places around the musicians on the grass. There were among them the most distinguished men of the tribe. Joe La Mousse, a descendant of Ignace, the Iroquois, grown to an honored old age, watched the younger generation with the simple dignity which became one of his years and rank. He possessed the richest war dress of all, strung with elks' teeth and resplendent with the feathers of the war eagle. He, with Charlot, met the Nez Perces and repudiated their bloody campaign. Francois and Kai-Kai-She, the judge, both patriarchs, and Chief Antoine Moise, Callup-Squal-She, "Crane with a ring around his neck," who followed Charlot to Washington on his mission of protest, moved and mingled in the bright patch-work of groups upon the green. But towering above the rest of the assembly, regal to the point of austerity, was a man, aged but still erect, as though his strength of pride would never let his shoulders stoop beneath the conquering years. He wore his blanket folded closely around him, and fanned himself with an eagle's wing, the emblem of the warrior. One eye was hidden beneath a white film which shut out its sight forever, but the other, coal-black and piercing, met the stranger gaze for gaze, never flinching, never turning aside. It was Charlot. Though an exile, his head was unbent, his pride unbroken.

Beneath a clump of cottonwood trees, around the tom-tom, a drum made of deer hide stretched over a hollowed section of green tree, sat the four musicians, beating the time of the chant with sticks bound in strips of cloth. Of these players one was blind, another aged, and the remaining two, in holiday attire, with painted lips and cheeks, were braves. One of these, seated a trifle higher than his companions, who leaned indolently over the tom-tom, plying his sticks with careless grace, possessed a peculiar magnetism which marked him a leader.

Of all that gathering, this Michel Kaiser was the one perfect full-blood specimen of a brave. It was he who, with suppressed energy, flung back his head as he gave the shrill cry and quickened the beat of the tom-tom until louder and louder, faster and faster swelled the chant:

"Come O! ye people! Come and dance!"

Suddenly a brave, painted grotesquely, dressed in splendid colors, with a curious contrivance fastened about his waist, and standing out behind like a tail, bounded into the ring, his hurrying feet beating to the tintinnabulation of sleigh bells attached to his legs. Michel Kaiser and the young man who sat beside him at the tom-tom, gave up their places to others, and after disappearing for a moment came forth freed from encumbering blankets, transformed with paint and ornament. A fourth dancer joined them, and the awe-begetting war dance began. The movement was one of restrained force. With bent heads and bodies inclined forward, one arm hanging limp and the other resting easily at the back, they tripped along until a war-whoop like an electric shock sent them springing into the air with faces turned upward and clenched fists lifted toward the sky.

This war dance explained many things. It was a portrayal of the glorious deeds of the warriors, a recitation of victorious achievement, a picture of battle, of striking the body of a fallen enemy — one of the greatest tests of valor. The act of striking was considered a far more gallant feat than the taking of a scalp. After a foe was shot and had fallen, a brave seeking distinction, dashed forth from his own band into the open field, and under the deadly rain of the enemy's arrows, struck with his hand the body of the dead or wounded warrior. In doing this he not only courted the desperate danger of that present moment, but brought upon his head the relentless vengeance of the family, the followers and the tribe of the fallen foe — vengeance of a kind that can wait for years without growing cold. By such inspiring examples, the young men were stirred to emulation. The dance showed, too, how in the past the storm clouds of war gathered slowly until, with lightning flash and thunder blast, the warriors lashed themselves to the white heat of frenzy at which they mocked death. The whole thing seemed to be a marshaling of the passions, a blood-fire as irresistible and sweeping as those floods of flame that lay the forests low.

The warriors ceased their mad career. The sweat streamed from their brows and down their cheeks as they sat beneath the shade trees in repose. Still the tom-tom beat and the chant continued.

"Come, O! ye people! Come and dance!"

They needed no urging now. What did they care for vespers and sermons when the ghostly voices of warrior ancestors, of forest dwellers and huntsmen, came echoing out of the past? Their spirit was aroused and the festival would last until the passion was quenched and their veins were cooled.

The next dance was started by a s..... It was called the "choosing dance," from the fact that either a man or a woman chose a partner for the figure. The ceremony of invitation was simple. The one who desired to invite another, grasped the individual's arm and said briefly:

"Dance!"

The couples formed two circles around the tom-tom, one within the other, then slowly the two rings moved 'round and 'round, with a kind of short, springing step, droning the never-varying chant. At the end of the dance the one who had chosen his partner, presented him with a gift. In some cases a horse or a cow was bestowed, and not infrequently blankets and the most cherished bead-work belts and hat-bands. Custom makes the acceptance of these favors compulsory. Even the pale-faced visitors were asked to take part, and the Indians laughed like pleased children to welcome them to the dance. One very old s...., Mrs. "Nine Pipes," took her blanket from her body and her 'kerchief from her head to give to her white partner, and a brave, having chosen a pale-faced lady for the figure, and being depleted in fortune by his generosity at a former festival, borrowed fifty cents from a richer companion to bestow upon her. It was all done in the best of faith and friendliness, with child-like good will and pleasure in the doing.

Then the next number was called; those who had been honored with invitations and gifts returned the compliment. After this was done, the Master of the Dance, Michel Kaiser, stepped into the center of the circle, saying in the deep gutturals of the Selish tongue, with all the pomp of one who makes a proclamation, something which may be broadly rendered into these English words:

"This brave, Jerome, chose for his partner, Mary, and gave to her a belt of beads, and Mary chose for her partner, Jerome, and gave to him a silken scarf."

Around the circumference of the great ring he moved, crying aloud the names of the braves and maids who had joined together in the dance, and holding up to view the presents they had exchanged.

The next in order was a dance of the chase by the four young men who had performed the war dance. In this, the hunter and the beast pursued, were impersonated, and the pantomime carried out every detail of the fleeing prey and the crafty huntsman who relentlessly drove him to earth.

The fourth measure was the scalp dance, given by the s....s, a rite anciently practiced by the female members of families whose lords had returned victorious from battle, bearing as trophies the scalps of enemies they had slain. It was considered an indignity and a matter of just reproach to husband and brother, if a s.... were unable to take part in this dance. The scalps captured in war were first displayed outside the lodges of the warriors whose spoil they were, and after a time, when they began to mortify or "break down," as the Indians say, the triumphant s....s gathered them together, threw them into the dust and stamped on them, heaping upon them every insult, and in the weird ceremony of that ghoulish dance, consigning them to eternal darkness, for no brave without his scalp could enter the Happy Hunting Ground. The chant changed in this figure. The voices of the women rose in a piercing falsetto, broken by a rapid utterance of the single syllable "la la," repeated an incredible length of time. The effect was singularly savage and strange, emphasizing the barbarous joy of the vengeful women. As the war dance was the call to battle, this was the aftermath. In pleasing contrast to this cruel rite was the marriage dance, celebrated by both belles and braves. The young s....s, in their gayest attire, ornamented with the best samples of their bead work and painted bright vermillion about the lips and cheeks, formed a chain around the tom-tom, singing shrilly. Then a brave with a party of his friends stepped within the circle, bearing in his hand a stick, generally a small branch of pine or other native tree. He approached the object of his love, and laid the branch on her shoulder. If she rejected his suit she pushed it aside, and he, with his followers, retired in humiliation and chagrin. It often happened that more than one youth desired the hand of the same maiden, and the place of the rejected lover was taken immediately by a rival who made his prayer. If the maid looked with favor upon him she inclined her head, laying her cheek upon the branch. This was at once the betrothal and the marriage. At the close of the festivities the lover bore her to his lodge, and they were considered man and wife.

After these figures had been repeated many times and twilight stole down with purple shadows over valley and hill, the music and the dancing ceased and the Indians held their feast. The fare was simple enough — canned salmon and crackers, wild berries and a drink made by the s....s, called "Indian ice-cream" — but they laughed over it and chatted as gaily as though the old times of bison banquets were come again. Yet amid the merrymakers there were those who did not share in the mirth. They were some of the older men; those with gray locks, wrinkled cheeks and hunted eyes.

I went to one of the young women, the daughter of Francois, whose convent education gave her a fair command of English, and asked her how the Indians felt about the opening of the reservation. She shook her head regretfully, and her glance sought out her father, Francois, toothless, white-haired, yet laughing with a group of the dancers.

"The young Indians do not care," she answered. "They gamble, and would rather have the money to lose than land, but the old men like my father, their hearts are breaking."

"Still your father smiles."

"His lips smile, but there are tears in his heart. In a few years he and the others of his age will be gone; then the change will not matter. It is a pity the white people could not wait a little while."

There was no bitterness in her expression or her tone — only infinite regret.

The Indians began to stir. They rose from the earth like ghosts from their graves, for the light was gone from the sunset skies and night was at hand. Through the evening calm, the monotonous chant shrilled weirdly, and the tom-tom vibrated with the regularity of a pulse-beat. And as that strange, unearthly measure swelled, then died in the engulfing night, it seemed as though the ancestral voices of these doomed children of the wild joined with them in a lament that even the weight of centuries could not still, for a wrong for which not even the promised recompense of the hereafter could atone.

Document 19

Eneas Pere Killed During
Fourth of July Celebration
July 9, 1908

Source: "Held for Murder," *Sanders County Signal* (Plains, Mont.), July 9, 1908, page 4, col. 3.

Editors' note: Another death during an off-reservation party. This one was at Plains.

Held for Murder

Dave Couture and Joseph Pain are in the county jail pending their preliminary hearing on July 20, at 10 o'clock a.m., in the justice court in Plains. They are charged with the murder of Eneas Pere, an Indian, who was stabbed about midnight of July 3. The affray took place at the stockyards where the Flathead Indians had gathered for the Fourth of July war dance. Shortly after the affair Officer George Wells was notified and on going to the tent where Eneas was, found Pain. He was arrested but denied having any knowledge of the crime. Eneas died Monday and was buried by the Indians that same evening.

County Attorney Schultz and Coroner Seward arrived Monday and investigated the matter and complaints were filed as stated. The coroner decided that it was not necessary to hold an inquest. Shortly after the cutting the victim was taken to the office of Dr. Hattery where he received medical attention, but the would [wound] was a fatal one, the Indian being disemboweled.

Both men have been accused of the crime and as the Indians are rather peculiar but little can be found out. It is alleged that Couture had Eneas down on the ground holding him in order that Eneas' wife could escape a beating that her noble lord had promised her. While in that position, it is asserted that Pain rushed out from a nearby lodge and his little knife did the rest. Couture claims that he had often held Eneas when he got on the war path and could always talk him out of the fighting notion.

The preliminary hearings promise to be long grawn [drawn] out as a large number of witnesses have been subpoenaed and the services of an interpreter will be required.

Pain says he is innocent of the crime and was in the tent for the purpose of trying to persuade his wife to return home.

No weapons were found on either men when arrested, but there are rumors of a bloody shirt and other evidence to warrant the officers in the belief that they have at least one of the parties.

Mr. Couture was arrested Monday night on his return from Camas. Both prisoners entered pleas of not guilty when arraigned before the local justice.

Document 20

Arrests for Having Booze on Reservation

August 18, 1908

Source: "Some Missoulans [sic] Given a Surprise," *The Anaconda Standard*, August 18, 1908, page 1, col. 5.

Editors' note: A special government agent collected evidence about liquor on the reservation and arrested a number of mixed blood tribal members and prominent white Missoulians.

Some Missoulans [sic] Given a Surprise
Arrested by Special Federal Agent for Having Booze on Reservation.
More Arrests Expected as Officer Is Hustling.

Special Dispatch to the Standard.

Missoula, Aug. 17. — A surprise was sprung here today when it was learned that Sam Cone, special agent of the government, has arrested 13 men of the community on charges of having sold intoxicating liquor to Indians on the Flathead reservation, or of having had the "booze" in their possession within the boundaries of the reserve. The investigation has been conducted quietly for some days by Mr. Cone, and he started to round up the men against whom he has evidence last Saturday, when a number were taken at Arlee, Sunday and today other arrests were made here. The case has created considerable interest on account of the prominence of some of the men now under bonds to appear before United States Commissioner W. P. Smith in a few days. The investigation is still being pushed, and a number of other arrests of well-known men are expected, according to the information given out by the special officer tonight.

One Gets Away.

The following is the list of those arrested up to a late hour tonight: J. M. Coudu, A. Marion, Nick Muscoes, Pasquale Palmicano, Henry Clairmore, Julian Ashley, James Raymond, Otis Worden, M. Wilburn, W. E. Milbury, Jack Cavander. The first six named were arrested on the reservation Saturday. An Indian named Michael Plant escaped from the officer at the time. Plant is a foot-racer of some renown and made a break for liberty and succeeded in dodging 32 bullets which the officer sent after him. The others were arrested in Missoula yesterday and today. Otis Worden is a brother of County Commissioner Tyler Worden, and is a grocer here. Wilburn is an organizer of the Industrial Workers of the World, who makes Missoula his headquarters. W. E. Milbury is a bartender of this city. Jack Cavander is a local electrician and A. Schmidt and Fred Anderson are well-known bartenders.

The investigation which is being made into the "booze" question on the Flathead reservation is in line with that which has been conducted by the government on other reserves in an attempt to stamp out the practice of carrying bottled goods to the Indians. Mr. Cone recently worked along the same lines at the Nez Perce reservation and as a result several prominent men were "pinched" and a number of heavy fines were imposed. Under the law a person can not carry liquor in any form on the reservation without laying himself liable. Most of those arrested furnished a sufficient cash bond to keep out of jail, but a few are now behind the doors of the county stronghold to await a hearing.

Document 21

Clairmont Brothers Arrested
for Liquor Violations
August 1908

Source: "Louis Clairmore Is Arrested," *The Daily Missoulian*, August 20, 1908, page 8, col. 4; "Clairmont Brothers Before Commissioner," *The Daily Missoulian*, September 1, 1908, page 2, col. 2.

Editors' note: Louis Clairmont was arrested and bound over to the federal grand jury for having alcohol on the reservation. His brother Henry Clairmont was discharged.

Louis Clairmore Is Arrested
Flathead Indian Is Added to List of Victims of Officer Cone.

Louis Clairmore, an Indian, was added to the list of Special Officer Sam Cone's victims last evening. Clairmore was brought in on No. 2 from the reservation by United States Deputy Marshal Heigler and was lodged in the county jail. He is to be charged with having liquor on the Flathead reservation. He was arrested yesterday morning on a warrant sworn out by Officer Cone. Those conducting the raids on the illegal liquor business on the reservation and watching for bartenders who sell whisky to the Indians are reticent as to their future plans. It is, however, said by them that they have numerous other arrests in prospect. Office Cone and his assistants will remain in Missoula for the rest of the month, in all probability.

At 2 o'clock this afternoon three of the men arrested by the United States officer will be arraigned before Commissioner W. P. Smith. Clairmore, Julian Ashley and James Raymond will be the first to have their hearing. The others will follow as rapidly as is possible.

* * * * * * * *

Clairmont Brothers Before Commissioner

Louis Clairmont, arrested at the Flathead agency early in August at the instance of Indian Agent Bellew, had his hearing before United States Commissioner Smith yesterday and as a result was bound over to await the action of the federal grand jury at Helena under bonds of $500. The bonds were furnished and the accused given his liberty. It was shown in the testimony taken today that the defendant had three gallons of whisky and a quantity of beer in his possession on the Flathead reservation.

Henry Clairmont, a brother of the above mentioned, who had been arrested on a similar charge, was discharged after a short hearing.

Document 22

Chief Charlo Repeats His Objections to
Opening the Flathead Reservation
October 6, 1908

Source: L. E. Milligan to Secretary Garfield, October 13, 1908, and Charles to Secretary Garfield, October 6, 1908, from file 70,266/1908 Flathead 308.2, Central Classified Files, RG 75, National Archives, Washington, D.C.

Editors' note: Pierre Pichette, a blind tribal member, sent this letter to the Superintendent of the Montana School for the Blind, in braille. The letter represented yet another effort by Charlo to have his complaints about the opening of the reservation heard in Washington, D.C. The letter is very hard to follow, but readers can get Charlo's general points.

Montana School for the Blind
Boulder, Montana, Oct. 13, 1908.

Secretary Garfield,
Department of the Interior,
Washington, D.C.
Dear Sir:—

A blind Indian Boy on the Flathead Reservation has sent me the enclosed appeal from Chief Charles [Charlo], to be forwarded to you. I have translated Chief Charles' letter litterally, and also enclose a brief typewritten summary of his claims.

Trusting you can find time to give this rather remarkable letter your personal attention, I am,

Very respectfully,
L. E. Milligan, Supt.

* * * * * * * *

October 6, 1908.

Secretary Garfield,
Department of the Interior,
Washington, D.C.

We respectfully appeal to you for a conference between a representative of your department and the Confederated Tribes on the Flathead reservation.

The Treatise which the Government has made with the Confederated Tribes, have been violated in the following respects:

1. White settlers have located on the Flathead reservation without the consent of the headmen of the tribes and we are powerless to dislodge them.

2. A new boundary line has been surveyed across the lower end of Flathead Lake cutting off part of the reservation, without consulting the Confederated Tribes.

Charles [Charlo],
Flathead Chief.

* * * * * * * *

October 6. 1908

Secretary Garfield,

We kindly appeal for through a council of the confederated tribes. Some oppositions were found very necessary to be controlled and promises made and offered to the confederated tribes through the treaties is found also very necessary to be attended by the Department, for as to our considerations we kindly ask help for them to be upheld by the Department.

No. 1. It is very well understood and familiar by all that it is prohibited for settlers to enter into the Flathead Reservation and settle without a consent of

Pierre Pichette, blind Salish historian
Source: Toole Archives, Mansfield Library, University of Montana, Missoula
detail from photo 82-22

the head men of the Confederated Tribes, and as we considered over it many such people that has no rights at all in the reservation are found to be referred and while others hired a lawyer to compose rights for them. And why did not they furnish evidences or witnesses to prove and compose their rights before the Head Men of the Flathead Reservation.

Now we kindly ask a question. Is a lawyer authorized to introduce and compose the rights of such people that we know has no rights at all in the reservation? It has been done before by a lawyer and it seems to us that those people without any rights were taken and thrown into a grinder by the lawyer and at last dropper [dropped?] out turned into Indians.

No. 2. For the new line situated so the furthest end of the northwest part of the Flathead Reservation. It has been announced to us so we all know very well the main boundary line of our reservation we have been considering by the new line which runs across dividing the Flathead Lake. The question is why and how was that new line located. Was it authorized without a consent of the Confederated Tribes to be situated and as for the part cut off from the reservation by the new situation line already mentioned, is it purposely done to be a loss to the Indians of a part of the reservation?

No. 3. Treaties of the Confederated Tribes. First treaty was made and signed by Governor I. I. Stevens and the Head Men of the Tribes.

Second treaty was made and signed by Governor Garfield and Head Men also.

Third treaty was made and signed by General H. B. Carrington and the Flathead Chiefs.

And through those treaties offers and promises were given for the benefit of the Indians and they were very gladly accepted. And we having been considering that why and how are not those offers delivered to the Indians yet. Or are these three men not authorized to make such treaties with the Indians, and if they are authorized it is time for the Department to attend to them and direct them as they were promised.

On your arrivance on 1907 on the month of July and that friendly speech you made before the Indians promising your help as to whatever you may be able to, so we do not hesitate to ask for your kind help, also we wish you to favor us for you to deliver our writings to the United States President. We also ask of him his kind help to acquire these matters controlled.

Our writings is concluded with wishes for your kind people help and hoping to hear a joyful answer to our desires.

Yours affectionate friend,
Charles [Charlo], Flathead Chief.

Document 23

Cooper & Courville

Sanders County Signal (Plains, Mont.) December 31, 1908, page 4, col. 6-7.

Cooper & Courville

The Plains
Meat Market

Fresh Meats and Sausages
And everything usually kept in a first-class
and up-to-date meat market. Everything
cool and clean.

Retail Department Lately Opened

Fish, When in Season

Document 24

Special Indian Agent Endorses
Agent Morgan's Work
January 30, 1909

Source: Thomas Downs to Commissioner of Indian Affairs, January 30,
1909, from file 9,444/1909 Flathead 150, Central Classified Files, RG 75,
National Archives, Washington, D.C.

Editors' note: White government officials were very pleased with Agent Fred
C. Morgan's efforts to enforce the government's regulations on the reservation
relative to adultery, alcohol, and gambling. Morgan was much younger than
Samuel Bellew, his predecessor, and moved aggressively, despite resistance from
many tribal members.

Department of the Interior,
United States Indian Service,
Flathead Agency, Jocko, Montana,
January 30, 1909.

Subject: Relative to conditions
at Flathead Agency.

The Honorable Commissioner
of Indian Affairs,
Washington, D.C.
Sir:

I desire to call your attention to the good work being accomplished by
Fred C. Morgan, the newly appointed Superintendent of this Reservation.
Mr. Morgan is a young man full of ambition, pluck and energy. When he
took charge of the reservation, two months ago, things were in a deplorable
condition; drunkenness and immorality being openly practiced by the Indians
without any apparent effort at control by the proper authorities. Mr. Morgan
at once started a reformation movement, using all the force at his command
to arrest and punish the offenders. Owing to his efforts order and discipline
are rapidly taking place. The good work he is doing is most commendable,
and I trust your Office will render him all the assistance you can, consistent
with the rules and regulations. In this connection your attention is called to

the insufficient clerical force in the agency office. Mr. Reynolds, a very efficient man, being the only clerk, and the volume of work sufficient to keep at least three men busy. Almost all of Mr. Morgan's time is, and will be for the next five or six months, required in the field, in restoring order.

Your Office recently authorized the employment of another clerk and a stenographer. With this additional help I think the work can be easily accomplished. These additional clerks should be men who are familiar with the work, and for this reason Mr. Morgan will ask for the transfer of Mr. H. S. Allen, now clerk at the Blackfeet Agency, Mr. Allen having signified a desire to be so transferred.

I trust your Office will grant this request, as it will certainly be a great help to Mr. Morgan.

Very respectfully,
Thomas Downs
Special U.S. Indian Agent.

Fred Morgan, Flathead Agent/ Superintendent, 1908-1917
Source: *The Daily Missoulian*, Dec. 12, 1915, ed. sec., p. 1, col. 1-7.
Thanks to Frank Tyro, SKC Media.

Document 25

Ka-ka-she Tries to Carry Complaints
to Washington
February 15, 1909

Source: Fred C. Morgan to Commissioner of Indian Affairs, February 15, 1909, from file 12,042/1909 Flathead 056, Central Classified Files, RG 75, National Archives, Washington, D.C.

Editors' note: Even as late as February 1909, tribal leaders made desperate attempts to have their complaints against allotment heard in Washington, D.C.

> Department of the Interior,
> United States Indian Service.
> Flathead Agency, Jocko, Montana,
> February 15, 1909.

Subject: Visit of Kakashe
& Jackson Sundown
to Washington.

The Commissioner of Indian Affairs,
Washington, D.C.
Sir:

In connection with my letter of February 11, 1909, regarding the visit of Ka-ka-she to Washington, I have the honor to state that on the 12th instant Ka-ka-she came to my office and stated that he desired to take with him one Jackson Sundown, whom I had positively forbidden to leave the reservation, for the reason that according to his own statement he is not legally married and when requested by proper authority to get married he insolently and impudently refused to do so. Jackson Sundown seems to be a sort of leader among the drinking and gambling element. Upon stating to Ka-ka-she my reasons for refusing to permit Jackson to accompany him on this trip he promised to and did select another interpreter in the presence of Chief Charlot, Judge Louison, Special Agent Downs, and myself. This interpreter, Joe Pierre, was satisfactory to me. Later they went to Missoula from which place Pierre was returned to the reservation and Jackson taken, which was in direct violation of my order and their agreement.

Should this delegation be received by your Office I feel that it would be a serious set-back to the discipline I am trying to establish, as it is the boast of Jackson's supporters that they could and would send him in spite of the orders from this office.

For the above reasons I respectfully request that the delegation be not received.

Very respectfully,
Fred C. Morgan
Supt. & Spl. Dis. Agt.

I heartily concur in the above recommendations.

Very respectfully,
Thomas Downs
Special U. S. Indian Agent.

Judge Baptiste Kakashe, Pend d'Oreille
Source: Photograph Archives, Montana Historical Society, Helena, Montana,
detail from photo 954-528

Document 26

Francois Chassah Murders Antoine Nenemay in Domestic Dispute
March 1, 1909

Source: "Story of an Indian's Revenge," *The Kalispell Journal*, March 1, 1909, page 1, col. 2.

Editors' note: Indian domestic disputes continued to spill over in violence, even as the reservation moved towards being opened by the government.

Story of an Indian's Revenge

The story of a terrible wrong and the revenge for that wrong, had just been brought to this city by United States Marshal Major Junius Sanders, who has returned to the city after an exciting trip to the Flathead Indian reservation for prisoners, says the Butte News.

The marshal brought five prisoners, three charged with whiskey selling, two Chinemen and a half-breed, one Indian, charged with assault with intent to kill, and the principal prisoner, Francois Chassah, a murderer.

On Novembrer [sic] Francois Chassah, a Flathead Indian, with French blood in his veins, stole in the dead of night to the tepee of another Indian, Antoine Nenemay; found his wife in the company of Antoine, and murdered him in cold blood. Francois placed the muzzle of a rifle at the head of his enemy and blew the man's head off.

But the sympathy of the Indians and all those who know the story of the terrible deed and the events leading up to it is with Francois and not only once, but again when the beautiful French-Indian s.... of Francois had come home begging forgiveness after she had run away with the bad Indian, Antoine, and her husband had forgiven and forgotten everything, even promising not to kill Antoine, for the s.... said the he was not so much to blame as herself.

Things went happily for some months after the return of the wife of Francois. Antoine was far away and nothing had been seen or heard of him. Then one night in November Antoine stole back again into the camp and when a chance presented itself he came to the tepee of Francois and begged the wife to fly with him again. She resisted for a time, but finally yie[l]ding to his entreaties went away with him into the dark.

Soon Francois returning missed his s..... There was no one to cook the evening meal, to smoke with him the evening pipe. He suspected at once what was wrong. His wife was gone again. Inquiry developed the information that an Indian boy had seen Antoine prowling around some minutes before. Without a word to anyone, Francois returned to his small log cabin, where he kept his guns, and taking his longest rifle he set out on the trail of the fleeing pair.

All that night he traveled toward the north where the trail led into the deep woods and toward morning he came upon the fresh-made camp. Antoines tepee was there, put up by his own s...'s hands, while the wife stealer looked on, thinking of the angry husband back at Jocko. Francois stole up and looked in. They were both there. Antoine rolled up in the middle of the tent in all the blankets, the s.... off in one corner shivering with the cold. With a catlike motion and the glitter of hate in his eye, Francois placed the muzzle of his gun at the head of the thief and spoke to him. The other opened his eyes and just as he realized in that one awful moment that he was on the verge of death, Francois pulled the trigger and blew Antoine's head almost from his shoulders.

The s.... awoke, terrified, and looked at Francois with the look of a frightened doe. Franicos [sic] raised his gun as if to shoot her down. She never moved. She was frozen stiff with terror. Then he lowered his gun and said one word, "dog," and turning on his heel went away. Some time later he retur[n]ed to Major Morgan, the agent at Jacko, and gave himself up. His s.... has never been heard from since, but some Indian came along and buried the body of Antoine. Francois Chassah is held without bond and awaits a trial for his life at Helena. He will plead the higher law.

Document 27

Charlot's Complaints About Agent Morgan

March 31, 1909

Source: Mr. Charlot to Secretary of the Interior, March 31, 1909, and
Fred C. Morgan to Commissioner of Indian Affairs, May 8, 1909, from file
27,058/1909 Flathead 154, Central Classified Files, RG 75, National Archives,
Washington, D.C.

Editors' note: The first letter is an example of the efforts of Chief Charlot
and other tribal leaders to get Washington officials to pay attention to their
complaints about Agent Fred Morgan's reform efforts on the reservation. The
original is hard to follow so paragraphs and some periods have been added to
the manuscript. On the same day this letter was written to the Secretary of the
Interior, Charlot also wrote an almost identical letter to the Commissioner
of Indian Affairs. The second letter reproduced here is Morgan's explanation
and defense of his actions. Morgan's letter is more literate and readable than
Charlot's, but it represented only one side of the story and should be taken
with a grain of salt. Morgan was making a special effort to end adultery and
drinking on the reservation. He thought that Indians trying to protect their
rights were agitators and particularly complained of Pascal Antoine and Henry
Matt. He also noted that tribal objections to allotment and the recent murder
of four Indians by a Montana game warden added to the unhappiness of many
tribal members.

March 31, 09

Secretary of the Interior Washington D.C.

as I become sensitive enough I lenriad and was infoned by my father flathead
chief Victor aboud their Kindnesses and well behaviars and kinds treatments
to the whites. the first white peoples seen by the flathead tribe was at Rosses
hole. the flathead Chief at that present time was three eagles. these seven whites
were seen by the flathead. they were permetted enter in to the camting ground
of the tribe without harm or damage under the acts of the head Chief. as they
arivearrened safly. robs were spread out for them to sit on. flathead Chief three
eagles then said to his tribe and children that such people as these whites not to
be Killed or interfered and always be Kind friends and treat them right always.

after the death of three eagles, Peter Sh-De-moo was then appointed by the tribe to be head Chief. while Peter Sh-De Moo was head chief of the flathead he gave equally at advises to his tribe and children as three eagles. then after death, Peter Sh-De-moo, my father was appointed head Chief of the flathead. he also firmly Kept the Kindnesses of the two dead chiefs and after the death my father I was appointed head Chief of the flathead for the first dead head chief was my arand father second dead Chief was my uncel third head Chief was my father Victor. so I firmly stand and keeped the Kindnesses of the three dead head chiefs to the whites, we flatheads at this present time do not mistreat or harm white at all for we Kindly Keep the words of the chieves and now we are surprised aroused by his acts and treatments to us.

first complaiments a prisoner under the care of a Govern. police escaped. the Indian Agent called the police in to the office and told him he has to be locked in Jail and police replied first said to the Agent we have to notfy the judges first. the Indian Agent said the Judges has no business aboud It. go or I will shoot you.

second complainments. the time when Baptist Ke-Ke-Shee and his interpreter were ready for their tripe to Washington D.C. on dudy the Indian Agent and half breed named Alex. Matte prevented the interpreter and Kept him in Jail for a day for not to been Christian. when Baptist Ke-Ke-Shee and his interpreter met togather again Baptist Ke Ke Shee took six other men along with him as far Missoula for he was afaraid that his interpreter may be arrested again. this six man stayed with him for several hours at missoula before he left. there six mans on their way home on the train one of them was Killed by the train. this event was the fault of the Indian Agent and Alex Matte if they would not prevent and arrest the interpreter no such thing would happen.

third complaiments one fool blood Indian man was Called in to the office by Agent and told why are you making so many talks about me. the man replied that he was not disoturbing any thing only helping his tribe and that he was rights to do so. and Indian Agent said to him that if he still Contioes such talking that he shall be reffared from the reservation. is the Indian Agent authorized by the department to refer Confedereted Indians from the reservation with out any wrongs found to the Indian.

we Kindly want you to investiagate in our Complainments for we are all anxious to get red of our Agent for we want Kind one that will treat us right

hoping our writing asking for your Kind help will be received with stasfation. Please notify us before long aboud our Complainments.

I remain yours truly friends
flathead Chief Mr Charlot
Jocko P. O. Montana.

* * * * * * * *

Department of the Interior,
United States Indian Service,
Flathead Agency, Jocko, Montana,
May 8, 1909.

Concerning Flathead
conditions.

The Honorable,
Commissioner of Indian Affairs,
Washington, D.C.
Sir:

Replying to Office letter of the 28th ultimo, Education-Administration, 27058-1909, EAF, I have the honor to submit the following:

1. What offences you refer to the Police Court. Would the case of a Government policeman who allowed a prisoner to escape come before it?

The Indian Court at this agency is conducted as nearly as possible in accordance with the Rules and Regulations. It is my desire and aim to at all times conform with the regulations. At times cases come up for which there are no provisions in these rules. Such cases I try to decide on their own merits, and to be just to all concerned. And for some of these cases I refer to the state laws.

In regard to the policeman (Paul Charley) who let the prisoner (Sohnia) escape, I have to state I was under the impression at that time that it was proper to refer the matter to the Indian Court. Since receiving your letter of inquiry and reading the regulations more closely it seems that the jurisdiction of the court is perhaps not broad enough to cover the conduct complained of. There was no punishment inflicted upon the policeman, it being my idea to have him disciplined by being put in charge of the jail for a short period of time, he remaining on duty as a policeman. At no time was he incarcerated. If the instructions under which I am working are not broad enough to allow me to use some discretion in regard to maintenance of discipline among those under my charge I would respectfully request full information as to what course to pursue in case of violation or infraction of the rules and regulations, or a disobedience of orders and instructions given by me. I did in the matter what I thought best for the maintenance of discipline. It is my desire to keep clearly within the scope of my authority in my efforts to conduct the affairs of this agency, but escapes from the jail are too frequent (there have been four since I assumed charge, but one of which has been re-arrested) and in this case the policeman was given particular instructions to guard his prisoner. This prisoner is the one who was since re-arrested, after an attempt on my life. He is now in Helena, awaiting trial before the Federal Court for assault. The offence for which he was arrested, and put in jail, was drunkenness. After his escape I learned that he was also guilty of adultery.

When Sohnia escaped from the jail the policeman was ordered to re-arrest him, but seemed to make no effort to locate him, and flatly refused to obey my orders. It was then that he was brought before the Indian Court, and detailed — not imprisoned — to look after the agency jail for six days. It was through wilful neglect on his part that Sohnia escaped. I am certain he could easily have found this prisoner, for a little later I learned where he was staying, and on going to the house and telling Sohnia to come with me he grabbed a rifle and pointed it at me, threatening to shoot. I succeeded in calming him, however, and, as above stated, he is now awaiting trial before the Federal Court.

For a more definite reply to that part of the question "what offences you refer to the Police Court," I will only say that at present there are in agency jail four persons serving sentences for living in adultery; one for desertion and non-support of his wife; and one for drunkenness. And these are not the only classes of offenders, as is shown by the reward offered by licensed trader G. H. Beckwith, for information that will lead to the arrest of parties or party who set fire to hay, buildings, etc., copy of which I enclose with this letter. But a couple hours ago I received word from Mr. Beckwith that last night some one broke into and burglarized his store, and that some of the Fathers' buildings at St. Ignatius Mission had also been entered. It is only a couple of weeks ago that three parties were convicted by the Federal Court for selling liquor to Indians, and one for introduction of liquor. I have three cases set for a hearing before the U.S. Commissioner tomorrow, for introduction of liquor. Besides Sohnia, whom I have previously mentioned, there are awaiting trial before the Federal Court at Helena one person accused of murder; two for horse stealing; and three for introduction of liquor.

> 2. What the facts are in the case of the Interpreter who was put in jail for one day at the time he was ready to come to Washington with Baptiste Ke-ke-shee. It is said that Ke-ke-shee thought it necessary, in order to prevent the re-arrest of the interpreter, to take six men with him as far as Missoula, and that one of these men was killed by a train while on his way home.

Office letter of December 12, 1908, Education 81329/08, JHD, Subject: Conditions on Flathead; encloses a copy of letter sent the same date to Rev. L. Taelman, S.J., St. Ignatius Mission, in answer to a letter from him relative to moral matters on the reservation, and instructs me "to act with discretion, and not to involve them (the mission people) or Father Taelman in such investigation as you will make of the charges which he has preferred, unless it becomes necessary in the interests of justice."

The evil of which the Father complained was widespread on the reservation, there being many more than the cases which he reported. In the past there had been no attempt to punish such offenders. While I feel that among the very old Indians, who have married according to the Indian custom, and lived together for many years, there may be some excuse, yet there is none for the young educated Indian who knows better, and who, in many cases, deliberately deserts the wife to whom he is legally married, and without even procuring a divorce, lives in open adultery with another woman.

Most of these cases I have taken up. It was necessary to confine some of the offenders in jail. A few of these have been making all manner of threats (I have been reliably informed by an Indian, who did not want his name mentioned, that three different parties had stated they would shoot me on sight) and doing all they could to interfere with my work. As to whether or not I am succeeding in my efforts to suppress this evil I would respectfully request that your Office write Father Taelman for another report. I will state, however, that the mission people have in no manner been spoken of, or brought into, my work for the abatement of this evil.

Jackson Sundown was an offender whose name was not on the list submitted by Father Taelman. He was the interpreter whom Kakashee intended taking to Washington, and who had accompanied Kakashee on such a trip a short time previous. I informed Kakashee that I would not permit Jackson to accompany him as interpreter, as he was living in adultery, was a leader among the gambling and drinking element, and not a proper person to represent the tribe in Washington. Kakashee then stated he would take another interpreter. When the party left the agency I instructed a policeman to see that Jackson did not go with Kakahsee. Jackson's confinement in jail was for but one night, and due to a misunderstanding of my order by the policeman, as the next morning I learned that he had placed Jackson in jail. I immediately released the latter. He then went to Missoula, where he took the place of the interpreter whom Kakahsee had promised me to take, and accompanied Kakashee to Washington.

Missoula is but 27 miles from the agency. The Indians who accompanied Kakashee there I believe went solely for the purpose of getting drunk, for, as nearly as I can learn, all returned in an intoxicated condition. Two, Pascal Antoine and Kaltome, came home on train No. 5, which is due at Arlee at about 11 P.M. Instead of coming to this station they got off at a small flag station called Schley, some distance below Arlee. Both were drunk. They had a small quantity of liquor with them. They were seen hanging around the station, and ordered away by the station agent, who told them that there would be a train in a short time, and it was a dangerous place for them to loaf. From all appearances Kaltome wandered back to the track, laid down and went to sleep, was run over by the train and one leg cut off. This must have happened about two A.M., and he laid there until about four or five A.M., when he was found by parties going home from a dance. They immediately notified this office, and in company with Dr. Heidelman, the agency physician, I went to the cabin of Lassaw, where Kaltome had been taken. While the injury was being dressed Pascal Antoine came in drunk, creating some disturbance, and wanting to fight. It was necessary for me to arrest him and bring him to the agency jail, where he was imprisoned for the second time since his return to the reservation, he having been been [sic] absent for about five years. I understand that he was on the Sisseton reservation, got into trouble, and was ordered off by the Agent there. There was some talk that it was Pascal who was responsible for Kaltome being on the track; that there were injuries on Kaltome's head, and finger marks on his throat. However, a careful investigation by the physician and myself did not reveal any such marks.

I will also state that Pascal Antoine is one of the principal agitators around the agency, attending councils, creating dissatisfaction among the older Indians, who normally are very peaceful in character. I think the information received by your Office was inspired by this man, Joe Pierre, and Henry Matt. Joe Pierre served a sentence in jail for returning to the reservation drunk at the same time as Pascal Antoine and Kaltome did, he being one of the men who accompanied Kakashee to Missoula. He (Kakashee) is also an old offender. On several occasions he has been found helplessly drunk by the policeman at St. Ignatius Mission, where Kakashee resides, and on account of his extreme age, and feeble condition, has been taken care of by the policeman until sober.

Henry Matt has been in four drunken fights within a year, two since I assumed charge. His last offence was drunkenness, and severely beating one Emmanuel Curley, at St. Ignatius Mission. For this he was arrested. The cases against Pascal Antoine, Joe Pierre and Henry Matt were tried by the Indian Court during my absence, Special Agent Thomas Downs being present and officiating in my place. I would respectfully suggest that your Office ascertain his opinion of those cases, and the incidents at that time; also, his opinion of conditions on the reservation at the time I assumed charge.

Henry Matt, although I have no absolute proof in all cases, has been creating trouble and dissention ever since his imprisonment. At the time of his punishment he stated that the Government had no right to punish him, and made the boast that he would have Special Agent Downs fired for his part in the trial. He did not deny his guilt; he simply contended that — in his own words — "the Government had no right to punish one of the leading men on the reservation."

Referring again to Office letter submitting list of Indians living in adultery, furnished your Office by Father Taelman, you are advised that in this list are the names of John Gongras and Emily McDougal. I warned Gongras against this practice, and as the woman was not a member of this tribe I ordered her off the reservation. She returned, and was again ordered to leave. Returning again (to Polson) she was brought to the agency by the policeman stationed at that point. She stated that she intended going home as soon as some money, which she expected, came. As she was not a member of this tribe I did not know what jurisdiction I had in the case, being unable to find anything in the regulations to cover the matter. I was not sure that I could imprison her, but as she had no place to stay I told her she could remain at the jail until her money came. Later she stated she could get work at Evaro or Missoula, and I allowed her to go. She was away but a few days, however, when she returned, with a money order on the local post office, which was the money she had been expecting, she said. She had this cashed, and has left the reservation. I wrote your Office about this case, asking that I be wired as to how to proceed. After she had left the reservation I received a message advising me to take the matter up with the state courts.

I enclosed herewith copy of statement from her, taken by the clerk, Mr. Allen, just before she left the reservation. This shows one of the cases where I have conclusive proof of the efforts of Henry Matt to make trouble.

In the copy of the interview sent with Office letter of November 13, 1908, Land 69971-1908, WMW, the second complaint the Indians had was:

> That they did not want the reservation opened or allotted;
> that none of the headmen or chiefs agreed to the opening of
> their lands and want the country retained for their children in
> order that they may hunt and fish as did their parents.

The fourth complaint is:

> That Joe Dixon has signed the names of their headmen
> and many members of their tribe to a petition to have the
> reservation opened and allotted; and that the headmen and
> others whose names are attached to the petition did not sign it
> and knew nothing about it.

Here is the principal cause for dissatisfaction. The old time Indians, the full-bloods, are bitterly opposed to it. They are still holding councils (two the past week) trying to devise some means for preventing the opening. Your Office can readily understand what trying work it is to have to tell them that their reservation must be opened, and at the same time try to show them the advantages the opening will have for them; to tell them that their children, born after a certain date, cannot be allotted, and at the same time keep them contented. One of the sorest points with the old Indian, and a matter he cannot comprehend, is why, with a large amount of surplus land on the reservation, to which he claims absolute ownership, his (in his words) little babies are to be robbed of land rightfully belonging to them, in order that it may be saved for some incoming white man.

When your Office realized that such men as Henry Matt, Pascal Antoine, Joe Pierre, and others, in the furtherance of their own selfish interests, and their desire for revenge against me for punishing them for their misdeeds, are playing upon this discontent of the old-time Indian, you can more readily understand that no matter how hard I try to smooth matters for them, how patiently I listen to their grievances, it makes a difficult task more difficult, and renders it impossible to entirely elim[i]nate in the short time I have been in charge, all the dissatisfaction and discontent.

3. Whether Indians are expressing dissatisfaction with the conduct of affairs, and, if so, what their complaints are.

To this I must answer **Yes**. Justice to myself compels me to say that in the past the laws of the reservation have not been enforced. Offenders who are now being punished for their misdeeds, and who in the past had escaped punishment, are expressing much dissatisfaction with the conduct of affairs. I have shown heretofore the cause, principally, of dissatisfaction among the older Indians. Another reason is the election of a business committee to represent the tribe in place of the headmen who had formerly transacted tribal business. The council which elected this committee was composed of more than 300 representative members of the reservation and only 13 opposed the selection of the business committee. The mixed-bloods, who form a majority of all the Indians on this reservation, are represented on the committee, they comprising four of the nine members. A very few of the older Indians do not like this, they holding that the old full-blood should transact all tribal business.

Another cause was the reservation of reservoir sites by the U.S. Reclamation Service, and the request that the allottees in these sites relinquish and select lands elsewhere. Until about the first of April they had refused to do this, and it is due entirely to the efforts of this office that they were finally persuaded that it was for their best interests to do so. They were quite bitter against the Reclamation people. I had reliable reports that most of this feeling was caused by outside parties, they telling the Indians that the Reclamation Service would have to pay any price they asked, and as some of the Indians stated they would not relinquish unless they received $20,000.00 and $30000.00 for their relinquishments, I am inclined to think that this was so. At any rate, I had a talk with some of those parties, and informed them that if I could secure sufficient evidence as to who was doing the agitating I would revoke their licenses, and put them off the reservation. Two days later I received a letter from U.S. Commissioner Bailey, of Polson, copy of which is enclosed, showing that my talk had produced the desired effect.

The U.S. Reclamation Service is also having trouble in securing labor, caused largely by agitators near the agency, who are telling the Indians that if they will refuse to work they can force the Reclamation Service to pay higher wages. At present the force on the Jocko project is threatening to go out on a strike. The matter of wages paid by U.S.R.S. was brought to the attention of this office by the Indians, and it is our opinion that the wages paid are very fair; in fact, many white people are only waiting for an opportunity to secure work.

On March 24, last, your Office was written relative to the killing of four Indians on Holland Prairie by the Deputy State Game Warden, to which you replied under date of April 27, 1908, Land-Uses, 72298 and 24518/08. The Indians here insist that at the time the Stevens treaty was made they were told that they could hunt and fish at any time and place they saw fit; and now that they are told that this privilege only gave them the right to hunt and fish off the reservation in common with the citizens of the state, and subject to the state laws, they feel that they have not been fairly dealt with, and have been wrongfully deprived of their hunting grounds. Since this killing threats have been made that "they would get an equal number of white men."

Referring to the forepart of my letter, wherein I state that there is nothing in the Regulations governing certain cases that arise, I beg leave to inform your Office that under date of Apr. 21, last, I wrote your Office asking how to proceed in such a case; whether or not I had authority to go off the reservation and bring back to the reservation escaped prisoners from the agency jail, and also other Indians, members of this tribe, for offences committed here. Near Missoula is an Indian camp which is made a refuge for any offender against the rules of the reservation. I know that one, and possibly more, of the prisoners who have escaped from the jail are at this camp. I enclose copy of letter received yesterday morning from a member of this reservation, asking that I come and arrest some of the parties there. I respectfully request information as to what course to pursue in this case.

I agree with your Office "that a good deal of trouble can sometimes be avoided by giving the Indians straightforward explanations of any difficulties which may arise, especially of any act which might otherwise arouse their suspicions." It is almost unnecessary to inform your Office that the Indian is very suspicious, and that just at this time conditions are probably harder than they have ever been before. I assure your Office that it has been my endeavor to do the right thing, and to work for the best interests of the Indian; but try as I may, it is impossible, at this particular time, and with the conditions such as they are, to avoid some dissatisfaction.

In this letter I have tried to show things just as they are. If your Office desires further information I respectfully ask that an inspecting official be sent. I am confident he would uphold me in what I have done.

I wish to assure your Office that it has been my endeavor to do in every case what I thought right and proper, and with as little annoyance and embarrassment as possible to your Office.

Very respectfully,
Fred C. Morgan
Supt. & S.D. Agent.

[Enclosures 1 and 3 with letter are not reproduced here.]
Enclosure No. 2:

Flathead Agency, Jocko, Montana,
April 8, 1909.

I, Emily McDougall, certify on honor that while I was staying at the police quarters at Flathead Agency one Henry Matt told me that as I was not a member of the reservation Mr. Fred C. Morgan, the Superintendent, could not keep me there. He advised me to enter suit against Mr. Morgan for false imprisonment. Later Mr. McClure and one of his sons told me the same thing. A few days ago, while in Missoula (where I had gone to look for work) Henry Matt came to me and tried to persuade me to see a lawyer and sue Mr. Morgan. I told him to mind his own business; that I knew what I was doing. At no time while I was at the police quarters did I consider it imprisonment. Mr. Morgan told me I could stay there until I got my money from home, which I expected, and with which I intended paying my way home. Later he told me that if I could find work he would let me go, and this he did, as on Monday, March 29, 1909, I told him I thought I could get work at Evaro, but that if I did not I would go to Missoula. Mr Morgan loaned me a horse to go to Evaro, gave me carfare from there to Missoula, and a letter to the Salvation Army Captain asking him to help me find work.

(Sgd) Miss Emily McDougall.

Witness:
(Sgd) H. S. Allen.

Enclosure No. 4:

Missoula, May 3, 1909.

Indian Agent, Ravalli.

Please come out west of town right near Chinamans ranch as soon as you can. Tillie and Geb are making all the trouble they can for me, drinking every night and beat me and trying to sell my tent and horses. I do not even sleep in my tent at night. Cant on account of them making such trouble and trying to kill me. Tillie owns ranch by Mission and has a husband and son there named Joe and husbands name is Chimime and they think you cant do any thing with them and they are not afraid of any thing. I am not drinking myself at all and cant even get a chance to work in the day time or sleep at night for this woman making such trouble here in my tent. If you could please help me by getting this woman away I would be much obliged to you. You know I told you before if I had any trouble I would let you know so I am writing to let you know how she is acting now. She wants to take my boy away from by force and of course I do not want him to go with her. I want you to help me in this so she will leave my boy alone because she would soon kill him. Tillie was in jail here for 10 days and as soon as she got out again the same day she began to drink worse than ever. Black Sam came in and tryed to make them behave and they beat him with a stick and rocked him and nearly killed him right in my tent, so if you could come right away and help me I will be much obliged to you. Its white people live right near here that are writing and they know all about the trouble I have had.

(Sgd) Joe Gaive.

Copied May 8, 1909.
HSA.

Document 28

Charles Allard, Jr., Starts New Stage Line

May 2, 1909

Source: "Allard Stages," *The Daily Missoulian*, May 2, 1909, page 8, col. 2; "Flathead Stage and Express Line," *The Daily Missoulian*, July 19, 1909, page 12, col. 1.

Editors' note: Charles Allard, Jr., started a new stage line through the reservation in 1909.

Allard Stages.

Charlie Allard will run a stage line across the reservation this year. This announcement will recall to old-timers the days when another Charlie Allard — father of this Charlie — operated a stage line over this same road. That was in the days when what is now Flathead county was merely the north end of Missoula county, when there were several towns up there but when only one of them was ever heard of outside the immediate family circle, and that town was Demersville, which was loud enough and busy enough and boisterous enough to make up for any shortage in the number of towns. Demersville was a peacherino, a regular lalapalossa; it was at the head of navigation on the Flathead river, and the steamers which ran up there connected at the lower end of the lake with the stage lines which ran from Ravalli, one of which was the famous Allard line. There were thousands of fine horses in the Allard herds, and from their number were recruited the animals that drew the old Concord stages and made overland records that caused the tenderfoot to wonder, while they were being made, if he would ever complete his journey alive. There were rival lines and the speed contests between these four and six-horse outfits were more like the mad dash of a battery of light artillery than the movement of stage coaches. Those who ever rode in one of these stages will never forget the experience. And now, by purchase of the Weightman line, Charlie Allard has come into possession of the old line. He will equip it with new Concord stages and there will be as fine a lot of horses in the service as were ever seen anywhere. There will be a new record soon.

* * * * * * * *

Source: "Flathead Stage and Express Line," *The Daily Missoulian*, July 19, 1909, page 12, col. 1.

Document 29

Tribal Members Buy Stock in Polson Bank

June 3, 1909

Source: "A Strong Institution," *The Kalispell Journal*, June 3, 1909, page 4, col. 3.

Editors' note: Three tribal members, Wm. Irvine, Chas. Allard, and Mike Matt, were stockholders in the Polson bank. The typesetting for this article was not very carefully done. The errors have been left in the text without using sic.

A Strong Institution
The First National Bank on the Reservation is Estaplished at Polson by Local Capitalists.

When C. B. Harris, president of the Kalispel National Bank, came into the Flathead several years ago, he made the trip overland from Ravalli to Polson across the Flathead Indian Reservation, and he was so well impressed with the splendid country that was soon [to] be opened to settlement that he made up his mind there would be an excellent opening for a National bank in that country, and beleiveing that Polson would be the principal town of that section, he at once commenced proceeidngs for the establishment of the bank. It took many months to unwind the red tape that had to be gone through with, and not until last March was the institution finally ready for business, and then had to be operated as a private bank temporarily.

Last week however, the charter for a National Bank was received, and the bank is now operating as the First National Bank of Polson. A meeting of stockholders will be held in a short time to organize when it is expected that Mr. Harris wil[l] be put in as president and A. W. Pipes, who has been with the bank since its opening, will be made cashier.

Besides Mr. Harris a large number of the best known capitalists of the upper valley are interested, the list of stockholders containing the names of such men as W. N. Noffsinger, J. V. Harrington, Morris Bartleson, H. S. Milbank, J. T. Peacha, W. E. Wells and othres [sic]. Aside from these many of the prominent men of the reservation have sufficient faith in the bank that they have taken stock heavily, including J. L. McIntire, Ober & Gregg, Wm. Irvine, Chas.

Allard, Mike Matt, and other gentlemen who do not care to have their names mentioned.

The business of the bank has been at least fifty per cent greater than was anticipated by the founders, and is a revalation to an outsider who has no idea of the volumn of business carried on on the reserva[t]ion. The bank is admirably equipped to handle any volume of business, as their vault and safe equipment is the same as the Kalispell bank, which is the best to be had any place. From the banking experience of the men behind the First National Bank of Polson, and the immense country that will open up tributary to that town, it is not too much to predict that that institution will become one of the strongest of the financial houses of western Montana.

Document 30

Tribal Leaders Invite All
to St. Ignatius Celebration
June 29, 1909

Source: "And All His Tribe," *The Kalispell Bee*, June 29, 1909, page 1, col. 6.

Editors' note: The Indians of St. Ignatius invited all their Indian and white friends to come to the Fourth of July celebration at St. Ignatius.

And All His Tribe

A Missoula man has received the following unique invitation to celebrate:

"The Indians of St. Ignatius are going to have their annual Fourth of July celebration at St. Ignatius, as usual, beginning Monday, July 5, and lasting until Friday, July 10 — five days — and expect to have a better time than ever before, and hope that you can come and help to make this a big success. They would like to have all their friends come and make camp Saturday so that all be in readiness to begin Monday morning to carry out the program. Please extend this invitation to all members of your tribe and all visiting Indians.

"Ki Ki She.
"Little Andrew.
"Big Johnny Finley.
"Chas. Mullman.
"Lomie Joseph.
"Committee,"

Document 31

Isaac Camille Dies in Accident

July 27, 1909

Source: "Horse Drags Boy to His Death," *The Daily Missoulian*, July 27, 1909, page 1, col. 6.

Editors' note: The tragic 1909 death of a young tribal member made it into the Missoula newspaper.

Horse Drags Boy to His Death
Isaac Camille Is Killed When Animal He Has Roped Runs Away.
Body is Found in Rocks.
Youth Is Thought to Have Startled Steed and to Have Become Entangled in His Lariat — When Discovered Young Man Is Still Alive, but Fails to Regain Consciousness.

Word was received in Missoula early yesterday of the tragic death of Isaac Camille, one of the best known boys on the Flathead reservation. The boy — he was fifteen years of age — was dragged to death on Sunday afternoon by a horse he had roped. No one saw the accident, which is almost unexplainable as the horse that caused young Camille's death was known as a gentle animal.

How It Happened.

It is thought that Camille startled the horse in some way when he threw his lasso and that it started to run as the noose settled around its neck. Whether the lariat was around the young man's waist or twisted about his wrist is not known, as his body was so badly bruised that an investigation was fruitless. The tragedy had as it scene the vicinity of the Camille home, on Post creek, about seven miles northeast of St. Ignatius Mission.

A Riderless Horse.

The first intimation that the boy's father, Louis Camil[l]e, had of the death of his son was when the horse dashed up to the ranch home with its trailing rope. A search discovered the still-breathing body of the youth lying in the rocks of the creek bed, stripped of very vestige of clothing, cut and mangled horribly. The rope had been loosened when the body had struck a boulder of unusual size. It is evident that the body was thrown many feet from the boulder by the shock, judging from the blood and brains left on the big rock. The boy was unconscious and died within an hour after having been found.

Well Known.

Isaac Camille, although only a boy, was one of the best known horsemen, of the reservation. He was known as a daring, brilliant rider and an expert roper. Many have been his feats and his has always been the luck of the seemingly reckless rider. His friends find it difficult to comprehend just how he could have become entangled in his lasso or why a horse that has always been gentle should have run away. The boy was known to every resident of the reservation and had many, many friends. Besides his father and mother, Mrs. [sic] and Mrs. Louis Camille, he is survived by a sister.

Document 32

Frenzy of Whites Applying for Underpriced Land on Flathead August 4, 1909

Source: "Like a Circus Day in Busy Missoula," *The Anaconda Standard*, August 4, 1909, page 5, col. 5.

Editors' note: The frenzy of white people registering for Flathead Reservation land in 1909 made it obvious that the land was offered at bargain prices. In all, 80,762 prospective homesteaders registered in Missoula and Kalispell for chances to get Flathead lands. In 1910, the names of 6,000 of the 80,762 applicants were called at the Missoula and Kalispell land offices, but only a little over one thousand of those 6,000 appeared to begin the process of filing for Flathead Reservation land. On November 1, 1910, the remaining "surplus" lands were opened for general homesteading on a first come, first served basis. The rush for land indicated most of the white homesteaders expected to buy the land for less than what it was worth. Later in the twentieth century, the U.S. Court of Claims decided the tribes had received only $1,783,549 for $7,410,000 worth of land — 24 cents on the dollar. Many tribal members did not follow the newspapers in 1909, but word of the frenzy must have spread around the reservation.

Like a Circus Day in Busy Missoula
More Than Fifty Thousand Registered to Date.
They Come in Trainloads
Coaches Crowded and Every Passenger Must Look Out for His Own Comfort — Official Word from Superintendent Witten.

Special Dispatch to the Standard.

Missoula, Aug. 3. — The following telegram, relating to the closing of the registration for Flathead lands, was received at the United States land office here today and is the final word from the superintendent of the opening:

"Register and receiver, Missoula, Mont. Applications may be sworn to prior to midnight on Aug. 5; must reached Coeur d'Alene before 9 o'clock a.m. on Aug. 9. Give to press. James W. Witten, superintendent."

With two more days yet to run the registration for Flathead lands in Missoula passed the 50,000 mark here today. The rush expected at the last end of the period has materialized and the Garden city today and tonight had the appearance of a circus day or a Fourth of July. Every train on both the Northern Pacific and the Milwaukee roads was loaded with registrants. Standing room was at a premium in many instances and requests for reservations in any direction were met with broad smiles and a shake of the head at the ticket offices. Butte and Anaconda sent big crowds today, but the main rush was from eastern points, people arriving breathless with excitement and in fear that they would be too late to make their applications. There was no trouble along this line, however, and the simplicity of the registration and the dispatch with which the crowds were accommodated continued to be a great surprise to those who were not fully advised as to the plan.

Estimate About Right.

There is now no question but what the estimate made in the Standard some 10 days ago that better than 60,000 would register for the Flathead in Missoula alone will be reached within the next two days. Dan Arms of the land office said: "You can safely say that there has been to date between 4,000 and 5,000 more people registered in Missoula than has been reported by the notaries. I make this estimate not so much from the record kept at the postoffice, but rather from the records of the number of envelopes which have been used by the notaries. The notaries may destroy and fail to account for the blanks for a number of cases, but scarcely a single envelope has been wasted, and on checking up the number at the land office this afternoon we find about this difference."

The result of the count up to 4:30 this afternoon is as follows: Previously reported, 49,939; today's registration, 4,182; total 54,121.

Document 33

Hotel DeMers

The Plainsman, August 26, 1909, page 3, co. 1-3.

HOTEL DeMERS

LOCATED AT

Camas, Montana

This hotel is located on the Flathead Reservation
and is the Headquarters for visitors who
come from cities to spend their vacation. Some of the most wonderful hot springs in
the U. S. are
here.

T. G. DeMERS,   -   -   PROPRIETOR

Document 34

Reservation Town Lots Go on Sale

November 1909

Source: "Watching the Sale," *The Weekly Missoulian*, November 19, 1909, page 2, col. 4; "Flathead Townsites Sell Well," *The Daily Missoulian*, November 22, 1909, page 3, col. 2-4.

Editors' note: Duncan McDonald witnessed the sale of town lots in Arlee, Ravalli, Dixon, Ronan, and St. Ignatius. The list of buyers indicated he and a number of other tribal members purchased lots in the new reservation towns.

Watching the Sale

Duncan McDonald came down from Ravalli yesterday to be present at the auction sale of town lots on the reservation. He was an interested spectator at the sale and watched the progress of business at the land office with interest. "No," said he in answer to a question from a Missoulian man, "I have not come to buy any lots, but to watch others buy them. I wanted to see how the sale went and I wanted to feel the public pulse in the matter. It seems like the beginning of the breakup of the reservation now that these sales are going on; the surveys and the appraisement and the allotment, all were a part of it, but they were so far ahead that we didn't realize their significance. But this lot sale, that is business, and the reservation will soon be a thing of the past."

* * * * * * * * *

Flathead Townsites Sell Well

With each town filled with men who are boosters to the core and who are possessed of the boundless enthusiasm of the homeseeker who has ended his pilgrimage and who is laboring to make his home the best in the state, it is no wonder that the people of western Montana are beginning to sit up and take notice of the five new towns, Arlee, Ravalli, Dixon, Ronan and St. Ignatius, which passed out of the hands of Uncle Sam last week. The result of the townsite sale passed all hope and dreams. It was a marvel to those who saw it and to those who have been following similar sales throughout the country. Never before has the little Missoula land office seen such a sight as it

witnessed last week. In times past it has seen perhaps, events which were more
dramatic but none which were more gratifying and encouraging. Prospectors
and lumbermen have in times past filled the room in their eagerness to file
their claims, but they were there to get temporary holding only. During the last
summer thousands passed through its doors to register for the land drawing on
the reservation but these people, most of them, were trying to get something
for nothing. They were drawn by the gambling spirit rather than the hope of
securing a home or making a business investment. Last week the land office
saw business men who were looking for a safe investment and who planned
to make the property which they bought a place of business excitedly bidding
against each other. It saw the old residents of the reservation bidding their
savings for lots in the towns where they had been born and in which they had
always lived. The people who bought property on the reservation last week are
going there with a spirit which promises much to the new towns and which
can do nothing but make the Flathead valley the finest and most prosperous
in the state.

The buyers themselves are enthusiastic — a glance at the records will show
that one and all they are convinced of the future of the valley. "It is as favorably
located as any other in the country," said one purchaser, "its climatic conditions
are the same as those of the Bitter Root. Its soil is wonderfully good and the
opportunities for the rancher are inestimable."

Among the names of the purchasers are many business men who are known
in Missoula and who intend to erect stores and other places of business in
the new towns. Certain lots in each townsite have been sent aside for school
buildings and the Methodist church of Missoula has purchased lots in each
town making it certain that there will be places of worship there before very
long.

From a financial standpoint the sale was equally successful. The prices
which the lots brought show as nothing else could the interest which was taken
in the sale. Judging from this standpoint the sale interest was great. Arlee,
which was appraised at $2,935 sold at a total of $3,270. Dixon was appraised
at $2,607 and sold for $8,329, nearly three times its set value. Ravalli went
at about double its appraised value, the set price being $1,830 and the selling
price $3,413. Ronan, the little town situated in the very heart of the reservation
surrounded by the most beautiful mountain scenery in the state and set in the
midst of rich farming lands, sold the best. This town was appraised at $2,345
and sold at $8,699, better by nearly a thousand than thrice the set value. St.
Ignatius was appraised at $3,783 and sold for $6,045.

A great many of the purchasers bought varying amounts in each town.
There were about an even 100 individual purchasers, however, as follows:

Duncan McDonald, D. Bergen, C. H. Haven, C. C. Rentfro, T. L. Bateman, S. O. Worden, W. H. Smead company, Joseph Morgan, Mrs. Gleim, Dr. Farnsworth, Thomas Ethel, Otto Shipparin, Joseph McDonald, Joseph Morgeau, Mr. Madson, Henry Pastoll, William Kelley, Mr. Dennison, T. Lacasse, Warren McNeil, G. H. Beckwith, Mr. Sawyer, Mrs. Carter, J. C. Bailey, J. R. Latimer, J. E. Lemire, Jacob Brouchman, Tony Cobell, C. P. Sawyer, R. S. Holland, F. W. Redick, A. L. Demers, H. Parlotte, K. O. White, Charles Schmidt, L. B. Bunch, J. S. Bergh, F. D. Everett, I. F. Hersel, A. M. Frank, Albert Moog, Joseph Mosier, John Kiley, Charles Norton, W. H. Ferguson, Gus Olson, N. C. Adler, Otto Shipright, Marion Hoffstat, Mr. Conture, John T. Bowser, William Simons, W. O. Priest, Dr. Oettinger, J. R. Daily, C. H. Kettlewell, Laren Madison, J. F. Olson, Joe Descants, Daisy McConnell, Harry England, Joe Michaud, Gustav Dubrille, J. B. Beauchemin, Mr. Durand, F. C. Thompson, Andy McGee, J. S. Gould, Joseph Grenier, Jr., George Steinbrenner, Ed DeMers, John Matt, C. Stilliar, William Engle, J. A. Lemire, Rev. J. W. Tait, A. C. Maillem, H. L. Fayette, M. J. Benedict, Charles Hendricks company, A. Sutherland, Arthur Biedalue, Mr. Stinger, A. M. Sterling, Emma Sutherland, Mr. Buckner, C. A. Thompson, George Godfrey, Joseph Bouchard, D. F. Olson, Eli Paulin, Swift Corville, N. McGee, Gilbert La Buff, F. E. Bonner, A. K. Tallefston, W. W. Dunlap, D. Bergen, George Caddick, E. H. Rathbone, J. M. Dawns.

Document 35

A Last-Minute Tribal Protest Against
Opening Reservation
December 28, 1909

Source: Chief Antease, et. al., to Secretary of the Interior, December 28, 1909, part of file 70,266/1908 Flathead 308.2, Central Classified Files, RG 75, National Archives, Washington, D.C.

Editors' note: Right up to the opening of the reservation in 1910, tribal leaders consistently protested against opening the reservation without the consent of the tribes.

Polson, Mont. December 28, 1909

To the Honorable Secretary of the Interior,

Washington, D.C.

Sirs:—

The Whites are flooding in here, and they are taking all kinds of privileges here hunting, fishing, and prospecting this Indian Reservation. This reservation has been set aside for the tribes before going here and not for the Whites; we released the balance of the country to the Whites and we have not interfered with them on the lands we agreed we would let them have, but with our White friends they never cease to crowd us, they are here now right amongst us contrary to the treaty. With the Whites it looks to us like the Government pays no attention to us but instead encourages the Whites to impose upon us. There is a few things which we will demand from the Government before the Whites come on this Reservation, in this we want a settlement with the Government in regard to two strips of land taken away from us by the Whites or the government itself, we don't know how the Whites do these things. But since the treaty there has been taken away from us two large strips of land, the one is where Kalispell is built; our line according to the treaty extended to Columbia Falls to the North but is now at Dayton creek. The Whites are on this Northern portion of our Reservation and we never received a cent for this part of our country; we want a settlement now before anything else takes place. We can't see why our country should all go to the Whites for nothing and us be satisfied, we are not satisfied the way these things are taking place. And there is another thing which we are going to explain to you and which we want you to explain to us, we are informed that the government has cut off of our Reservation a large piece of country and has turned it into a Forest Reserve, if this is the fact what are we going to get out of this part of our country? Are we obliged to let the government have the land for nothing or not? We would like to know the results on this strip of our country. The government knows and we know that our boundry line included the Swan River country, starting from Columbia Falls on the North East to the Skunk prairie on the South East. This part of our country has been taken away from us and we have not received a cent for the same, now we ask a settlement for these tow [sic] strips of our Country before the Whites get in here again. If they are going to take our country like this and us receive nothing, that is just like taking away our lives, and they might as well take away our lives and be done with it. We seek a reply on these questions, I am the chief Antease, acting according to the wishes of the Reservation people.

Awaiting your reply,
Chief Antease, ([blank]) His mark.
Kusto
Batse
George Chief Hat
Williams
Alex Andrew

Chief Antease is acquainted with the parties on this Reservation all the lines conserning it.

Chapter 5

Documents of
Salish, Pend d'Oreille, and Kootenai
History Between 1910-1911

Document 36

Indian Takes Whiskey for Medicine

January 7, 1910

Source: "Consumptive Indian Sent to Jail," *The Daily Missoulian*, January 7, 1910, page 7, col. 2.

Editors' note: Alcohol was illegal for tribal members, but it could also be used as a medicine.

Consumptive Indian Sent to Jail
Law Makes It Impossible for Court to Do Otherwise
— Will Get Pardon.

Helena, Jan. 6. — (Special.) — There have been many instances in the federal court from time to time of the hardship and injustice imposed by the law relating to whisky peddling to Indians, but no more striking instance of its general viciousness and harm was ever given than this morning when William Deschamps, a halfbreed Indian, pleaded guilty to introducing a half-gallon of whiskey on the Flathead reservation July 9, last.

Under the law, the court is allowed no discretion, it cannot take into consideration the time that a prisoner has been in jail while waiting trial, nor can it consider any extenuating circumstances. The minimum sentence is 60 days in jail and a fine of $100, equivalent to 90 days in jail in all, and this sentence was imposed on Deschamps by Judge Hunt.

Deschamps is a consumptive. He is in the last stages of the disease. While in court this morning his emaciated frame was racked and torn by violent coughing. His eyes had that feverish brightness peculiar to people who are far gone with tuberculosis, and the pallor of his sunken cheeks was accentuated by the hectic flush above the cheek bones.

Deschamps explained that he took the whisky on the reservation for his own use, his physician having prescribed it for him. With him it was not a question of law, but one of living. Replying to questions of the court, Deschamps said that he slept little at night, fits of coughing disturbing his slumbers. He has been afflicted with the disease seven years. His condition has grown worse all the time.

Judge Hunt said that it would be a crime to confine Deschamps with the other prisoners at the county jail and expose them to the disease, but under the law he could only impose the minimum penalty and then suggest to the marshal that Deschamps be kept in isolation at the county jail so that the other prisoners do not become infected with the disease.

Judge Hunt directed that Deschamps be examined by the government physician and he assured Deschamp's attorneys, D. J. Heyfron of Missoula and O. W. McConnell, that if his physical condition was shown to be what it seemed, he would be glad to sign a pardon and would do what he could to have Deschamps released as soon as possible. District Attorney Freeman also said that he would be glad to sign a pardon.

If the law were amended so that the minimum penalty was left to the discretion of the judge, the court this morning would not have been forced to send Deschamps to the county jail, where the other prisoners will be exposed to the disease and where also there is every possibility that the building itself will become tainted with tuberculosis germs.

Document 37

Death of Chief Charlo

January 11, 1910

Source: "Chief Charlot Journeys to Happy Hunting Ground," *The Daily Missoulian*, January 11, 1910, page 1, col. 1-2, and page 4, col. 3; "Chief Charlot," *The Daily Missoulian*, January 11, 1910, page 4, col. 1; "Remains of Chief Are Laid to Rest," *The Daily Missoulian*, January 13, 1910, page 1, col. 2-3.

Editors' note: Chief Charlo died just months before the Flathead Reservation was thrown open to white homesteaders. He had fought against the opening, but was spared watching the final act. In 1910, he was a prominent Montanan and his death made the headlines.

Chief Charlot Journeys to Happy Hunting Ground
Famous Old Indian Passes Away in His Little Home on the Reservation.
A Son of Rulers and a Born Aristocrat
A Lifelong Friend of the Whites the Old Man Suffered Many Wrongs at Their Hands Which Embittered Him but He Remained True to His Principles and Died as He had Lived, a King.

Just after the birth of yesterday, while the night yet wrapped the earth in darkness, the spirit of Charlot, hereditary chief of the Flatheads, took flight to the Happy Hunting Ground. The proud old chief — a born aristocrat — gave up the fight reluctantly, stern and stubborn to the very end; he faced death as unconcernedly as he had faced the foes of earthly mould in the 80 years of his life; the journey to the home of the Great Spirit was a fearlessly undertaken as had been a walk to a council fire, where Charlot sat at the head of his chieftains.

In the modest little frame house back of the agency at Jocko, where Charlot had lived all the years since his removal from the Bitter Root, he passed away. Death came at 2 o'clock yesterday morning; it was not unexpected, as the old chief had been for weeks wasting away, yielding stubbornly but surely to the relentless assault of age. There had been no acute illness; it was just the wearing out of the sturdy frame that had for four-score years buffeted the hard blows of fate and the deceit of supposed friends.

Funeral Wednesday.

There was no one with Charlot when he died except his immediate family. The arrangements for his funeral have been made and the burial will take place Wednesday noon at the agency. Several of Charlot's Missoula friends, including Major Catlin, Judge Woody and Judge Sloane, will attend; there will be a great concourse of Indians, as the old chief was the most celebrated figure on the reservation, Burial will be by the fathers of the Catholic church.

Charlot never regarded with favor the opening of the reservation; his unhappy experience in connection with the departure of his people from their ancestral home in the Bitter Root had made him suspicious; he had never fully believed that his tribe would be squarely treated in the present opening, and, had it not been for the assurance given by his old friends, Judge Sloane and Major Catlin, it is doubtful if he would have given even the grudging assent which he accorded to the allotment of lands. It was, perhaps, the kindliest act of fate in all Charlot's life that he was taken away before the reservation was opening and the tribal life of his people ended. He died a chief, as he had lived.

A Son of Chieftains.

Charlot was hereditary chief of the Bitter Root Indians; he was the son of old Chief Victor and the grandson of Three Eagles, the chief who met Lewis and Clark when they entered the Bitter Root valley at Ross' hole on their trip across the continent. He was about 80 years old; he did not know, himself, his exact age.

Speaking last night of Charlot's life, Judge Woody said: "I don't think he was quite eighty, though he may have been. I had him on the witness stand once in a Bitter Root land case and I asked him how old he was. He said he didn't know. Then I asked if he was present at the great council in Grass Valley, when the Stevens treaty was signed — that was July 18, 1855 — and he said he was. I then asked if he was a boy or a man at that time and he said: 'I was a man. I was married.' That would probably make him close to eighty."

At the time of the Stevens treaty, Charlot's father, Victor, was chief. That treaty, signed at Grass Valley, defined the present boundaries of the Flathead reservation and the five confederated tribes were assigned to this reserve as their home. Victor's people, however, were exempt from the agreement; they had acquired homes in the Bitter Root and most of them had become farmers after their fashion. They were allowed to hold these lands.

The Garfield Treaty.

Upon the death of his father, Charlot succeeded to the chieftaincy; he was head of his tribe when General Garfield came out to make the treaty of 1872, which provided for the relinquishment of the Bitter Root lands by the tribe and the transfer of the people to the Jocko valley. The lands were to be sold

Chief Charlo, Salish
Source: Photograph by John K. Hillers, Bureau of American Ethnology,
Washington, D.C.
Photograph Archives, Montana Historical Society, Helena, Montana,
detail from photo 954-526

by the government and the proceeds were to go to the owners as recognized at the time of the removal. This treaty was signed by all of the head men but Charlot; he always insisted that he did not sign it, though the government representatives claimed that he had done so.

This experience embittered the chief. He had always been a warm friend of the whites; he had prevented trouble many times when warfare threatened and had many intimate associations with his white neighbors. He insisted that he had not signed the treaty and he refused to be bound by it. He would not leave the Bitter Root. There were 40 families of his tribe who remained with him and stuck to their Bitter Root homes.

The rest of the tribe went to the reservation. The government named Arlee as chief and this further embittered Charlot. But the Indians never recognized this appointment; Charlot was always their chief.

The grudge which Charlot bore on account of this incident lasted until a few years ago. His only belief was that somebody had forged his name to the treaty; that was natural, as he knew he had not signed it, and all the government agents declared he had signed it. It was in 1904 that the matter was cleared up. Judge Sloane was visiting Charlot at the agency and the chief showed him a certified copy of the Garfield treaty. The question of the supposed forgery was under discussion and Judge Sloane looked at the document with interest.

"Charlot," said he, after he had looked at the paper, "you never signed this and it does not say here that you did."

That was the happiest news that Charlot had had in years. For 32 years he had been told that he had signed the treaty and for the 32 years he had insisted that he had not. The explanation was after all, simple. When the treaty was signed, the clerks of General Garfield had written the names of Charlot and his headmen at the signatory place on the document. Then each of the Indians, except Charlot, had made his mark — his tribal signature — opposite his written name. But there was no mark against Charlot's name. The government men had taken it for granted that the written signature was Charlot's own; the old chief knew that his mark had never been placed on the paper by himself.

He Loved Home.

Until 1891 Charlot and the 40 families lived on in the Bitter Root. The old chief, always an eloquent orator — was never so eloquent as when he was describing the Bitter Root and his love for its mountains and his attachment to the place where reposed the bones of his ancestors. But he became morose brooding over the indignities which he felt had been heaped upon him. The settlement of the valley crowded the white man close upon him and his people; their wonted freedom was circumscribed; there was not the happiness for him and his tribe that there had been in the old Bitter Root. Father Ravalli, Charlot's friend, had died; the ties were loosening that bound him to his ancestral home.

To Jocko.

In 1891 came Major Carrington for another council with Charlot. This pow-wow was successful. Arlee had died and the government persuaded the old chief to resume his place amongst his people. He and the 40 families moved to the Jocko, where, close under the mountains, the old chief ended his days.

His last few years of life were pleasanter than the preceding decade had been. He understood better and the explanation of Judge Sloane of the treaty signatures cleared up a matter that had weighed heavily upon him. He had, too, found a friend whom he could trust in Major Morgan, the present superintendent of the reserve. He felt more reconciled than he had ever been to the relentless advance of the whites.

Tribute of a Friend.

Charlot had, as has been stated, many warm friends amongst the whites. Oldest of these, in point of acquaintance, are Major Catlin and Judge Woody. When a Missoulian reporter yesterday told Major Catlin of the death of the old chief, the major was deeply affected. "I knew Charlot for a good many years,["] said he, "and he was as good a friend as I ever had. It was in 1868 that I met him first; that was at Stevensville and during all the years of my residence in the valley our friendship grew. His ranch was on the west side of the river, next to the Silverthorn farm. He was not much of a rover, even then, and he came to town only once a fortnight or so. But he always came to see us. He was a splendid man, physically and mentally, and he was thoroughly honest. He was reserved to the point of sternness and he was as haughty as a hereditary chief should be. He felt his pride of ancestry and never forgot it. When I was allotting the reservation lands I had my last intimacy with the old man. He was failing rapidly then. I am sorry to hear of his death, but I expected it; I knew he could not last long.

Judge Woody's Eulogy.

"Chief Charlot was one of the most remarkable Indians I never met," said Judge Frank H. Woody yesterday when he was told of the old man's death. "He was honest and straight as a string. His love for the whites was second only to his love for his own race and his dealings with the settlers were always of a character which bred respect and admiration. I had him as a witness in a law-suit once and his straightforward, intelligent answers were a revelation to me. My acquaintance with him dates back a long way. I have never known him to do anything which would in any way detract from his dignity. He was an aristocrat, and he knew it, and he made all with whom he came in contact appreciate the fact. I am sorry to hear of his death, for he was a wonderful Indian, the last great character of his race."

From Judge Sloane.

Judge Sloane was another warm friend of the old chief. Speaking last night of his associations with the old Indian, the judge said: "I have many pleasant and interesting recollections of the old man, but the pleasantest is of the day when I told him and showed him that his signature had never been attached to the Garfield treaty. That lifted such a load from his heart that he smiled and shook my hand. He had been under a cloud for more than thirty years and it had been raised. I don't believe I ever did anything for anybody that afforded me greater satisfaction than this simple deed for old Charlot. He was stern, but he was a true friend, and when you got to know him there was nothing that he would not do for you if he liked you. He was a power for good amongst the Indians."

The Last Days.

Major Morgan of the reservation, speaking last night of Charlot's last days, said: "He failed rapidly toward the last. For several weeks he could not eat much of anything and I was in the habit of taking him a bowl of soup each day. It was an attention which he clearly appreciated and, after he had overcome his unwillingness to be under any obligation to anybody, he enjoyed the broth. The last time I saw him was at 3 o'clock Sunday afternoon. I went up to his house and I could see that he was very low. But he looked up as I leaned over the bed, turned partly over and extended his hand to mine. 'Goodbye,' he said. That was the last I saw of him."

The question of the succession to the chieftaincy remains to be settled. Until now it has been a hereditary office and it would, under that rule, go to Martin, Charlot's son. But there is talk amongst the Indians of the election of either Moise or Louison, who are the head men or subchiefs. Both are good men; Moise is younger and more progressive. It may be that the Indian bureau will seek to prevent the continuance of the tribal government after the reservation opening, but this is not likely.

* * * * * * * *

Chief Charlot.

Charlot, hereditary chief of the Bitter Root Indians, erroneously called Flatheads, is dead. He was every inch an Indian, reserved, taciturn, haughty, self-contained and, at times, resentful. But to those who broke through the crust of his reserve he was known as a loyal friend, as steadfast in that role as when he played the foe. Charlot suffered much; he was deceived and cheated, he was maligned and mistreated; his pride was hurt, but he suffered, most over the wrongs that were inflicted upon his people. Some of his personal grievances he forgave, but he was resentful to the very end against those who had, according to his belief, robbed his people. He was proud and he despised deceit. He had some warm friends amongst the whites; these he trusted to the limit. But to his last breath he cherished a fierce hatred of the men who lied to him and who drove him from his ancestral home in the Bitter Root. And where is the white man who would not have done the same?

* * * * * * * *

Remains of Chief Are Laid to Rest
In the Shadow of the Rugged Peaks Beneath the Cross, Body of Charlot
Is Consigned to Its Eternal Sleep.

In the shadow of the rugged peaks that tower above the valley which was his last earthly home, beneath the cross whose follower he was all his life and amidst the scenes in which he had for many years been a commanding presence — the mortal remains of Charlot, hereditary chief of the Flatheads were laid in their eternal sleep yestereday morning with the solemn rites of the Catholic church.

At 7:30 o'clock Father De La Mott of St. Ignatius mission celebrated mass in the little church at the Jocko agency; burial was an hour later. An unexplained change in the hour of the service disappointed many who had planned to be present at the services. From all parts of the reservation came Indians, as late as noon, the announcement having been made that the funeral would be held at that hour. From Missoula, Major Catlin, Judge Sloane and Artist E. S. Paxson — friends of the old chief — arrived at 11:30.

There would have been hundreds of Indians and whites at the service at noon; as it was, there were scores who had learned of the change in the hour and had hastened to pay their tribute of respect to the old chief.

Following the burial, the subchiefs and many of Charlot's tribe met at Charlot's home. All of the belongings of the departed chief were taken from the house and piled on the ground in front. There they were burned, while a solemn chant was sung by the braves who filled the little house and swarmed about it.

This ceremony was in progress when the Missoula men arrived. Too late for the funeral, they sought to pay their respects to the aged wife of the dead chief and to express to her their sympathy. With them was Michel Revais, the aged blind interpreter of the agency; to the old woman, Michel delivered the message of the white friends of her consort, presenting her with the flowers which had been taken to place on the chief's bier. The old interpreter explained to the widow the significance of the flowers and she was visibly pleased.

When the Indian guests departed, the white visitors had another talk with Charlot's widow. She was able to express to them her appreciation of their presence and to Artist Paxson she granted permission to take any or all of the photographs which her husband had gathered in recent years. Some of them Mr. Paxson brought home for use in a work which he contemplates.

"We had an interesting visit," said Major Catlin last night. "Major Morgan had a conveyance for us at the station at Arlee and we were taken quickly to the agency. There, everything possible was done for us. While we were sorry that we could not reach there in time for the church funeral, we were glad that we went, as we were able to express to the widow and the tribe some of the respect in which their chief was held by the whites who knew him."

"There is not much talk about the succession," said Judge Sloane in answer to a question from a reporter last night. "Moise is the probable candidate unless the succession is determined to be hereditary. But the Indians are now too much cast down to consider the matter. They mourn sincerely the death of their chief."

Document 38

Tribal Member Arrested for Murder at Dance

January 11, 1910

Source: "Killed at a Dance By Redskin," *The Daily Missoulian*, January 11, 1910, page 10, col. 4.

Editors' note: Dances that resulted in violence received newspaper attention. Gatherings that were peaceful were not noted. In this case, Louis Scullina may have murdered Blackfoot Antoie in self-defense.

Killed at a Dance By Redskin
One Good Indian Well Planted, Is the Result of a Reservation Fight.

A warrant was issued by United States Commissioner Smith yesterday for the arrest of Louis Scullina, a fullblood Indian, who is now in jail at the Flathead agency, charged with the murder of Blackfoot Antoie, a Piegan halfbreed. The killing took place at Scullina's home on Camas Prairie, Thursday morning at 4 o'clock. A dance had been in progress which was attended by Indians from all parts of the reservation, amongst them Antoie, who had gone up from his home on Post creek, near the mission.

The remoteness of Camas Prairie from the agency delayed the news. As soon as it was received Major Morgan sent Policeman Fred Normandin from the mission. Normandin and one other policeman reached Scullina's house Saturday night and arrested him without trouble. He was brought back to the agency where he was given a hearing.

Scullina, Dave Couture, Francis Selpah, Jim Buckman and Leo Paul were examined as witnesses. All of these were at the dance at Scullina's and Buckman and Paul claim to have witnessed the killing. All of the witnesses agreed that the killing was in self defense. Their stories agree in all details.

Antoie Was Ugly.

Scullina had invited the Indians to a dance at his house. Blackfoot Antoie and his wife came from Post Creek. Antoie, who had a bad reputation, was quarrelsome and signalized his arrival at Camas by announcing that he intended to kill some of the Camas bunch before he left. That was a pleasant starter and Antoie continued to play his part along the lines laid down in his advance notices.

Scullina had a lame knee and didn't dance. About midnight he turned the dance over to Dave Couture and Francois Selpah as masters of ceremonies and climbed up to the upper room in his log house. Antoie continued his disturbance through the night but inflicted no personal injury upon anybody but his wife, Louise, whom he abused in sportive sideplay.

A Good Indian.

About 4 o'clock in the morning Antoie climbed up stairs to find Scullina. He found him lying on his blankets, fixing some eagle feathers with a knife. Antoie said he had come up to kill Sucllina, adding: "You're as good as dead now." With that he jumped upon Scullina before Buckman could hold him back, he having followed up stairs to prevent trouble. As Antoie jumped, Scullina pushed at him with the hand holding the knife. Antoie fell back in Buckman's arms, gasped a couple of times and died. There was a small knife wound just over the heart.

Antoie was buried, Scullina was arrested and is now held at the agency jail. Antoie was a bad man by reputation; three weeks ago he nearly killed his wife by beating her with a club. Scullina used to be a good Indian but recently he has been drinking whenever he could get booze and has been ugly. Couture says there was a jug at the dance; the other witnesses say they didn't see any.

Document 39

Duncan McDonald Ponders Indian Future

January 28, 1910

Source: "M'Donald Deplores Conditions," *The Missoula Herald*, January 28, 1910, page 2, col. 4.

Editors' note: Duncan McDonald could always be counted on for some good quotes. He had definite opinions about reservation affairs.

M'Donald Deplores Conditions
Ravalli Man Declares Flathead Indian Is Given No Industrial Chance.
Redskin Is Restrained
Man Who Has Spent All His Life With Copper Race Believes
Each Should Be Given Liberty to Dispose of Allotment.

"I don't know what will ultimately become of the poor Indian," said Duncan McDonald this morning, "but under the present system exercised in his control he cannot become better; he can only grow worse."

Mr. McDonald is a resident of Ravalli, and has lived in this part of the country since his birth in 1849. Having some Indian blood himself, and having lived with and near them all his life, he is in a very good position to judge their needs and observe the difficulties under which they labor.

"There is no inducement held out to the Indian of today," he continued. "He is expected to live much in the same way as any other public charge and to be coddled and taken care of like a child and like any other being not thrown into the world to have the rough edges knocked off and learn the value of a dollar, he is rapidly becoming indolent and useless. He is not naturally lazier than his white bother. In every country and among all human beings we find two classes of men — the shiftless and the ambitious. Like all other races the Indian has these two classes. Some of our people will always be indolent and accomplish nothing, even as there are such characters among the white race. Others would be ambitious and accomplish great things if they only had the chance.

Should Be Allowed to Sell.

"The Indian now has an allotment of 80 acres, where he, a few decades ago, had the whole of this part of the state. That isn't so bad in itself. In fact,

Duncan McDonald
Source: Photograph Archives, Montana Historical Society, Helena, Montana,
photo 943-624

it would be right were he accorded the privileges of sale he should have. Of course, if they could sell their land there would be some among them that would throw the purchase price away in less than three months, but others would have money with which to go in business and probably become wealthy. But the government says, 'We must protect this class of Indians even if we sacrifice the prudent, the sagacious and energetic.'

"I ask you this: If all the land in the world should be divided into equal tracts and every man given an equal tract, how long would it be before the profligate and spendthrift would have neither land nor money to show for his allotment? The shrewd and economical man would have his land or the money and probably that of his shiftless neighbor. Why should not the government say, "We will allow no man to sell or mortgage his land. There are some among us who cannot transact their own business and we must protect them even at the sacrafice [sic] of the others."

Pratects [sic] Shiftless.

This is the policy the government carries out with the Indian — it protects the shiftless, the e'er-do-well, the shiftless, the ne'er-do-well [sic], and worker, the saver, and the careful. You take away all the incentives of ambition from us, and then you call us lazy and of no account. You give us a piece of land and then won't let us sell it. You keep our money from us for fear that we will spend it. And still you wonder why the Indian accomplishes little. Give him a chance to work out his own destiny.

"Stop coddling and spoiling him and make him stand on his own feet. When you do you will find that he is much like any other man. You will find some of us weak and incapable, but you will find others of us strong and competent, able to make a sustenance for ourselves and lay a tidy sum away for a rainy day."

Document 40

Martin Charlo Elected New Salish Chief

January 28, 1910

Source: "Indians to Elect New Chief," *The Daily Missoulian*, January 28, 1910, page 6, col. 5; "Son of Old Charlo Elected Chieftain," *The Anaconda Standard*, February 7, 1910, page 1, col. 5.

Editors' note: Duncan McDonald commented on a new law that would allow tribal members to sell two thirds of their allotments. Charlo's son, Martin, was elected as the new Salish chief.

Indians to Elect New Chief
Flatheads Will Choose Charlot's Successor and the Date Is Announced.

Duncan McDonald was in town yesterday from his home at Ravalli. He talked interestingly of conditions on the reservation. There is plenty of news there these days and the Indians share with the whites the interest in the approaching opening. Concerning the news that there is a probability that the Indians will be permitted to sell their allotments down to 20 acres each, Mr. McDonald said: "I believe it all depends upon the way the proce[e]ds of the sale are handled, whether this will be a benefit to the Indians or not. If the sales are made, as The Missoulian said, under the direction of proper advisers and if the proceeds are held in trust by the government, the sale may be a good thing. If, however, the money is given to the Indians to handle, it will not last them any time at all. I hoped you had a copy of the bill. It will have to be well managed or it will not be as good for the Indians as to hold and lease their lands."

Mr. McDonald says the death of Charlot affected all the Indians; even those of the other tribes relied upon the old chief for counsel and they miss him much. "Charlot used to talk to them just like a preacher," said Duncan. "He advised them and they always listened to him. His last instructions to his tribe were to elect an adviser from their own number. He knew that the tribal relation will be broken up as soon as the reservation is opened and that the title of chief will not mean what it has always signified. But he felt that they should have one of their old men delegated to counsel them as they would listen to one whom they had thus chosen.

Martin Charlo
Source: Photograph Archives, Montana Historical Society, Helena, Montana,
photo 954-501

"Thus the chieftaincy of the tribe ceases to be hereditary. Charlot's son will not be chief; the man chosen may be called chief but he will be only a counsel. There are several candidates for the position; it seems certain that the tribe will heed the advice of Charlot. But there are not many of the old men who are fitted for the place; they are old and they are a thousand years behind the times; they have not the intellect of Charlot and will not be able to advise as well as he did.

"The election will be held the fourth day before Ash Wednesday. That has bene [sic] decided upon already."

* * * * * * * *

Son of Old Charlo Elected Chieftain
Flathead Indians Select Him for Place Held by Father.

Special Dispatch to the Standard.

Missoula, Feb. 6. — Martin Charlo, hereditary successor to the leadership of the Flathead tribe of Indians, was unanimously elected to that position, made vacant by the recent death of his father, Chief Charlo, by the council of red men which gathered at the Flathead agency for the purpose today. Practically all of the remaining members of old Charlo's band of Bitter Root Indians were present and only these had voice in the election, which proceeded practically without any opposition and only consumed a few minutes' time. It was evident that the election had been prearranged and was thoroughly understood to those who had a voice in the deliberation.

Chief Martin Charlo was born on the Missouri river near Helena 53 years ago. He figured quite prominently with his tribe and his father in the early fights with the Sioux, Crow and Blackfeet Indians, but since the civilization of the tribe was commenced he has not been conspicuous in its affairs and his life has been uneventful. During his life and chiefship of his father he probably did not wield even as much influence as sub-Chiefs Moise and Louson.

Document 41

John Matt Has Locating Business

February 1910 — January 1911

Source: *Lake Shore Sentinel* (Polson, Mont.), February 11, 1910, page 1, col. 5; "Cutler & Matt," *The Daily Missoulian*, April 17, 1910, part 3, page 7, col. 1; "John Matt," *The Daily Missoulian*, September 16, 1910, page 10, col. 6; "John Matt," *The Daily Inter Lake* (Kalispell, Mont.), October 14, 1910, page 7, col. 5-6; "Flathead Timber Land for Sale," *The Daily Missoulian*, January 28, 1911, page 11, col. 6.

Editors' note: John Matt had worked with the appraisal commission and later developed a business helping white homesteaders select land. He started the locator business in partnership with a white man named Cutler, but soon operated independently.

John Matt of Jocko was in town [Polson] for several days this week. Mr. Matt is in the locating business and is getting everything in readiness for the reopening of his office at Jocko. He handled about one hundred of the lucky ones last fall, and expects several times that number in the spring to go over the lands and pick out a claim. Mr. Matt was present at the election in Jocko last Sunday of a chief to succeed the late Chief Charlot, and he says that in talking with the men high up in the councils of the tribe he learned that there was considerable feeling against permitting the Indians to sell their lands, as it was the general opinion that the younger ones would only squander any money that they might receive for their lands.

* * * * * * * *

Cutler & Matt

Locators on

Flathead Lands

CITY OFFICE, 317 HIGGINS
AVENUE
F. N. TRUESDALE, Manager

Stage Office, Ravalli

To Homesteaders: Under our system we give you a complete tour of the reservation, checking off for you on our locating map, on which we give you every 40-acre tract subject to entry you may desire. We have in the field with you our Mr. Matt, who appraised all the land for the government, and whose knowledge of the reservation is complete and correct. In addition, we assist you at Kalispell and Missoula on filing days, as you may direct. We are prepared to care for you on arrival. Call at office for further information.

Source: "Cutler & Matt," *The Daily Missoulian*, April 17, 1910, part 3, page 7, col. 1.

John Matt

Locator of Flathead Reservation Land

Lifelong resident of reservation. Former commissioner of appraisement board.

Reliable information. .Moderate fee

Missoula Office:
327 NORTH HIGGINS AVE.

Source: "John Matt," *The Daily Missoulian*, September 16, 1910, page 10, col. 6.

JOHN MATT

Locator Flathead Indian Lands

Now is the time for all persons residing near the Flathead Indian Reservation to select homesteads. REMEMBER! Come at once with me and take a trip through the reservation and make your first choice.

DON'T WAIT UNTIL TOO LATE

Write or call and see me for further information

Office: RAVALLI, MONTANA

Source: "John Matt," *The Daily Inter Lake* (Kalispell, Mont.), October 14, 1910, page 7, col. 5-6.

Flathead Timber Land For Sale

I have 80 acres of fine saw timber on level ground; soil good, easy to get to; one mile from Schley station; one of my allotments. For further information write to

JOHN MATT, Jocko, Montana.

Source: "Flathead Timber Land for Sale," *The Daily Missoulian*, January 28, 1911, page 11, col. 6.

John Matt
Source: Virginia Matt Brazill, Arlee, Montana

Document 42

Leaders Oppose Bill to Allow Indians to Sell Most of Allotments February 15, 1910

Source: Antoine Moiese, et. al., to Secretary of the Interior, February 15, 1910, from file 99,865/1909 Flathead 013, Central Classified Files, RG 75, National Archives, Washington, D.C.

Editors' note: It seemed that Joseph Dixon could always come up with new ways to transfer Indian owned assets to non-Indian ownership. Tribal leaders understood the future costs of such sales.

Jocko, Montana, February 15, 1910.

The Honorable Secretary of the Interior,
Washington, D.C.
(Through the Commissioner of Indian Affairs.)
Sir:

We, the undersigned, members of the Flathead tribe of Indians, residing on Flathead Reservation, Montana, and representing the tribe, respectfully request that Section two of the bill introduced by Senator Dixon of Montana to amend the Act of April 23, 1903 [1904], providing for the survey and allotment of the Flathead Indian Reservation, be stricken out.

This bill provides that an Indian having an allotment of irrigable land may dispose of sixty acres of same. We believe that such a bill would cause the white people to get the Indians in debt, then sell part of their allotments and use the money to pay these debts. This would only make the Indians poorer. Also, we believe that 80 acres is a small enough piece of land for the Indians to make a living upon. We have no objection to a bill allowing the Indians having timbered allotments to sell their timber, but we do not want them to sell any of their land. We respectfully protest against the passage of the act as at present proposed.

Also, we respectfully request that an additional allotment of 80 acres of grazing land be made to each member of the tribe. The allotted land comprises only a small part of the reservation, and we feel that we are entitled to more of the reservation than we have received through allotment.

Very respectfully,
Antoine Moiese, his x mark
Louie Pellew, his x mark
Jerome Big Hawk, his x mark
Pattee Kakashee, his x mark
Charlowain, his x mark
Martin Chalwain, his x mark
Henry Chalwain, his x mark
Abel Telgosta, his x mark
Aleck Finley, his x mark
Que-que-cho, his x mark
Kayola, his x mark
Alex Matt, his x mark
John Matt
Louie Lumprey, his x mark.

Document 43

Tribal Members Invest in Dayton Businesses

February 24, 1910

Source: Excerpts from "Dayton Townsite Notes," *The Daily Inter Lake* (Kalispell, Mont.), February 24, 1910, page 8, col. 4-5; "Dayton Mercantile Company," *The Kalispell Bee*, April 19, 1910, page 4, col. 2; "National Banks for Somers and Dayton," *The Daily Inter Lake* (Kalispell, Mont.) April 1, 1910, page 4, col. 1-2.

Editors' note: Mike Matt invested in Dayton land and businesses, and Arthur Larrivee developed housing lots in Dayton.

Dayton Townsite Notes

. . . . . .

Arthur Larrivee, who owns land adjoining this town is making plans to have 40 acres surveyed into lots which will form the first addition. He has just completed a six room cottage which is now occupied by Mr. and Mrs. Oscar Bartch. . . . .

Ben Lawles of Kalispell and Chas. Frost, Jacob Knerr and Mike Matt of Dayton, beside establishing their general merchandise store have also incorporated for $20,000 to conduct general banking business. This capital is paid up and the bank will be under the direct charge of Mr. Lawles. The bank fixtures have been ordered and are expected to reach here soon. Mr. Frost is now in Chicago purchasing the stock for this company's store. It is understood their new stock will be very complete. Besides groceries, dry goods, men's furnishings and hardware they will have carriages, farm wagons and farm implements. . . .

Y.

Feb. 20th, 1910.

* * * * * * * * *

Maxime "Mike" Matt
Source: Carol Kuntz, Pablo, Montana

Dayton Mercantile Company
Notice of Intention to Increase Capital Stock.

Notice is hereby given in accordance with a resolution of the board of Trustees of the Dayton Mercantile Company, a corporation, organized and existing under and by virtue of the laws of the State of Montana, that a meeting of the stockholders of said Dayton Mercantile Company, has been called by said Board of Trustees, to be held on the 31st day of May, 1910, at ten in the forenoon, at the office and prinicpal [sic] place of business of said Dayton Mercantile Company, at Dayton, Flathead County, Montana, and that the purpose of said meeting is to consider and act upon the proposition that said Dayton Mercantile Company increase the amount of its capital stock from $20,000 to $75,000, for the purpose of extending and increasing the business of said corporation.

By order of the Board of Trustees of the Dayton Mercantile Company, said corporation.

Dated this 11th day of April, 1910.

— J. B. Lawlis.
— Charles Frost.
— Mike Matt.
— Jacob Knerr.

Trustees of Dayton Mercantile Company, a corporation.

* * * * * * * * *

National Banks for Somers and Dayton

Somers and Dayton are to be favored with national banks according to an application filed by two groups of men, in each case headed by C. B. Harris, president of the Kalispell National bank. At Dayton, the building to be occupied is now nearly ready, and as soon as fixtures arrive, the bank will be opened and operated as a private institution pending the receipt of the charters. Each will be capitalized for $25,000. The incorporators are: First National bank of Somers; C. B. Harris, J. B. Lawlis, A. H. Moberly, P. C. McStravick and R. P. Austin; for the First National bank of Dayton; C. B. Harris, C. I. O'Neil, J. S. Knerr, Charles Frost, Mike Matt, John Herman and J. B. Lawlis.

Document 44

Tribal Members Invest in Polson Bank

March 18, 1910

Source: "Polson's Second Bank Opened for Business," *The Lake Shore Sentinel* (Polson, Mont.), March 18, 1910, page 1, col. 5.

Editors' note: Charles Allard, Jr., and J. O. Dupuis were among the investors in the new Polson bank.

Polson's Second Bank Opened for Business
Directorate of the New Institution Is Made Up Largely of Local Men.

Last Saturday the Flathead County State Bank sent its announcement to the public proclaiming its readiness for the transaction of business in its line.

The directorate of the new bank with the exception of Aug. Peterson, is made up of local men whose abilities are so favorably known as to need no comment. Mr. Peterson is cashier of the First National bank of Harvey, N.D., and is also president of several national and state banks in the states of Minnesota, North Dakota and Montana. He is president of the Polson bank, J. A. Trow vice president, and Walter W. Brant cashier.

Associated with these men in the enterprise are several prominent financiers of the west and middle west, including J. S. Pomeroy, cashier of the Security National Bank of Minneapolis, Minn.; J. M. Keith, president of Missoula Trust and Security Bank; H. C. Keith, president of First National Bank of Kalispell; John O. Hanchett, S. S. Renfew and J. J. Reiner, capitalists of Harvey, N.D., and O. E. Osthoff, H. M. Billesby and R. J. Graff of Chicago. The local stock holders comprise the names of F. L. Gray, C. M. Sutherland, Charles Allard, J. A. Trow, J. O. Dupuis, F. P. Browne, Arthur D. Maynard, and W. W. Browne.

The building occupied by the institution is at the corner of B and Third streets. Its location and construction are well adapted to the needs of the business, and the interior equipment is in every way modern and up to-date, the counter being of quarter sawed oak and having three marble slab dealing plates. The other articles of furniture match nicely the interior fittings and counter, the whole interior being admirably lighted through ample-sized windows from two sides.

The construction work and organization was begun last fall and has continued through varying conditions until the completion has been effected, and now Polson has another institution that will be of material use to the city and in which its people may well have a pardonable pride.

Document 45

Tribal Member Complains
About Boundary Survey
March 23, 1910

Source: Angus P. McDonald, "Memorandum Regarding Flathead Reservation," March 23, 1910, from file 27,727/1910 Flathead 304.3, Central Classified Files, RG 75, National Archives, Washington, D.C.

Editors' note: For many years the tribes sought to correct a mistake in the survey of the southwest corner of the reservation boundary. The claim was finally settled for a cash payment in the twentieth century. The question of missing payments for the tribal chiefs under the 1855 treaty was also still outstanding in 1910.

Memorandum Regarding Flathead Reservation
March 23, 1910

From an examination of the maps and plats showing the Flathead Indian Reservation in Montana, made by me with Mr. Angus P. McDonald, it appears that the maps of the Office and the maps showing the reservation as given in Royce's Cession are correct insofar that they follow the description of both the cession and the reservation given in the Treaty of July 16, 1855, with the Flathead Indians, except that the description of the southern boundary of the reservation is not definite when it come to the description of the SW corner thereof, there being no definite point given in the description from which to locate said SW corner.

Mr. McDonald says that the older Indians are positive in their contention that the reservation was not surveyed strictly in accordance with their understanding of the description as given in the treaty, thus depriving them of considerable land which they feel should have been included in the reservation but which was not. The suggestion was made by Mr. McDonald that, in view of the necessity for satisfying the Indians, it would be wise, even at the expense of the tribe, to cause a careful investigation of this old matter to be made as promptly as practicable with a view to determining exactly where the Indians think their reservation boundaries ought to be, so that this old matter can be adjusted, and if their contention is found correct a claim made for compensation.

This matter ought to be adjusted as promptly as possible in order to prevent another such tragedy as happened last year when a number of Indians were killed while in the forest reservation adjoining the Indian reservation, on the supposition and in the full belief that they were on their own lands. This is the second time that Indians have been exterminated on lands in the same region when they believed themselves to be well within their rights and on their own reservation. A proper adjustment of this matter would prevent any such occurrences in the future.

Another matter which Mr. McDonald desires to call attention is the claim of some of the Indians who are heirs of the old head chiefs of the tribe, that the salaries stipulated to be paid the head chiefs by Article V of the Treaty were not fully paid to them, but in many cases only a partial payment was made. He asks that this matter and any other questions that may arise when an inspector is sent to the reservation be carefully and fully investigated.

Angus P. McDonald

Document 46

Duncan McDonald Named Tribal Judge

April 17, 1910

Source: "New Tribal Judge Named," *The Daily Missoulian*, April 17, 1910, page 7, col. 2-3.

Editors' note: Duncan McDonald supported Flathead Agent Fred Morgan's reform agenda on the reservation and acquiesced to the allotment policy.

New Tribal Judge Named

An important change in the tribal affairs of the Bitter Root tribe of Indians [was] made yesterday at the Jocko agency. Lewison, who has been judge for a long time, was deposed from his high office and in his stead Duncan McDonald will henceforth officiate. The action was taken after the return of Major Morgan from a tour of duty which had taken him away from the agency for some days. Since the death of Chief Charlot, Lewison has been a disturbing factor in tribal matters and has created considerable dissatisfaction among the Indians. He was one of the candidates for the chieftany [sic] when the tribe elected a successor to Charlot and was disappointed that he was unsuccessful in his aspirations. He is one of the older men of the tribe and has held the judgeship for many years. Lately his influence has been all for the bad and it has been the cause of so much trouble that the change became a necessity. Duncan McDonald, the new judge, is the best known man of Indian blood in the northwest. He is thoroughly educated, a man of high natural intelligence and thoroughly in sympathy with the Indians and imbued with the spirit of fair play. He has been for years one of the most trusted advisers of the Indians and his influence will, it is certain, be potent for good in the tribes. The accompanying portrait of Duncan McDonald was taken upon the occasion of the visit of Secretary Garfield to the agency; this was one of the rare occasions when Duncan donned his Indian garb. His dress is one of the very few real Indian costumes in the tribe; it is made in the old Indian fashion and according to the Indian regulation.

Document 47

Louison Complains About Actions of Agent Morgan April 18, 1910

Source: Chief Louison to Commissioner of Indian Affairs, April 18, 1910, and Chief Clerk to Chief Louison, April 28, 1910, from file 33,159/1910 Flathead 056, Central Classified Files, RG 75, National Archives, Washington, D.C.

Editors' note: Louison complained about being fired from his position as tribal judge. Tribal leaders were also upset about the new reclamation project which was being built with tribal money and mostly benefitted the white homesteaders.

Arlee Mont.
Apr. 18, 1910.

Commissioner of Indian Affairs,
Washington D.C.
Dear Friend

All the Indians on this Flathead Indian Reservation are not satisfied of the assistance of their Agent Fred C. Morgan.

Mr. Morgan do not assist the Indians as he ought to, he travels a great deal and he is hardly at his Office or said tribe's Agency during the time he has been here. Mr Morgan has been with us as an Agent for the pass of two years, and he has not done anything to benifit the Indians on this Reservation.

Thirty-five years ago I was appointed by Indians and the Agent to be in position as Chief and Judge of this Reservation of Flathead Indians.

On April 16, 1910, I was relieved from the duty as Judge by the Agent Fred C. Morgan.

I wish to ask you to give an information, the reason why I was relieved from my duty as Judge.

I also wish you to give full information about the irrigated ditches and Canals on the said Reservation. In some parts of the Reservation needs the irrigation and some parts of it has plenty of water and the irrigation is not necessaryly.

Judge Louison, Salish
Source: Photography by F. A. Rinehart, National Anthropological Archives,
Smithsonian Institution, Washington, D.C.
photo 03545500 (Photo lot 59)

Further more I wish to ask you to give me the permit of making a trip to Washington D.C. on a visit to President and yourself.

Will enclose my letter by best regards to you all, whom in Indian Office from all your Indians of Flathead Reservation.

I remain Yours Truly
Chief Louison
Arlee, Mont.

* * * * * * * *

Apr 28 1910

Visit to Washington.

Chief Louison,
Through the Superintendent Flathead Indian School,
Jocko, Montana
My friend:

I have read your letter of April 18, 1910, in which you request to be allowed to visit Washington to discuss conditions on the Flathead Reservation.

While I am always glad to meet Indians from the various reservations to discuss with them important matters relative to their welfare, I see no necessity for you to visit Washington at this time, especially in view of the fact that the Secretary of the Interior on April 13, 1910, granted authority for a delegation of Indians from the Flathead Reservation with an interpreter to come to Washington to confer with the Office on matters of business concerning the respective tribes. It is probable that all of the matters you write about will be discussed with the delegates, and that they will be able to give you full information on their return home.

Your friend,
(Signed) C. F. Hauke.
Chief Clerk.

Document 48

Zephyre Courville Invests
in Plains Mercantile Store
April 29, 1910

Source: "Have Faith in Plains," *Sanders County Democrat* (Plains, Mont.), April 29, 1910, page 3, col. 5.

Editors' note: Tribal member and cattleman, Zephyre Courville, invested in a meat market and later a mercantile store in Plains.

Have Faith in Plains
Prominent Young Business Men Organize Mercantile Company

Pinning their faith to Plains and the adjoining country George Cooper, Z. Courville, Dave Clements and H. J. Morrison, well-known business men of the city, have formed a company to be known as the Sanders County Mercantile company. The articles have been filed with the clerk and recorder and the new firm is in active operation.

The company is capitalized for $50,000 and its life is to be forty years. It will combine the Cooper & Courville Meat Market and the Morison & Clements Merchandise store. The new firm will engage in the wholesale and retail butchering business, hay grain, produce and everything that is carried in an up-to-date department establishment.

As soon as the material can be secured a modern building 50x100 will be constructed on the sight [sic] where Waller's barbershop and the market now stands. The plans of the building call for concrete blocks, pressed brick and a large plate glass front, with a full basement.

Messrs Morrison and clements came here about a year ago and purchased the Kruger & Peterson store and by their courteous treatment of customers retained the patronage of the old store and as the population increased added to their list of friends. Mr. Morison for a long time was connected with the M. M. company at Missoula and Mr. clements made scores of friends when he was with the De Borgia Mercantile company. Both gentlemen are progressive business men and in every respect most desirable citizens.

George cooper has friends all over Sanders county, having been almost raised here. He and Z. courville became owners of the Russell Meat Market a little over a year ago and have been doing a splendid business. Mr. courville and Mr. cooper are so well acquainted in the valley it is almost needless for the Democrat to introduce them to the public. The first named is a prominent cattleman of the reservation and by the shrewdness, and honest dealing, with his neighbors has amassed a small fortune. For years these gentlemen have watched Plains and have come to the conclusion that no better place could be found to get good returns for an investment.

Document 49

Prospectors on Reservation and Delegates to Washington May 5, 1910

Source: "Indians Plan to Select Envoys," *The Daily Missoulian*, May 5, 1910, page 1, col. 6; "Proceedings of General Council of Indians of Flathead Reservation, Held at St. Ignatius, Montana, on Monday, May 9, 1910. . . .," and Fred C. Morgan to Commissioner of Indian Affairs, May 10, 1910, from file 47,604/1909 Flathead 056, Central Classified Files, RG 75, National Archives, Washington, D.C.

Editors' note: The reservation was opened to white prospectors to file mineral claims, and tribal members met in council to elect six delegates and an interpreter to go Washington, D.C., and negotiate with the Indian Office.

Indians Plan to Select Envoys
General Council Is Called for Monday, May 9, at St. Ignatius Mission.
Delegates to Capital
Flathead, Pend d'Oreille and Kootenai Tribes Are to Name
Representatives and Interpreter — Lure of Gold Draws Hundreds of
Prospectors to the Reservation.

(Staff Correspondence.)

Ravalli, May 4. — A general council of the Indians of the Flathead reservation has been called for next Monday, May 9. The session of the tribes is to be held at St. Ignatius and will begin at 10 o'clock in the morning. The purpose of the convention of the red-men in the mission town is the selection of six delegates and one interpreter to go to Washington for a conference with the officials of the Indian office. The official call, which is signed by Major Fred Morgan, superintendent of the reservation, says that the delegates are to take up Indian affairs with the government bureau. Two delegates are to be chosen from the Flathead, two from the Pend d'Oreille and two from the Kootenai tribes. The Indians are very much interested in the coming election, which has been advertised from one end of the reserve to the other, and there will probably be a large attendance.

Gold's Lure.

The lure of gold is drawing hundreds of prospectors to the Flathead, the rush beginning Monday morning. Before daylight a small party had started from Ravalli for the hills, and a similar outfit left Arlee at the same time. From Polson and Ronan — from all the towns on the reservation, as a matter of fact — comes reports that the country is overrun by mining men. All sorts of rumors of rich strikes are heard on every hand, but the rhapsody of the optimist is almost invariably counterbalanced by the Jeremiad of the pessimist. There are those who believe that the reserve is to be found rich in ore, principally gold and copper, but there are many old-time prospectors who believe that the metal found will not be in paying quantities. Certain it is, however, that the territory is to be given a thorough test, that every gulch and creek bed that looks at all promising will be examined as with a microscope.

Two Stories.

There are two stories that are typical of the reservation right now. The first is that of an old man — his name is supposed to be Patrick McGee. It is said that McGee, an old-time prospector, came onto the reservation 34 years ago and found what he considered a claim of fabulous value. He was chased from the reservation by the Indian police. In good order Patrick retired, vowing that he would return, should the tract ever be opened to the white man. Thirty-four years afterward — last Monday — he was back and his was one of the first claims to be filed. He is now 82 years of age, and he has carried the secret of his prospect on the reservation through the principal mining camps of the world.

Here is the other story. Joe Grenier and J. T. LaCasse returned to Ravalli Monday night with seven nuggets of gold, found within a few miles of this town. The nuggets are small, very small, but the two men claim that they have located a good placer claim. Both are experienced and much weight is attached to their statements. The claims of the old man and Grenier and LaCasse are close together.

* * * * * * * * *

Proceedings of General Council of Indians of Flathead Reservation, Held at St. Ignatius, Montana, on Monday, May 9, 1910, for the Purpose of Selecting Six Delegates and One Interpreter to Visit Washington, D.C., Under Authority Granted by the Secretary of the Interior on April 13, 1910, No. 30610.

The council was called to order at 10:55 A.M., by Superintendent Morgan, with Duncan McDonald acting as temporary interpreter. The following notice, calling the council, was read to the assembled Indians:

Notice

A General Council of all the Indians of Flathead Reservation
is hereby called to meet at St. Ignatius Mission, Montana, on
Monday, May 9, 1910, at 10 o'clock A.M., for the purpose of
selecting six delegates and one interpreter to visit Washington,
to confer with the Indian Office on matters of general interest
to the tribes. Two delegates each will be selected from the
Flathead, Pend d'Oreille, and Kootenai tribes.

(Sgd) Fred C. Morgan,
Superintendent.

Flathead Agency, Jocko, Montana,
April 30, 1910.

A motion by Hector McLeod, seconded by Wm. Irvine, to adjourn until
one P.M., was adopted by the council.

Council reconvened at 1:50 P.M. Called to order by Superintendent
Morgan, who stated that nominations of interpreters to act during the council
would be considered.

Duncan McDonald was nominated by Chas. Allard;

Alex Matt was nominated by Duncan McDonald;

Baptiste Marengo was nominated by Mose Delaware.

The vote for two interpreters resulted as follows:

Duncan McDonald, 86; Baptiste Marengo, 63; Alex Matt, 31. Duncan
McDonald and Baptiste Marengo declared elected to act as interpreters during
the council.

Superintendent Morgan stated to the council that they had been called
together for the reason that the Secretary of the Interior, through the Indian
Office, had granted authority for six delegates — two from the Kootenai tribe,
two from the Flathead tribe, and two from the Pend d'Oreille tribe — with
one interpreter, to visit Washington for the purpose of conferring on matters
of interest to the Indians of the reservation, and that the council should select
the persons they wished to represent them.

The Superintendent asked that nominations be made for three judges of
the election.

Martin Charlo was nominated by Alex Big Knife;

Antoine Moiese nominated by Chas. Allard;

Thomas Antiste nominated by Duncan McDonald.

No further nominations being made, the council voted that Martin Charlo,
Antoine Moiese and Thomas Antiste act as judges during the election, there
being no objection to any of the nominees.

Nominations being then in order for delegates to Washington, the following nominations were made for the Flathead tribe:

Martin Charlo, by Big Hawk;
Baptiste Marengo, by John Decker;
Duncan McDonald, by Hector McLeod;
Antoine Moiese, by Basil Finley;
Mose Delaware, by Joe Deschamps;
Louie Pierre, by Duncan McDonald;
Victor Vanderburg, by Eneas Concow;
Charlie Cooper, by Chas. Kicking Horse;
Sam Resurrection, by Pierre Lamoose.

The following nominations were made for representatives of the Kootenai tribe:

Antiste, by Peter Finley;
Mose Auld, by Hector McLeod;
James Sloane, by Henry Clairmont;
Chas. Allard, by Mose Delaware;
Bazil Finley, by John Decker;
Wm. Irvine, by Mack Couture;
George Riley, by Andrew Bullhead;
Lassaw, by Eneas Concow.

The following nominations were made for representatives of the Pend d'Oreille tribe:

Michel Pablo, by Wm. Irvine;
Joe Dupuis, by Henry Clairmont;
Paul Sh-lako, by Charles Cooper;
Eneas Concow, by Chas. Allard;
Charlie Michel, by Hector McLeod;
Alex Matt, by John Decker;
John Finley, by Baptiste Marengo;
Frank Ashley, by Joe Deschamps;
Alex Finley, by Antoine Pariseau;
Martin Chalwain, by Duncan McDonald.

Duncan McDonald made the following motion, seconded by Chas. Allard, and adopted by the council, there being no objections:

"That the nominees of each tribe receiving the highest number of votes be declared elected to represent their respective tribes."

Each person attending the council was allowed to vote for two persons to represent each of the three tribes.

The vote resulted as follows:

To represent the Flathead tribe:

Martin Charlo,	58;
Duncan McDonald,	55;
Antoine Moiese,	50;
Baptiste Marengo,	21;
Chas. Cooper,	8;
Sam Resurrection,	8;
Victor Vanderburg,	5;
Louie Pierre,	5;
Mose Delaware,	3;
Pierre Lamoose,	3;
Louison,	1.

To represent the Kootenai tribe:

Chas. Allard,	71;
Thomas Antiste,	62;
George Riley,	19;
Mose Auld,	19;
James Sloane,	17;
Wm. Irvine,	9;
Bazil Finley,	8;
Lassaw,	6;
Koostatah,	3.

To represent the Pend d'Oreille tribe:

Charlie Michel,	48;
Michel Pablo,	46;
Joe Dupuis,	36;
Alex Matt,	26;
Eneas Concow,	19;
Paul Sh-lako,	12;
John Finley,	10;
Frank Ashley,	2;
Martin Chalwain,	16;
Alex Finley,	1.

Martin Charlo and Duncan McDonald, for the Flathead tribe; Chas. Allard and Thomas Antiste, for the Kootenai tribe; and Charlie Michel and Michel Pablo, for the Pend d'Oreille tribe, having received the highest number of votes cast for representative of the respective tribes, were declared duly elected.

It then being in order, the following nominations were made for interpreter to accompany the six delegates to Washington:

Baptiste Marengo, by Mose Delaware;
Mose Auld, by Lassaw;
Peter Irvine, by Mack Couture;
Loma Bad Road, by Chas. Allard.

There being no further nominations, the matter was placed before the council, and the following vote resulted:

Mose Auld,	23;
Baptiste Marengo,	15;
Peter Irvine,	1;
Loma Bad Road,	14.

Mose Auld, having received the highest number of votes, was declared duly elected.

Flathead Agency, Montana,
May 9, 1910.

I certify on honor that the above is a true and correct record, taken by me, of proceedings of general council held at St. Ignatius Montana, on May 9, 1910.

H. S. Allen
Clerk, Flathead Agency.

Flathead Agency, Montana,
May 9, 1910.

I certify on honor that I was present at the general council held at St. Ignatius, Montana, on May 9, 1910, and that the foregoing is a true and correct report of the proceedings.

John H. Heidelman
Physician, Flathead Agency.

Flathead Agency, Montana,
May 9, 1910.

I certify on honor that the foregoing record of proceedings of general council held at St. Ignatius, Montana, on May 9, 1910, is true and correct.

Fred C. Morgan
Superintendent.

* * * * * * * *

Department of the Interior
United States Indian Service
Flathead Agency, Jocko, Montana,
May 10, 1910.

Delegation.

The Honorable,
Commissioner of Indian Affairs,
Washington, D.C.
Sir:

Referring to office letter of April 22, 1910, enclosing copy of an authority granted by the Secretary of the Interior on April 13, 1910, for the visit to Washington, D.C., of a delegation of two Indians from the Kootenai tribe, two of the Flathead tribe, and two of the Pend d'Oreille tribe, and one interpreter, I have the honor to report that on April 30, 1910, I issued a call for a general council to be held at St. Ignatius Mission on Monday, May 9, 1910, for the purpose of electing the delegates. There is herewith enclosed copy of the proceedings of this council, and I respectfully request that same be approved, and that the six delegates and one interpreter chosen by the general council be authorized to visit Washington.

Martin Charlo, Charlie Michel and Antiste are full-bloods, while Michel Pablo, Chas. Allard and Duncan McDonald are half-bloods. Mose Auld, interpreter, is a half-blood Indian and Chinaman.

About 200 Indians attended the council, the full-bloods being in the majority, many of the mixed-bloods (who constitute a majority of the Indians of this reservation) not being able to be present owing to the fact that they were busy plowing and putting in their crops. One hundred and ten Indians voted, of whom 59 were full-bloods and 51 mixed-bloods. Many of the older full-blood Indians refused to vote, owing to the fact that they claimed the mixed-bloods should not be represented in the delegation, and should have no voice, or vote, in the selection of the members of said delegation.

I would respectfully request that your Office advise me when this delegation is desired in Washington, in order that I may inform the members and have them prepared for leaving here.

I would also request that your Office advise me whether the expenses of this delegation is to be reimbursed them after the trip has been completed and upon presentation of sub-vouchers, or is there any way whereby I could advance money to certain members of the delegation, as, in my opinion, the three full-bloods, who are practically penniless, would have a great deal of trouble in raising the necessary amounts of money.

Very respectfully,
Fred C. Morgan
Superintendent.

Document 50

White Prospectors Flood Reservation

May 11, 1910

Source: "Mineral Locations Numerous," *The Daily Missoulian*, May 11, 1910, page 2, col. 2.

Editors' note: Duncan McDonald had been a trader and operated a hotel and other businesses, but also had a continuing sideline of prospecting over the years. His financial success in prospecting seemed to have been limited. McDonald also commented on his upcoming trip to Washington, D.C.

Mineral Locations Numerous
Duncan M'Donald Tells of the Stampede for Gold
on the Reservation Lands.

Duncan McDonald, judge of the Flathead tribes, is in the city, having come down from the reservation last night. He confirms the reports that have been current about the activity in locating mineral land on the reservation since the opening and says that the stampede shows little sign of abatement.

"The hills about Ravalli before daylight on the morning of the opening, looked like a Fourth of July illumination,["] said Mr. McDonald last night. "There were lanterns moving everywhere, all the way down to Dixon. Many locations were made and the locators are s[t]ill at it. Some of the notices are posted in rediculous [sic] places.

"Two or three years ago," continued Mr. McDonald, "I was riding out from Ravalli with Dr. Heide[l]man, the agency physician, when I noticed a hole that had been freshly dug in the hillside. I at once thought somebody had been prospecting, as I had known of mineral in that hill for a good many years. So I left the doctor and hastened back to my home for the necessary equipment. Then I hurried to where I had seen the hole. It was there, all right, freshly dug and there were some faint traces of mineral. While I was wondering who had been digging there, I noticed two things. First, I thought the hole had some of the appearance of a coyote den. Second, I saw a camp of Crees down at the foot of the hill. I went down there and asked the Indians if they had been digging and they showed me some young coyote pelts; they had dug out the den and captured the coyotes for the bounty. I was up there the other day and I found that somebody had posted a location notice at that old coyote hole. That ought to make a good mine; the Crees made money out of the digging they did there.

"Some years ago there was what looked to be a rich bit of float found along the river above Dixon. Above it was a ledge of barren quartz but the man who found the float thought it came from that ledge. When the opening came, he took one of his old friends — a Missoula man whom you know well — and showed him the ledge. It didn't look good to the Missoula man and he said so. I was along and when the Missoula man asked to see the float and it was shown, I was able to tell him where the ledge cropped out a mile or so away. It was peculiar rock, streaked with black, and easily recognized. The prospector said the black streaks were rich in gold and silver. So some claims were located on the ledge and the matter was to be kept a secret. Like all secrets it leaked out and during the next few days that vein was followed all the way down to Dixon and located. The locators think they have something good but I saw an assay certificate of the black rock and it runs a little over twenty cents to the ton. There will be some abandoned claims there when it is known how the assay went."

Mr. McDonald has some specimens of galena that look good; he found them on the reservation and he is going to see what there is in the lead that he has discovered.

As to the election at the mission, which was mentioned in The Missoulian's special news yesterday, Mr. McDonald said, "It is not easy for Pablo and me to leave for the trip to Washington and we don't like to take it, but we are going — and we are going because we feel that it is time the Indians had proper representation in the councils at Washington. For years they have been sending old, prejudiced men, ignorant Indians, who have done the tribes no good and who have made a mess of things generally. The vote of the Indians which defeated the discontented element, shows they are tired of it."

Document 51

Hotel Demers

The Plainsman, May 26, 1910, page 5, col. 5-6.

Hotel DeMers
Camas, Mont.

Headquarters for Stage Lines
running to Plains on the West
and Dayton on the East.

Stage Three Times a Week to
Dayton. Daily Stage to Plains,
Except Sundays.

Rates $1.50 up   T. G. DeMers, Prop.

Document 52

Flathead Reservation Delegation to Washington

June 1910

Source: "Ready to Go East," *The Daily Missoulian*, June 7, 1910, page 12, col. 2; "Indian Delegation to Washington," *The Daily Missoulian*, June 8, 1910, page 14, col. 3; "Indian Delegation Starts Home," *The Daily Missoulian*, June 20, 1910, page 2, col. 1.

Editors' note: The June 1910 delegation to Washington, D.C., mixed official business with tourist sites in the East. No transcript of the negotiations has been found.

Ready to Go East.

Duncan McDonald came down from Ravalli yesterday morning and spent the day in Missoula. This morning he will be joined by Major Morgan and the members of the delegation which goes to Washington to discuss with the Great White Father matters which pertain to the Indians in connection with the reservation opening. The delegation, it will be remembered, was chosen by the council of the tribes last month. Duncan McDonald received the highest vote and had the support of the best element; his selection guarantees that the cause of the Indians will be properly presented. The party will go east on No. 4 this morning. "I have not been in Washington for seven years," said Mr. McDonald yesterday. "There are some pleasant things about the trip but it is very tiresome and the ride is so long and hot at this time of year that I do not anticipate much pleasure. There are, however, some important matters of business that must be talked over and it is best that they should be discussed by men who know the conditions and are disposed to be fair. I hope to be able to do something for my people."

* * * * * * * * *

Indian Delegation to Washington
Representatives of Flatheads Start on Their Way to Capital.

A delegation from the Flathead Indians passed through this city on No. 4 yesterday morning on the way to Washington. Indian Agent Morgan, who is accompanying the delegation, when asked in regard to the objects of the trip, said that the definite reason for which the delegation was called to Washington had not been mentioned, but that it was more than likely that the boundary question would come up at the meeting. Duncan McDonald, sub-chief of the tribe, said that he did not know why the party had been called to Washington. "But," said the chief, "I am going to Washington with the firm intention of doing all I can for the Indians. I know Uncle Sam is poor, but the Indian is a whole lot poorer, and I will try to the best of my ability, to wrest the last possible nickel from the reluctant grasp of the government. I regret greatly that Sam Ressurection cannot accompany us on this trip; we shall miss him very much."

The party was composed of Duncan McDonald, William Irvine, Charles Allard, Chief Antiste, Charles Michelle and Moses Auld.

* * * * * * * *

Indian Delegation Starts Home
Flathead Representatives, After Pleasant Visit, Leave Washington.

Washington, June 19. — (Special.) — Led by Indian Agent Major Morgan, the Flathead Indians tonight turned their faces toward Montana. They will stop one day to view Niagara and then head straight for home. The entire delegation with the exception of Charles Allard, who left for New York, called on Senator Dixon at the capital this afternoon. They expressed their appreciation of the courtesies extended them during their visit and related with enthusiasm their experiences while in Washington. They told of their visits to Mt. Vernon, Arlington, the Washington monument and the capitol — for they had visited every point of interest in the city. At the monument old Insiste [Antiste], the Kootenai chief, flatly refused to ascend in the elevator unless the rest of the delegation made the trip in safety first.

After his comrades had come down the old Indian went up and thought the view "almost exqual [sic] to top Mission mountains."

"George Washington heap big man to have such big tombstone," he remarked. At the navy yard the Indians looked long and hard, and the sight of 2,000 men making cannon for Nncle [sic] Sam. When they were told that a big 13-inch gun before them would carry a shell from St. Ignatius to Polson, Charlie Mitchell remarked that he "would like to have it on Wild Horse Island."

Duncan McDonald and Billy Irvine each occupied the chair of Vice President Sherman and of Speaker Cannon, a recess having been given for the moment. The rest of the delegation insisted that Duncan McDonald try his hand at presiding in the supreme court, being chief justice of the reservation.

There was no chance there, however, and he went away disappointed.

The Indians met the commissioner on Indian affairs and discussed reservation matters with him. They expressed themselves as being well pleased with their visit and left for home in high spirits.

Document 53

Tribal Members Attend Circus In Missoula

August 14, 1910

Source: "Indians at Circus Heap Good Time," *The Daily Missoulian*, August 14, 1910, page 2, col. 2-3.

Editors' note: Special events like the circus brought many tribal members to the big city for a day.

Indians at Circus Heap Good Time
Streets Were Dotted From Early Morn with Groups of Redskins.

The circus has come and gone, and there were heap big Indians here. The two railroads brought carloads to Missoula. The various Indian tribes represented were the Flatheads, Pend d'Oreilles, Kalispells, Nez Perce and Coeur d'Alenes. Some of the oldest citizens saw Indians they have never seen before. The Coeur d'Alenes are not well known here. They came on the new Puget Sound road. All wore picturesque clothes. The blankets, the handkerchiefs and the moccasins were full of color. Some few carried dark brown tastes in their mouths from the night before. Ten or twelve had to pay fines for being drunk and down before they got to see the elephant, but, as a rule, they were right side up with care.

Early yesterday morning, long before the streets began to be crowded, Indians planted themselves along Higgins avenue, dropping down in groups on doorsteps, wherever they found them convenient, and sitting there hour after hour, apparently listless and satisfied. A few of them leaned against awning poles and other supports, with legs crossed, and hands folded. All were waiting — as they seemed to be doing most of the time — for something. Nothing excited them. Everyone of them appeared to be fixed for life.

A Trio.

Among the first to locate was a trio — two bucks and a s..... It became attached to the steps of the Western National bank. The s.... of the party wore a green handkerchief on her head, black and white blanket, a red skirt and yellow moccasins. The men were covered from neck to heel in green blankets and wore large, light tan hats. Their apparel was new and fresh looking. They remained there half the morning, silently and indolently watching the passing throng. Now and then one or all of them would say "Huh!" when a redskin acquaintance passed. Some time up in the day a man and his woman came along, traveling out in the street, sheep fashion, the husband six or eight feet in advance of his wife. They walked blocks that way. "Huh!" they grunted to the trio at the bank. "Huh!" responded the three. This was all the conversation they indulged in. The lord and master of that couple had the ends of his hair done up in green silk, and slouched along with his hands in his trouser pockets.

At the southeast corner of the Florence hotel two elderly s....s, the one fat and full-faced and the other lean and wrinkled, stood nose to nose, jammed in a corner, talking neighborhood gossip. Both were clad in red.

In Court.

But, back on Stevens street, between Front and Main, quite a different scene was being enacted. Judge Small was dealing out justice to the ones who had fallen victims to the old Indian enemy, firewater. John Lumprey, Joe Badrode, Bucks Peon, Antoine, Martsley, Bighawk, John McDonald, Saul Gavin, Peter Adams, Joe Turnage and Jim Buckman were fined, permitted to pay up and go to see the parade. Badrode was a little the worse for wear. He had lost his blanket and was hardly presentable. His fat sides — and they are as fat as those of Mark Twain's shot-fed toad — stood out over his tight little trousers.

"Your blanket," said Chick White, "is somewhere else, not at the jail."

"Huh! Dom blanket!" was the short reply.

Later, however, when seen on Higgins avenue, he was robed in his beautiful pea green blanket; his chubby face just as round as ever, and his smile just as sour.

The happiest Indians were the little ones with their hands full of circus day toys. Most every small boy or girl had a gaudy balloon. The manufacturers of the tiny airships had colored some especially for the sons and daughters of the red men.

A S.....

A lone s...., wearing a bright red handkerchief, a brown and red blanket, a red velvet skirt, and tan moccasins, stood an hour or longer in front of the Grand theater. She seemed to be in a deep study. Other Indians passed and bowed, but she welcomed not their salutes. A smiling buck, in passing, tarried a moment to pay his respects, but she encouraged him not.

"Pocahontas must be pouting," suggested a bystander. "She cares not for attention."

Standing on the curbstone, eagerly watching the parade, was a mother and her papoose. The baby was not old enough to take it in, but the woman was enjoying everything. Among the interested spectators near her was Joe Lamoose, one of the most graceful as well as persistent dancers on the Flathead reservation. There was a downcast look about his face. He would rather have been in war bonnet and dress suit doing a dance to the tone of "Hey Ho!" Circuses do do [sic] not enthuse him.

Effigy.

None of the Indians liked the effigy on the Uncle Sam wagon. As it passed they murmured in one voice, "Huh!" with a contemptuous rattle to it. The horses and the highly colored wagons and uniforms delighted them.

During the day two got in serious trouble. One fell, head foremost to the basement of the Montana block, and was rendered unconscious and had to be taken to St. Patrick's hospital, where he remained in that condition the rest of the day. He had been drinking heavily. Michael Stevens was his name.

Pascale Antoine was arrested by Detective McDonald and locked up on a horse-stealing charge. He, it is alleged, sold beasts that belonged to another.

Judge Small was merciful to the Indians who fell by the wayside Friday night. He let them out on fines leaving each money enough to go in the circus on, and they seemed very appreciative.

Document 54

Indians Required to Have Hunting Licenses on Reservation
August 1910

Source: "Indians Must Have License," *The Missoula Herald*, August 17, 1910, page 6, col. 2; Charles E. Redeker to Commissioner of Indian Affairs, August 26, 1910, and Second Assistant Commissioner to Charles E. Redeker, September 3, 1910, from file 71,147/1910 Flathead 302, Central Classified Files, RG 75, National Archives, Washington, D.C.

Editors' note: Montana state moved aggressively to take control of hunting on the reservation after the opening — even by tribal members. Needless to say, tribal leaders were very upset.

Indians Must Have License
Ruling of Attorney General Galen Is of Interest Generally.
May Have Good Effect
Useless Slaughter of Game May Be Prevented — Likely That Indians Will Not Take Kindly to Game Warden's Order.

Making it clear that all persons, including Indians, must procure a license before being permitted to hunt or fish within the state of Montana, Attorney General Albert J. Galen has submitted the following:

Helena, August 15, 1910.

Mr. Henry Avare, State Game Warden, Helena, Mont. Dear Sir: Replying to your request for an opinion as to whether or not Indians are required to obtain a license before they may be permitted to hunt or fish within the state of Montana, I will say:

By the act of congress, April 23, 1904 (35 U.S. St. L. P. 302) all the Flathead Indian reservation situate within the state of Montana was directed to be surveyed for the purpose of being disposed of under the general provisions of the homestead, mineral and townsite laws of the United States, to be opened to settlement and entry by the proclamation of the president; the president's proclamation has heretofore been issued and the land embraced within the said reservation opened to settlement under provisions of this act. By the act referred to, and the president's proclamation, the Flathead reservation was abolished.

Section 1976, laws of Montana, 1907, as amended by the act of the 11th legislative assembly, provides:

"Every person who is a bona fide resident of the state of Montana, under the provisions of section 1976 of this code, who desires to hunt, kill or catch any of the game animals or game birds, and desires to take, kill or catch any fish in any of the streams of this state, must first obtain a license therefor by paying the officer issuing such license the sum of $1."

Indians residing within the former limits of the Flathead Indian reservation in the state of Montana are residents of this state.

Since the Flathead Indian reservation was abolished I am of the opinion that any Indian or other person desiring to hunt or fish within the bounds of what was formerly the Flathead Indian reservation, in the state of Montana, is required to first obtain a license under the provisions of section 1976, as above quoted. Yours very truly,

Albert J. Galen.
Attorney General.

Mr. Avarre [sic] has a number of the copies of the opinion in his possession and he is taking them to the Flathead reservation with him, where he will supply them to his deputies.

It has always been the custom of Indians on the reservation to hunt and fish without a license. In fact, all who have a strain of Indian blood in them, and who have allotments under the regulations adopted by the government, have been practically conceded this right, the white settler alone taking out licenses at the different points where they are kept for sale by the game warden's deputies. It will be a hard matter to make the Indians understand the meaning of the new order of affairs, but it will undoubtedly be accomplished, for the Indians of the reserve, while they submit grouchily to the many new conditions which have arisen since the white farmer came to the reservation, do not kick up any fuss, and finally bow to the inevitable, if their head men say it is all right.

* * * * * * * *

The Shawnee Fire Insurance Co.
of Topeka, Kansas
Chas. E. Redeker,
Agent
Polson, Montana, Aug. 26, 1910.

Hon. Commissioner of Indian Affairs,
Washington, D.C.
Sir: —

At the request of Chief Thomas Antiste of the Kootenai tribe of Indians, and in the interest of the Indians resident on the Flathead Reservation generally, this protest is made against the decision of the Attorney General of Montana, requiring the indians to procure hunting and fishing licenses. The enclosed clipping will explain the cause of the present grievance. The Indians have not the money to expend in licenses, moreover by habit they consider that the untrammeled right to hunt and fish belongs to them, and should this order be brought into effect it will work a hardship upon the Indians as well as making them feel that almost their last treasured privilege is being taken away from them.

I believe that such a ruling as that of the Attorney General of the State should not obtain, personally I believe that the State in this transgresses its rights in attempting to impose this act upon them. The Chief urges you to favor the Indians by replying to this letter at once, as their hunting season is near at hand.

Very respectfully,
Chas. E. Redeker

* * * * * * * *

Sept 3, 1910

Rights of Indians
to fish and hunt.

Mr. Charles E. Redeker,
Polson, Montana.
Sir:

Your letter of August 26, 1910, written at the request of Chief Thomas Antiste of the Kootenai tribe of Indians and in the interest of the Indians residing on the Flathead Reservation generally, protesting against the requirements of the State of Montana that licenses by obtained by Indians who desire to hunt and fish, has been received.

It was clearly decided in the case of Ward vs. Race Horse (163 U.S. 504), that the rights of Indians to hunt and fish within a state irrespective of treaty stipulations or provisions are subordinate to the state laws.

Section 1976, Laws of Montana, 1907, as amended by the Act of the 11th Legislative Assembly of the State of Montana provides that persons who desire to hunt and fish in the streams of the state must first obtain a license therefor. The Office is of the opinion that this provision applies to Indians as well as other residents of the State of Montana.

With the settlement of the state by homesteaders and the rapid increase in population it is necessary that restrictions be placed upon hunting and fishing in order to preserve for future generations such game and fish as now remain within the borders of the state. The Indians should be willing to comply with the laws of the state made as well for their benefit and protection as well as for the white people and the Office can see no good reason why the Indians should not comply with the game and fish laws of the state as same as the other laws.

Very respectfully,

(Signed) C. F. Hauke.

Second Assistant Commissioner.

Document 55

Forest Fires on Flathead Reservation in 1910

August 1910

Source: "Fires Dead," *The Daily Missoulian*, August 31, 1910, page 10, col.
2

Editors' note: As in the rest of the Northern Rocky Mountain Region, the 1910 forest fire season was unusually bad on the Flathead Reservation.

Fires Dead

Major Morgan was in town last night from the reservation with the good news that the fires which have caused trouble up there are all out. "There has been comparatively little damage done," said he. "When we consider the extreme dryness of the forests and the favorable conditions for a big fire, it is remarkable that the blazes have been confined to such small areas. The fires have been kept out of the most valuable timber on the reservation and much of the forest that has been burned over has not suffered commercially. This gratifying result is due to the efforts of the soldiers who have worked willingly and zealously wherever they have been assigned. Officers and men have vied with each other and, even before the rain came, the fires were well under control. You can safely say now that the fires are out. There have been no fatalities, but Captain Bates of the Twenty-fifth infantry, who is in command of E and H companies, had a narrow escape at Perma. With 50 of his men, Captain Bates was fighting an ugly fire in the hills when the blaze flanked the company and nearly cut off the only way of retreat which lay through a narrow gulch. The fire in the rear was discovered just in time, and the men got out all right; but it was a close call. The rains have finished the work of the soldiers in fine shape. It if had not been for the organized fight, the loss in the timber would have been incalculably greater than it is."

Document 56

Indians Visit Buffalo Bill Show

September 3, 1910

Source: "Red Men," *The Daily Missoulian*, September 3, 1910, page 12, col. 2.

Editors' note: Many tribal members were drawn to the Buffalo Bill Show in Missoula in 1910.

Red Men

The day brought, also, the Indian, in all his glory and with all his family. For today is the date of the Buffalo Bill show, and Mr. Indian has been waiting and watching for it, lo, these many days. In instances, he stayed home from the three circuses that have been here already this season, in order that he might come down from the reservation in royal style to say farewell to Buffalo Bill. Buffalo Bill is the idol of the Indian — he and his show. The Flatheads, Kootenais, Coeur d'Alenes, Kalispells, Pend d'Oreilles and the rest of the reds in this part of the country never knew Colonel Cody as a foe, and they have not inherited the dread of him and the fear of his prowess that the plains Indians hold. They know him as the big showman, the handsome dresser, the daring rider and the boss of the most interesting aggregation of attractions that could be brought together to tempt an Indian. So he came down to Missoula yesterday with his wife and his children, and they are all waiting this morning for the big show to begin.

Document 57

Duncan McDonald Attends
Homestead Selection
September 1910

Source: *The Missoula Herald*, September 9, 1910, page 6, col. 5.

Editors' note: Many tribal members were outraged at the forced allotment and opening of the reservation. Other Indians may have been spectators to the process, but only Duncan McDonald was noted in the newspapers.

Duncan McDonald, a prominent representative of the Flathead Indian tribe of Ravalli, is among the many visitors in Missoula today. Mr. McDonald is also an interested spectator at the local land office where the selection of Flathead land is taking place.

Document 58

Indian Policeman Drowned

September 20, 1910

Source: "Indian Policeman Drowned in Lake," *The Kalispell Bee*, September 20, 1910, page 1, col. 3.

Editors' note: An Indian policeman fell into Flathead Lake and drowned after drinking alcohol.

Indian Policeman Drowned in Lake

Antoine Paraiso, the Indian policeman who brot [brought] to Kalispell, last Wednesday, the Bonners Ferry Indians who were arrested on a charge of kidnaping, fell from the deck of the "City of Polson" just as she was leaving the narrows Thursday evening, and drowned before he could be rescued.

Paraiso was on the upper deck with a number of white men when it commenced to sprinkle rain. The others went below, but the Indian insisted on staying on top, and it is thot that he fell overboard and before a lifeboat could be lowered and assistance reach him he had gone down for the last time, and was only recovered after dredging the lake for some time. While in Kalispell, the Indian had imbibed quite freely of fire-water, and when the boat left Somers he was plainly under the influence of liquor. He sobered up some on the trip, and his friends, who had been watching him closely, believed he was all right. But when the boat left Rollins he opened a new bottle, according to the story of passengers on board, and by the time the narrows was reached, was again in bad shape.

There were no eye-witnesses to the accident, but it is believed that, after his companions had gone below, Paraiso had decided to do likewise, and in making the descent had fallen over into the water. The accident was discovered in a few minutes after it happened, and a life-boat was let down and Ben Cramer, one of the passengers, attempted to save the drowning Indian, but could not reach him in time. The body was recovered the following morning.

Paraiso had been in the Indian police service for a number of years and was always considered as trusty an Indian as there was on the reserve. He was well thot of, especially around Polson, where he had a wide acquaintance. He leaves a wife and nine children.

Document 59

History of Forced Opening
of Flathead Reservation
October 2, 1910

Source: "Opening of Flathead Reservation Marks End of Strenuous Endeavor," *The Daily Missoulian*, October 2, 1910, page 4, col. 1-3.

Editors' note: Joseph Dixon owned the *Missoulian* in 1910 and that paper was very pro-Dixon. Note that Dixon used an obscure section of the 1855 treaty, which probably had not been explained to the chiefs in 1855, to justify the opening. Dixon made no attempt to get the informed consent of the chiefs. Land sales to whites were under federal laws designed to convey public lands to white homesteaders for less than the real value of the land. To add to the outrage of tribal leaders, in 1908 Dixon added a provision for an irrigation project that would be paid for with tribal money received for the sale of tribal lands and timber. The irrigation project mostly benefited white homesteaders rather than tribal member farmers. In 1916, the tribal funds taken for irrigation construction were returned to the tribal account and the construction costs were made a lien on the irrigated lands, including both homesteads and allotments.

Opening of Flathead Reservation Marks End of Strenuous Endeavor
Men Who Favored Change and Development of Big Valley Worked
Hard and Long to Get the Bill Through Congress
and Make Present Situation Possible.

Seven years ago this fall Joseph M. Dixon, then fresh in the lower house of congress, introduced the original bill which proposed to open the Flathead Indian reservation. A few days ago — on September 29, to be exact — the last names were called on the list of eligibles and the last selections of land made, and the last formality enacted in connection with the opening proclamation issued by President Taft. All of which goes to show that the opening of a reservation is not boys' play; that it is a man's job in the full sense of the term, and that it can not be accomplished in a day.

It was early in the session of the fifty-eighth congress that Congressman Dixon first took up the matter of the Flathead opening at Washington. He had drafted a bill and introduced it, and the same had been referred to the proper committee when he was one day called before it to give some information concerning the agreement or treaty that was in existence which might give the government a right to survey and open the Indian's domain. In discussing this and other early circumstances in connection with the opening bill, Senator Dixon talked interestingly a few days ago.

Up a Stump.

"I want to confess," said the senator, "that when I was called upon the first time to back up my eagerness to open the reservation with some authority which made it proper and lawful for the government to take such action, that I was simply up a stump. In my eagerness in planning the opening I had overlooked that important point.

"I have never told this before, but it is a fact that I had to ask more time from the committee and went back to study up the Indian treaties and find a plan of action. I finally got out the old treaty made with the confederated tribes at the time the Bitter Root reserve was exchanged for the Flathead. This was made by Governor Isaac I. Stevens on July 16, 1855. In reading through this I ran across a paragraph which gave me a peg to hang my hat on. I gathered this in with great glee and the next day carried the big book up to the committee, and read it off in as telling a manner as was possible. While there remained some question in my own mind as to whether it would be sufficient, it satisfied the committee and led to the passage of the original opening bill."

The Peg.

The article of the treaty is the sixth one, and reads as follows:

"Article 6 — The president may, from time to time, at his discretion cause the whole or such parts of such reservation as he may think proper to be surveyed into lots, and assign the same to such individuals or families of said confederated tribes as are willing to avail themselves of the privilege, and will locate on the same as a permanent home, on the same terms and subject to the same regulations as the treaty with Omahas, so far as are provided in the sixth article of the same may be applicable."

The treaty with the Omahas contained the general opening provisions which were applicable in the case of the Flathead reservation in connection with the section quoted.

The Dixon bill was introduced in the fall of 1903. It passed the house on February 21 following and the senate some time in April. The original bill provided for the survey and classification of the land, and held the general opening provisions. It was a new departure in the plan of opening. It was fashioned after no other. It was simply forged in Congressman Dixon's own blacksmith shop. The provision relating to the personnel of the commission to appraise and classify the land put the work into the hands of two representatives

Joseph Dixon
Source: "Governors of Montana" [poster]
(Historical Library of Montana, no date)

Joseph Dixon walking over the Flathead Reservation
Source: Created by Robert Bigart with material from political cartoon in
Anaconda Standard, September 4, 1904, editorial section, page 1.

from the Indians, a special agent from the Indian office, and two from the outside. This gave the red man better representation than he ever had before and made the bill popular with the Indian's supporters. Theodore Roosevelt said: "That is the fairest Indian bill I have ever seen." The Indian office liked its general make up so well that it was adopted as a standard form.

Irrigation.

It required three years to get the surveys completed, and it was about that time when Mr. Dixon conceived the idea of putting a portion of the reservation under irrigation. He talked the matter over with Director Newell of the reclamation service and Engineer H. N. Savage, and the gentlemen expressed their willingness to help if the Indian office could be persuaded to join in the scheme. It had to be done through the Indian office and as an irrigation scheme, not as a reclamation project. To advance his cause Senator Dixon three years ago succeeded in getting a meeting of Secretary Garfield, Director Newell, Engineer Savage and Commissioner of Indian Affairs Leupp in Missoula, and all made a trip across the reservation, spending two days there. The possibilities of the reclamation proposition won the approval of all the officials from Washington. That winter there was tacked on the original opening bill the irrigation proviso, it appearing theoretically to be for the purpose of watering the Indians' land.

No Money

This done all was ready to proceed but there was no money available. None could be asked from the reclamation fund, for it was not a reclamation project. The Indian office had none which could be used. To overcome this the Indian service simply borrowed Engineer Savage and other reclamation engineers and the government loaned the Indians $50,000; which was to be paid back by the proceeds of timber sales, town lot sales, and a share of the land sales, another amendment having been made to the original bill to make this possible. As a supplemental scheme this amendment also provided that the president should reserve all power sites on the reserve for use in the irrigation scheme, and which also might be leased, to help pay for the irrigation work. Instead of selling the timber outright, the Flathead Indian lands were included in a special reserve, handled outside the forest service. It also provides for the opening to settlement of any timber land of agricultural value after the timber shall be cut.

With this $50,000 available the preliminary work was commenced upon the reclamation project, and Engineer Savage reported one of the finest schemes in the whole country. The following year an additional loan to the Indians of $250,000 was secured and last winter $250,000 more was loaned.

More Money Needed.

As the whole irrigation scheme on the reserve is to cost, when complete, about $3,000,000, it became necessary to figure an additional income to pay back this borrowed money to the government aside from that provided by the sale of timber and town sites. Last winter a scheme was evolved to survey the unallotted lake frontage into lots of from two to five acres in extent to be sold as summer homes. About 800 of these small tracts will be available along 15 miles of lake front. The survey of these lots is now in progress and is to be finished this fall. This will bring in, it is estimated, fully $100,000. With these amounts available in the near future, the timber sales growing greater each year and more town sites and water power to be sold and leased, the prospects look favorable for ample funds, so that the project can be carried right along to completion without delay.

Other Changes.

Besides these changes mentioned in the original bill, there were numerous others of smaller scope, but which all go to make the bill more perfect and absolutely fair to all concerned. The university land grant for a biological station was reserved, as was also a grant to the Catholic institution at St. Ignatius. Camas Hot springs were reserved for the public, and the prohibition clause, to keep liquor off the reservation for 25 years, was attached. Another small matter was a clause protecting the Indians' water rights.

When all was ready President Taft Taft [sic] issued his opening proclamation on May 22, 1909. This provided for a registration in Missoula and Kalispell of all those who wished to secure a Flathead farm, and then for two selection periods the names of 3,000 of the successful registrants to be called each time and given an opportunity to select lands, the lists to be prepared, and the names called in the order of the drawing.

Registration.

Registration commenced in both Missoula and Kalispell on July 15, 1909, and closed on August 5 following. H. J. Rossi of this city was the first man to have his signature regularly acknowledged by a notary. The total number to register during the period was 80,762, of which 6,62 [56,625] were taken in Missoula and 24,137 at Kalispell.

The registration slips were all mailed to Judge J. W. Witten, at Coeur d'Alene City, Idaho. Judge Witten was the superintendent of the opening and held a drawing at that place for the Flathead, Spokane and Coeur d'Alene reserves. On August 12, 1909, the Flathead drawing took place. The big cans, containing the sealed enverlopes [sic] were opened and the yellow papers scattered over a platform erected in the open. Little Miss Christina Donlan, daug[h]ter of Senator and Mrs. Donlan of Missoula, drew the envelopes, and 6,000 were selected as drawn.

Classification.

The whole Flathead reservation contained practically 1,425,000 acres. Of this 222,109 acres were allotted to the Indians, leaving a balance to be opened for settlement of about 1,200,000. This was surveyed and classified as follows: Agricultural lands of the first class, 40,229 acres; agricultural lands of the second class, 75,109 acres; grazing land, 336,189 acres. The remaining is timber and mineral areas. The agricultural and grazing lands were appraised at from $1.25 to $7 an acre.

The first selection period, when those holding numbers would have a chance to select lands and offer filings under the opening proclamation, started in Kalispell on May 2 and in Missoula on May 9 of this year. During that period from the list of 3,000 names called there were 830 to select and file on homesteads.

The second opportunity to file opened in Kalispell on September 1 last and in Missoula on September 8, continuing to and including September 29. In Kalispell there were 90 filings taken and in Missoula there were 119 selections made. The chance for more land under the opening regulations have passed. No more names will be called, but the remaining lands of the reserve will be thrown open to entry under the general homestead laws on November 1 of this year.

From the figures above it can be seen what a small proportion of the reservation has been settled upon. The last selection and filing period especially lacked interest. When it is known that under the irrigation system alone there are 1,600 farm units that were thought valuable enough to irrigate, it can be seen that there must be left hundreds of valuable farms, within the territory that was formerly the Flathead Indian reservation. There should be rich opportunity here for the homesteader on the first day of November.

The reclamation project on the Flathead is not a myth. Already 12,000 acres are under water, the ditches having been operated this season. There will be 20,000 acres under the ditch next spring, and perhaps the whole system, which is to over 150,000 acres, will be completed in the third or fourth year. The reservation is a coming country. It must prosper. Its opening was a great thing for western Montana, and to those who assisted in working out the splendid plan and who have helped carry through the provisions of the opening act, Missoula and western Montana owe a debt of gratitude.

Document 60

Duncan McDonald's Prize Potato

October 17, 1910

Source: "Duncan's Big Spud Is a Dandy," *The Daily Missoulian*, October 17, 1910, page 2, col. 3.

Editors' note: Duncan McDonald had a talent for generating publicity. His large potato also testified to the fertility of the farms on Flathead.

Duncan's Big Spud Is a Dandy
Four-and-a-Half Pound Potato Comes From M'Donald Farm at Ravalli.

"Dear Sir: this potato is my own raising, without water, and it is for your dinner. Yours truly,

"Duncan M'Donald."

This letter, under Ravalli date, was received yesterday by the editor of The Missoulian. The letter was attached to a box which containtd [sic] the biggest potato ever seen by any of The Missoulian force, all of which members examined it yesterday.

The big spud was weighed after there had been a proper number of guesses made as to its "heft" and it turned the scales at four and a half pounds. It is a clean, big spud, without blemish, and is a beautiful testimonial to the fertility of the Ravalli farm of Mr. McDonald.

The McDonald garden has been famous for its products for a good many years and its crop this season is reported to be unusually good. The potato which was received at The Missoulian office yesterday is in the humdinger class and would be placed on exhibition were it not for the fact that Mr. McDonald sent it to be eaten. It will make a good dinner.

Document 61

Indian Rider Injured in Accident

October 21, 1910

Source: "Reservation Rider Seriously Injured," *The Daily Missoulian*, October 21, 1910, page 4, col. 4.

Editors' note: Horses and horse races were a part of the tribal and American culture in the early twentieth century. Accidents could be serious.

Reservation Rider Seriously Injured

Kalispell, Oct. 20. — (Special.) — John Couture, a half-breed from Polson, who was one of the winners in the Indian races at the county fair here last week, is suffering at the Catholic hospital here with a broken thigh and hip and severe dangerous internal injuries as the result of an accident at the race track Saturday afternoon. The fact that he had been injured did not leak out until today, as it occurred while the horsemen were having a little race carnival of their own after the close of the fair.

Couture's pony, which he was riding bareback, suddenly turned from the home stretch into an opened gap in the inside inclusure, the turn being so sudden that its rider was hurled with terrific force against a fence post. Couture was riding a small, thin sorrel, which had been the fastest horse in the running, but which had frequently caused much merriment by stopping to buck while he was making the circuit of the track. It is doubtful whether Couture will recover.

Document 62

State Claims Control of Pablo Buffalo

October – November 1910

Source: "Notice Is Served Against Big Hunt," *The Anaconda Standard*, October 31, 1910, page 8, col. 6; "Buffalo Men Will Confer," *The Daily Missoulian*, November 14, 1910, page 10, col. 4-5; "Big Buffalo Hunt Is All Off," *The Daily Missoulian*, November 15, 1910, page 7, col. 3; Assistant Commissioner to Fred C. Morgan, December 5, 1910, from file 92,843/1910 Flathead 170, Central Classified Files, RG 75, National Archives, Washington, D.C.

Editors' note: In 1910, Montana State moved aggressively to grab control of wildlife and affairs on the Flathead Reservation. In this case, the Indian Bureau defended Pablo's ownership of the outlaw buffalo on the reservation.

Notice Is Served Against Big Hunt
Special Dispatch to the Standard.

Missoula, Oct. 30. — Deputy State Game Warden W. W. McCormick of this city returned home tonight from the Flathead reservation, or what once was the Flathead reservation, where he went yesterday to serve notice on Michael Pablo, once the "Buffalo King" of the world, that the state game warden would not permit the shooting of any buffaloes on the range. The action of State Game Warden Avarre [sic] followed an opinion from Attorney General Galen who had been informed that Howard Douglas, commissioner of the dominion parks in Canada, had announced a buffalo hunt for the purpose of killing off some of the unruly bulls of the Pablo herd yet remaining on the reservation, they having prevented the capture of about 75 of the animals which were yet to rounded up and shipped to Canada.

The attorney general in his opinion pointed out that the Flathead reservation had been opened by the government and was no longer a reserve, but comes now within the jurisdiction of the state.

Some Misunderstanding.
There is some misunderstanding about the status of the bison in question. Pablo sold to the Canadian government buffalo for $250 a head, delivered at the dominion park. Therefore, the Canadian government does not lay any

claim on the animals until they have reached their destination. Hence the unruly beasts are either wild and the property of the state, or controllable and Pablo's.

Warden McCormick upon his return tonight stated that he had served notice upon Michael Pablo, that the old buffalo king took the matter very kindly, and said that he had no disposition to overstep any of his rights in the matter. He said however, that the plans for the buffalo hunt had been grossly misrepresented because it had only been planned to kill several head of old and unruly bulls. This would leave about 70 head yet to be corralled and shipped.

Mr. Pablo stated to Deputy McCormick that he believed that the Canadian government had already violated some of the terms of the contract under which they were to receive his buffaloes and that it could not lay claim to the balance of the herd. He believed that it was a good opportunity for the government or the national buffalo society to secure the animals saying that he would be willing to make any reasonable arrangement for the disposition of the balance of the herd. In the meantime he promised that none of the animals would be hunted or shot.

* * * * * * * *

Buffalo Men Will Confer
Pablo, Douglas and Game Warden Avare to Talk Buffalo Hunt.

In Missoula today there is to be a conference between State Game Warden Henry Avare of Helena, Michael Pablo, of the Flathead reservation, once the "buffalo king" of the world, and Howard Douglas, commissioner of parks in the Dominion of Canada, the outcome of which will be watched with great interest by those who have become interested in the proposed buffalo hunt which was to have taken place on the reservation at about this time, the plans having been cut into by warning to desist from the state game warden. Howard Douglas has been in Missoula several days and Michael Pablo arrived late last evening. Mr. Avare is to come over from Helena on the first train today and the conference will probably be held some time this afternoon or evening.

Some days ago there was much talk started throughout the state over the report circulated that Howard Douglas had sent out word that he was bringing a crowd of hunters from Canada to proceed to the reservation and make merry with the others of the Pablo herd that have up to date, defied all attempts to round-up and ship them from their old stamping grounds.

Story Misleading.

This story grew to considerable proportions until it came to the attention of the state game warden and under considerable pressure that was brought to bear in the matter, Warden Avare notified Deputy Warden McCormick of this city to stop the proposed hunt. Mr. McCormick went at once to the reservation and served such notice on the owner of the herd, Michel Pablo. It was then that the true facts in the case became known. Mr. Pablo assuring the warden that his object in allowing the hunt was simply for the purpose of killing off a few of the outlaw bulls which could not be corralled and which led the rest of the animals into the wilds. He urged that those animals should be killed, now that the reservation is being settled, for they were mean and fierce and promised to do serious damage to man and domestic stock. He stated that this was his only object in inviting Mr. Douglas and his friends from Canada, as well as a number in Montana, to join in the hunt. Since Mr. Pablo expressed these sentiments it has been proven that he was correct for only a few days ago a big bull buffalo attacked a settler on his claim, chased him into his cabin and bunted his shack around off its underpinnings. It was also reported last evening that another settler had been attacked while on his claim near Dayton and was compelled to shoot the buffalo in self-defense.

Mr. Douglas Talks.

In speaking of his intentions in the matter, and of his interests in the proposed hunt, Howard Douglas said last night:

"I am very sorry that this matter has been so much garbled and overdrawn. I understand that Mr. Pablo has explained his invitation to me and a party of friends who were interested in coming down to see the country and enjoy the novelty. He had informed us that there were 15 or more head of old outlaw bulls over 20 years of age, with which something must be done and that the best plan would be to have them shot. No cows or young bulls were to be harmed. Under these conditions I was anxious to make the hunt for two reasons. It would rid the herd of the outlaw animals so that the balance could be rounded up and shipped and would also have a great experience for some of my friends who were willing to pay Mr. Pablo $250 for each animal killed, just to get the head. The report that Canadian government was sending men across the line to hunt buffalo put us in a bad light as we had no interests in the matter other than for the good of the cause. It is not a logical thought even, to say that the Canadian government would sanction or permit a slaughter of these animals after having expended so much money and time in getting together the fine herd that is being assembled in our parks. I am sure that there can be no blame attached to anyone when the whole matter is explained and I hope that the conferences here tomorrow will further perfect this explanation. I am of the opinion that these old outlaw bulls should be killed, whether they are hunted or not, as they are dangerous to the people who are now making their homes in that fine Flathead country. It seems also that something must be done to eliminate them before the rest of the herd of about 50 animals can be rounded up and shipped. It makes little difference which way the matter stands so far as the Canadian government is concerned. We expected and had hoped to get 30 or 40 more animals from the herd and this is as far as our interests extend."

From Conrad Herd.

Mr. Douglas announced last night that on his way from Canada he had stopped at Kalispell and purchased two cars, 28 head, of the Conrad herd of fullbloods. These are to be loaded today and tomorrow and probably shipped Tuesday evening. These animals are domesticated and almost as gentle and as easy to handle as ordinary cattle.

Mr. Douglas stated that by the first of the year the Canadian government would have assembled in its parks an even 1,000 buffaloes. To date there has been 704 head shipped to Canada from the Pablo herd.

With Mr. Douglas from Canada are W. S. Robertson, sheriff of northern Alberta, James Ross and K. C. McLeod, friends who came to witness the rounding up of the last of the herd. A. Ayotte, the Canadian immigration agent, was also of the party last night and will probably attend the conference to be held today.

* * * * * * * *

Big Buffalo Hunt Is All Off
Game Warden Avare Comes with New Decision —
Pablo No Longer Owns Herd.

Armed with a new opinion from Attorney General Galen, State Game Warden Avare arrived here late last night from Helena and immediately held a conference with Michel Pablo, owner of the once-famous herd of buffalo on the Flathead reservation, and Howard Douglas, commisisoner [sic] of Canadian parks, the subject of the conference being the proposed killing of a number of outlaw bulls of the remaining herd still running wild in the Flathead country. The result of the conference leaves the matter in a most peculiar condition, and is to the effect that all of the remaining buffalo, 75 in number, are "wild animals" and subject to the laws of the state of Montana. This means that they can not only [not] be killed, but that Pablo is no longer the owner of the animals and has no right to dispose of them, and cannot even round them up or put them within the confines of the Montana bison range, which has been established near Ravalli.

The following is the attorney general's opinion, rendered yesterday:

"Mr. Henry Avare, State Game and Fish Warden, Helena, Montana.

"Dear Sir: — In further advice of our letter of recent date to you concerning the slaughter of buffalo now ranging on what was the Flathead Indian reservation, I have to advise you that in accordance with our holding that these buffalo are wild animals and not the subject of private ownership, that section 8790 of the revised codes makes it unlawful to wilfully catch, trap or otherwise restrain buffalo, elk and moose, or mountain sheep within the state.

"You are therefore advised that if the renegade buffalo of the Pablo herd are restrained within a large enclosure, as you advised us might be done, that, nevertheless, they are still wild animals and are entitled to the protection of the game laws of the state.

"Yours very truly
"**Albert J. Galen,**
"Attorney General."

The section of the game laws referred to reads:

"Section 8790. That any person who shall wilfully catch, trap, or otherwise restrain, for the purpose of sale or domestication, or any other purposes, any buffalo, elk, moose or mountain sheep within the state, shall be deemed guilty of a misdemeanor and be fined not more than $500 nor less than $100, and shall be imprisoned in the county jail for a term not to exceed six months, or by both such fine and imprisonment for each offense committed, in the discretion of the court."

In the conference last night Michel Pablo was represented by Attorney Thomas C. Marshall. Everything was affable and in the best of spirit. Mr. Pablo was considerably disturbed by the decision, and it was decided that he and Mr. Marshall will go to Helena this evening and have a personal interview with the attorney general. The situation is very peculiar and while the decision is strictly according to the law, Mr. Pablo feels that it [is] very unjust to him — that he should suffer the total loss of the rest of his herd, as they have, under the decision, simply been taken over by the state. Under the decision, Mr. Pablo has had no right to dispose of a single buffalo since the Fathead reservation was officially thrown open and the territory became subject to state laws and regulations.

* * * * * * * *

Dec 5, 1910

Seizure of
Indian's buffalo.

Mr. Fred C. Morgan,
Superintendent Flathead Indian School,
Jocko, Montana.
Sir:

Your letter of November 18, 1910, regarding the herd of buffalo owned by Michel Pablo, an Indian of the Flathead Reservation, Montana, has been received.

The Office is unable to understand upon what basis or theory the authorities of the State of Montana are claiming the herd of buffalo or any of these animals, which are recognized now and have always been recognized as the personal property of Michel Pablo and his former partner, Charles Allard, the herd being the direct descendants of certain animals captured by Sam, a Pend d'Oreille Indian, and raised by the Indians as their personal property. They are in no sense wild beasts such as were so described by the common law, and hence the property of the community and subject to the laws of the State.

The Office notes you say that the claim of the State of Montana appears to be based largely on the question of jurisdiction, although the buffalo are now grazing upon tribal timber lands of the Flathead Reservation.

The Office can hardly believe that the State contemplates seriously the confiscation of the personal property of Michel Pablo, whether it be his buffalo, his cattle or other personal property.

You are requested to take the matter up at once with the proper State authorities, and call their attention to the understanding of this Office regarding the ownership of these buffalo, and ask that further steps regarding the taking of the animals without payment or due process of law cease and determine [sic]. In the event that the State attempts in any way to obtain possession of these buffalo in any manner other than that which is right and proper, you will at once wire this Office of the facts, and the matter will be called to the attention of the Attorney General, with a view to such action as may be warranted by the facts and the law.

In the meantime, and for use in case the subject reaches a critical stage, you are requested to procure and forward to the Office a statement of the exact origin of this herd of buffalo, its increase from time to time, and the sales of the surplus animals from time to time, and whether the State has by any direcot [sic] act or otherwise recognized the ownership of these animals in Pablo or Allard when the latter was living. Have any taxes every been paid upon these animals? Has the State ever purchased any of the animals from the persons owning them? The Office desires to have full information in the case, so that if it is necessary to bring the matter to the attention of the Attorney General he may be given such facts and circumstances as will enable him to take immediate action without the necessity of waiting for further information.

Very respectfully,
(Signed) F. H. Abbot.
Assistant Commissioner.

Document 63

Boundary Survey of Southwest Corner
of Reservation
December 5, 1910

Source: Fred C. Morgan to Commissioner of Indian Affairs, December 5, 1910, from file 49,688/1910 Flathead 304.3, Central Classified Files, RG 75, National Archives, Washington, D.C.

Editors' note: The map Morgan referred to was not in the file with this copy of the report. The official government survey of the southwest corner of the Flathead Reservation cut off some valuable timber and farming land along the Clarks Fork River. The claim for the lost land was not settled until the second half of the twentieth century.

(Copy)

Department of the Interior
United States Indian Service
Flathead Agency, Jocko, Montana,
December 5, 1910.

Boundary, Flathead
Reservation.

The Commissioner of Indian Affairs,
Washington, D.C.
Sir: —

Replying to Office letter of July 19, 1910, relative to the location of the western boundary line of the Flathead Reservation, I have to report as follows:

From an examination of the treaty of July 16, 1855, which defines the boundary line in question, it would appear that the southern boundary line is the watershed between the Missoula River on the south and the Jocko and Flathead rivers on the north. While the Missoula River is not mentioned in the treaty, it is probable that it is the stream referred to as the Bitter Root. It is my understanding that the Indians who made this treaty were living in the Bitter Root Valley at that time and it is only natural that they should consider the stream as being the Bitter Root even after its junction with the Missoula, up to the point where the Missoula joins with the Flathead to form Clark's Fork.

From all that I can gather, Clark's Fork is, and always has been known as such, *only* below the junction of the Missoula and Flathead rivers.

There is enclosed a map issued by the General Land Office, showing the Flathead Reservation. It will be noted that the southern boundary line is surveyed through ranges 19, 20 and 21. From the map it would appear that the line is unsurveyed to a point approximately in section 29, twp. 18, range 24. From here the line turns sharply to the north, crosses the Flathead River in section 6-18-24, and continues in a northerly direction to a point about nine miles south of the Dog Lake, or, approximately in section 19-19-24. The part from section 29-18-24 to section 19-19-24, is the part disputed by the Indians.

An examination of the records in the U.S. Land Office at Missoula, Montana, shows approved surveys covering the boundary line from the northwest corner of the reservation to a point in the northwest quarter of section 32-19-24, and in that part of section 6-18-24 lying north of the Flathead River. No record was found of a survey of the western and southern boundary on the south side of the Flathead River, but it is understood that a surveying party has been in the field, and the irregular curves in that part of the boundary line in dispute would indicate that at least some of the prominent points have been located. The maps of townships 18 and 19 in range 25 shows that the point of land between the Missoula and Flathead rivers is in Lot 2 of section 34-19-25, and that a well defined ridge extends from this point in a southerly direction through sections 3, 4, 10, 14 and 15 in township 18-24. It is also shown that a well defined ridge extends from the north bank of Clark's Fork, at a point directly opposite the junction of the Missoula and Flathead Rivers, through sections 35, 26, 25, and 24, and into section 19-19-24, connecting with the present surveyed line.

On the map enclosed there is indicated in red the approximate location of the western boundary line of the reservation as claimed by the Indians. A rough estimate of the amount of land in dispute is eleven thousand acres, the greater part of which is covered with valuable timber.

[Here Morgan gave a detailed account, including legal descriptions, of 15 filings on land in the disputed section, and 4 other claims which may conflict with part of the cut off portion.]

From the records of the Land Office at Missoula it would appear that the western boundary of the reservation is by the officials of that place, considered to be approximately as is shown in black on the enclosed map, for filings have been permitted on the south side of the Flathead River, above its junction with the Missoula, on land which, by virtue of the treaty of 1855, belongs to the Flathead Indians.

There is on file in this office a blue-print of the map of final location of the Northern Pacific Railroad across this reservation. This map, approved by the then Secretary of the Interior on January 16, 1883, shows the western boundary of the reservation to run approximately north 4° east from a point in the center of the main channel of the Clark's Fork, at a point about 5800 feet downstream from the junction of the Missoula and Flathead rivers. The report of the Commissioner of Indian Affairs, for the year 1883, on page XIX and XX shows that this map was approved, and that payment was made by the railroad company for a right of way to a point over three miles west of land they have taken up. Also, in the report of the Commissioner for the year 1882, page 103, it speaks of this map having been shown to the Indians, in which the right of way is defined as "and passing out of the reservation *at* or near the mouth of the Missoula river – – –"

Since it was the understanding at the time the treaty was made that the line ran to the junction of the Missoula and Flathead rivers, it seems that if the treaty means anything it refers to a point on the Clark's Fork of the Columbia River, and not to a point on the Flathead River, as shown on the enclosed map.

On a recent rrip to the land in question, in company with Duncan McDonald, who, no doubt, has a better idea regarding the topography of the country and the understanding the Indians have regarding the treaty than any other individual on the reservation, I saw the existing boundary line, and the one claimed by the Indians, the latter at a point on the Northern Pacific Railway and at the confluence of the Missoula and Flathead rivers.

Mr. McDonald pointed out the site of an early village which existed during the construction of the Northern Pacific Railway across the reservation. It was called "Last Chance" for the reason that it was built just west of the then supposed boundary line, and was the last point where one could secure liquor before going on the reserve. This town was located in the northeast quarter of section 28-19-25, or about one mile west of the confluence of the Missoula and Flathead rivers.

Many of the older Indians, Joseph Seepay, Antoine Moiese, Louie Vanderburg, Big Sam, Lassaw Kaltomee, and many others have the same understanding regarding the location of the line. So firm were the Indians in the belief that the disputed territory was theirs that they built homes for themselves along the river (Flathead) abandoning them only after they were informed by the Indian Agent that the land in question was open to homestead entry.

Several ranches have been developed along the river between the two lines in dispute, some of these ranches being worth several thousand dollars. On the land homesteaded by Harrison A. Robinson there has recently been cut six hundred thousand feet of yellow pine, worth approximately $3,000.00.

In order to have a more comprehensive view of the matter, I respectfully recommend that the Project Engineer in charge of the Reclamation work on this reservation be instructed to make a survey showing the topography at and between both of the lines in question, giving the areas of timber and of agricultural land involved.

Very respectfully,
Fred C. Morgan,
Superintendent.

Document 64

Duncan McDonald Wants Square Deal
for Indian
December 13, 1910

Source: "Duncan M'Donald Wants a Square Deal," *The Missoula Herald*, December 13, 1910, page 2, col. 2.

Editors' note: Duncan McDonald always liked to meet a reporter and express his views on tribal and national topics.

Duncan M'Donald Wants a Square Deal

Duncan McDonald, who was a Missoula visitor yesterday, does not like the way the white man complains.

"Why," said he, "he squeals about everything, and is never satisfied. That's the white man! He would take everything the Indian has. I have found that the idlers, the fellows who hang about the barrooms and pool tables, are the ones that make most trouble. That is my observation.

"Squeal, squeal, all the time!"

Mr. McDonald was rather bitter in his remarks. He made it plain that he did not believe that the Indian was getting a square deal in this world.

"They asked me," he continued, "if I objected to any one on the jury. I told them to stand aside any southern democrat."

"Why did you do that?" he was asked.

"Because, southern democrats are prejudiced against color, and race."

"If the white man will go to work with the land he has in our section of the state he will be all right," said the visitor. "Let him put the harness on himself and go to it. He need not be worrying about water. He can make stuff without irrigation.

"Look at my orchard! That shows what can be done. I have been digging at it for years.

"The water, I think, belongs to the tribes. The Indians are going to hold it. We will fight for it."

Mr. McDonald wore a fur cap and a fur-trimmed overcoat, and looked very picturesque. He has a strong face and talks well. His home is at Ravalli.

Document 65

Joe Pain Arrested for Murder

January 14, 1911

Source: "Murder Is Charged Against Indian," *The Daily Missoulian*, January 14, 1911, page 3, col. 2.

Editors' note: Alcohol fueled murders on the reservation were tried in federal court and frequently made it into the newspapers.

Murder Is Charged Against Indian
Joe Pain Held by Federal Officers — Body of Victim Is Examined.

On October 12 of last year Frank Lalacelle, a full-blood Flathead Indian, was killed near the Michel ranch, about three or four miles north of Dixon. Joe Pain, uncle of the dead Indian, was arrested and, after an inquest held at Plains, he was bound over to the federal grand jury. The body of Lalacelle was buried on the place belonging to his grandfather and until a few days ago it was allowed to remain in that resting place. At the instance of the federal authorities the body was exhumed and brought to Missoula to permit a thorough investigation of the remains with a view to ascertaining, if possible, the exact cause of death. This investigation was conducted at the Northern Pacific hospital yesterday morning, without resutling [sic] in any tangible evidence being found. The inquiry was conducted by Drs. W. C. Reddell and T. U. Trinwith of Helena, Dr. John H. Heidelman of the Flathead agency, who represented the government, and Dr. Green of the Northern Pacific surgical corps. The real incentive for the investigation was to find the bullet, which is said to have caused the death of Lalacelle. The missile was not recovered.

The Crime.

Reviewing the crime of last October, a reservation man who is conversant with all the facts connected with the murder and its subsequent developments, tells the following story:

A few days prior to the event, Frank Lalacelle and his uncle, Joe Pain, were employed repairing a house belonging to another Indian, named Magpie, living a short distance east of Perma. When the job was completed the men passed north across the river to Camas Prairie to seek Magpie in order to receive their pay. The employer was engaged rounding up some stock for

Michel, but arrangements were made by Magpie to have the men paid by order on a Plains storekeeper, the order to be given Lalacelle and Pain by Zaphire Courville, an Indian rancher who lives a few miles west of the Michel place. The order amounted to about $45, and with this Lalacelle went to Plains, where he secured a big supply of intoxicating liquor. Plains is about 25 miles southwest of the Michel place, and it was not until some time the following day that Lalacelle returned to the point where he was to meet his kinsmen. In the meantime he had picked up another Indian named Sonneal, and the pair had partaken freely of the liquid goods. Later in the day they located Pain and his s...., and the quartet imbibed freely, all, with the exception of the strange Indian, becoming more or less intoxicated and scrappy. Sonneal, as the party approached the Michel place, rode ahead and advised Michel of the condition of Lalacelle. Pain and the latter's s...., and the rancher instructed his advisor to order the drunken Indians to stay away from his place. Sonneal tied his horse to a haystack and proceeded to the place where the trio was engaged in a verbal conflict. He transmitted his message and Pain immediately left the party, himself going to Michel's, where he took charge of his 9-year-old son, who ahd [sic] been left on the ranch after the former visit when Magpie was being sought. With the boy he rejoined the other members of the party, Sonneal leaving immediately.

Shot Is Fired.

The quarreling kinsmen camped a short distance from the Michel home and during the night a shot was fired. The next morning the death-stilled body of Lalacelle was found with a hole through the region of the heart. The wound had all the appearance of having been made by a bullet, and at the inquest held on October 14 at Plains a verdict was returned to that effect.

The dead body was taken care of by Rancher Michel, who also notified Major Fred Morgan, the later at once proceeded to the scene of the tragedy and later arresting Joe Pain and his s.... on the road betwe[e]n the ranch and Dixon. Pain denied having any knowledge of his nephew's death, declaring with emphasis that he had left Lalacelle in a drunken sleep by the roadside. The s.... did then and has ever since maintained a stolid silence, but the son of the pair confessed that his father shot Lalacelle. Pain is to be tried in the Helena federal court very soon, and it was for the securing of positive evidence against him that his relative's body was exhumed, brought here and submitted to dissection.

Another Crime

On July 4, 1908, Joe Pain and Dave Couture were arrested for the murder of an Indian named Eneas Pierre at a celebration dance. Pierre having been disembowled with knives said to have been wielded by Pain and Couture. There was not sufficient evidence against the men and both were released.

In the present case Pain refuses to make a confession; in fact, he has become absolutely silent with the approach of his trial. The body of Lalacelle was forwarded to Dixon last night and will be reinterred there. Major Fred Morgan attended the investigation, and, with Dr. Heidelman, returned to the agency last night.

Document 66

Flathead Indian Students Travel to Carlisle Indian School March 26, 1911

Source: H. S. Allen, "Twelve Flathead Indian Students Have Enjoyable Journey to Carlisle," *The Daily Missoulian*, March 26, 1911, editorial section, page 1, col. 1-7, and page 5, col. 4.

Editors' note: Allen's account of chaperoning twelve Flathead Indian students to Carlisle Indian School in Pennsylvania gave a detailed description of an important event in the lives of these students. According to a caption on a picture published with the article, the names of the students were Peter Barnaby, Nicholas Lassaw, John Roullier, Louie Gingras, St. Peter Pierre, Frank Roeder, Ursula Vinson, James Kallowat, Annie Ducharme, Cecille Ducharme, John Bouchard and Joseph Pierre or Wah-wee.

Twelve Flathead Indian Students Have Enjoyable Journey to Carlisle

On the second day of March — the morning of that day — a crowd of 12 Flathead Indian boys and girls arrived at the Carlisle Indian school, tired and weary from the excitement and unusual experiences during the long trip from Arlee on their reservation, which place they left the Monday before. This was the largest delegation of students from the Flathead that has ever been sent to Carlisle. There were five full-bloods in the party and a number of them came from the Camas Prairie district, where heretofore it has been almost impossible to make any of the Indian school regulations effective. The youngsters started out on their journey in high glee, after once having made up their minds to go, and it was a novel experience for them all, a trip to Missoula having been as far from home as any of them had ventured before in their lives. It was interesting to watch them and see their expressions of wonder and delight as they were whirled along through a strange country, and the passengers on the train were much amused from association with the students.

Along the western end of the journey the Indians caused but little notice at the various stations where they would have an opportunity to leave the train and promenade the platforms for a few minutes. The people of the west have become too familiar with the Indian and his dress and habits to longer be curious at such sights. However, after Chicago was reached the students created sensations all along the rest of the route. Sometimes the Indians were compelled to take the brunt of jokes made at their expense, but at other times the white man, a stranger to western conditions, was humiliated by some retort of the students which exposed his ignorance, to the delight of his friends.

Just after leaving Chicago, James Kallowat, or "Jim," as he was called by all, humped-up in a seat, got on a sad, far-away look, and when asked what was the matter tears came to his eyes and he would not, or could not answer. Nicholas Lassaw, or "Nick," was a sure cure for the blues, however, and it was only a few moments until Jim was again thinking of the distance to Carlisle instead of the many miles between himself and Flathead. This was the only time any of the party became homesick.

Wah-wee (Joe Pierre) was the only long-haired-buck in the party. Before reaching St. Paul, contact with the passengers had had its effect, and he requested that his hair be cut. This was promised at the first opportunity. We were only 40 minutes in Chicago, and that time was fully occupied in keeping the party "corralled." The haircutting was therefore postponed. This was just as well, perhaps, for a picture of the party as they enter Carlisle was wanted, in order that it might be compared with pictures of themselves after finishing their terms and could be shown other reservation children to impress them with the difference a few years in one of the large government schools would make. There is nothing bad, and a great deal that is good, about Wah-wee, and he should make good. A picture of the moccasined, long-haired Wah-wee, as he entered the school, and (if all goes well) a picture of Joseph Pierre at the end of his five-year term, will show better than any article what the government is and has been doing for the Indians. Had his hair been cut at Chicago such a picture would not have been secured — but Wah-wee would have been saved some embarrassing incidents. One was when a young fellow asked him if he was a s...; another was after the arrival at Carlisle, when a little full-blood Indian, in audible and excellent, even if slangy, English said: "Gee! Look at the long-haired geezer." From the ready-to-dodge-if-he-does-it-again look on Wah-wee's face, his wincing at the remark, his humped-up back and slouching gait, his mental faculties were subject to a strain such as they have never experienced before, and at one and the same time he was probably praying for a shower of slippers and scissors and cursing the Flathead custom of wearing long hair.

Probably the most laughable incident occurred about one-half hour after the party had been turned over to the superintendent at Carlisle school. The call for supper had sounded, the pupils had lined up, two abreast, and in perfect step were marching to the dining hall. At the end of the line came the Flathead boys — but not two abreast or keeping step. They were in one compact body all slouching along in seemingly different steps. It would be impossible to tell just how ludicrous a picture they presented — but the laugh was tempered by the thought that in a year or two those same boys would be marching, erect and in time, and furnishing just such a contrast as had just been witnessed when new arrivals would succeed them at the end of the line.

Not all the laughable incidents were at the expense of the Indian boys, however. For every one on them they had probably two on the white people to whom they were objects of curiosity, or, more probably, living Indians of the type they (the whites) had seen in wild-west shows, featured in moving pictures or read about in the average novel, where the scene is laid in the west. There was a crowd constantly surrounding the boys. In fact, they were such an attraction that one conductor suggested charging admission into the car in which they were riding. Nick, perhaps, was the liveliest of the party. Among the jokes perpetrated by the Indians, usually headed by Nick, was the drawing on an old, soiled handkerchief of a buffalo, a horse, etc., with a common lead pencil, and the sale to a young fellow in search of something "real Indian" for a quarter. The Indians also had a good laugh over Nick's story about being with Buffalo Bill and receiving $5.00 per day for riding; that he was only going to Carlisle until the show started out in the spring. A small scar on his cheek, after he learned how the white people to whom he was talking were ready to believe and anxious to hear such stories, developed into a scar caused by being shot through the cheek with a rifle while engaged in a fight. Then, assisted by two Ohio gentlemen who were returning from a visit to the west and who were on the train the Indians boarded, worked such a fright into one of the waiters on the diner that he, when announcing meals, was afraid to enter the car the Indians were in for fear of being scalped.

It would require too much time and space to enumerate all the jokes played by the Indians. This would also be true of any effort to picture the surprise of the Indians at the many, and to them, marvelous things they saw, the distances they traveled and the constantly-increasing size of the towns until Chicago was reached, and after riding through Chicago of their readiness to take everything as a matter of course.

Such a trip, however, is not altogether a picnic for the escort. And the greater part of the work comes before the train is boarded. The gathering of such a party is not the work of hours or days, or even weeks. It requires the constant dinning into the ears of the children and parents by all the agency employes, principally the superintendent, of what an education will mean; of the difficulty the uneducated Indian of the future will have in making a living; then of the results obtained by a course in one of the large government schools and the effort the government is making to give free of cost an education to each Indian that will enable him to compete with the whites in the labor markets of the country. The selection of the school rests with the parents for all children between 14 and 18 years of age, and with the pupil for all between 18 and 21 years of age. This party, just entering Carlisle is the first large party from the Flathead reservation to ever enter that school, and was the result of the work, and hard work, of months. How well these pupils realized the opoprtunity [sic] the government was giving them is shown by the coming to the agency, voluntarily and several days before the party was to leave of five full-blood boys from Camas Prairie, which, perhaps has been less influenced for good by contact with the whites than any other district on the reservation. Slowly but also surely, the government is educating the Indians, and the results can be seen in the increasing number who not only have the ability and are fully competent to, but are competing with the whites in the different lines of endeavor.

The party just entering Carlisle seemed to realize fully what they were going for and actually seemed pleased at the thought that they would soon be learning some trade or study that would fit them to make their way through life. The Carlisle school is the largest Indian school in the country, is finely equipped and seems well adapted for the work of turning into useful self-reliant citizens the Indian pupils sent there.

H. S. A. [Allen]

Flathead Agency, March 24, 1911.

Document 67

Indian Dances at St. Ignatius Celebration

July 5, 1911

Source: "Indian Dances Mission's Feature," *The Daily Missoulian*, July 5, 1911, page 1, col. 2, and page 10, col. 5-6.

Editors' note: This detailed account of the 1911 Fourth of July celebration at St. Ignatius noted the Indian dancing, parades, concert, horse racing, baseball games, and pageant that were part of the event. Other tribal members took part in celebrations at Jocko and Ronan.

Indian Dances Mission's Feature
St. Ignatius Celebrates the Nation's Birthday in Fine Style.
Reds Please Big Crowds
War-Dance, Tribal Games and Pageant Are Presented by Aborigines —
Ball Game Won by Mission Team — Racing Program —
Five Hundred People Attend Celebration.

St. Ignatius, July 4. — (Staff Correspondence.) — Five hundred visitors from Missoula and the reservation towns filled St. Ignatius to overflowing today and helped the quiet little mission town to celebrate the birthday of the nation. It was the biggest celebration ever held here. From early morning until late at night there was something doing all of the time, and the big crowd was kept jolly and excited clear through. Despite the size of the visiting delegations, there was no overcrowding and the day was an enjoyable one for all.

The celebration began with a ball game between the Mission and the Moiese valley teams, in which the former won by a score of 12 to 6. In the afternoon came the Indian war dance and a long program of races. The Indians again performed in the evening, with games and a historic parade as features.

War Dance.

Despite the interest aroused by the other events it was the Indian war dance which drew the crowd and was the feature of the celebration. The Indians gave a splendid exhibition. Dressed in their brilliant costumes, painted guadily and decked with feathers, they performed tirelessly all afternoon the battle dances of their fathers. It was a pitiful performance in many ways. There, at the mission, the first seat of the white man in the Flathead, surrounded by curious hundreds of the palefaces, who have occupied their ancient territory, the red men went through the war dance which they were too peaceful to hold in the days of their strength and which is a hollow mockery now in the days of their submissive weakness. Still it was interesting enough as a specimen of old Indian life and when once whirling to the music of the tom-tom the dancers seemed to forget the presence of their spectators and the fall of their race.

The dance was slow in starting. Despite the insistent call of the tom-tom and the chanting of the players, the warriors stayed in their lodges for a couple of hours, painting and befeathering themselves, before they appeared for the dance. Then one by one they sauntered in, faces, chests, arms and legs painted red and yellow and blue, clad in brilliant costumes and covered with sleigh-bells; and to the tune of the oft-repeated chant of the tom-tom players and the squalling of the paleface papooses they began the movements of their peculiar dance. A few more than a score of braves took part in the dance and long after the crowd had left to watch the races the sound of their yells and the sighing of the players came from the camp.

After the arrival of all of the dancers old, grey-haired Chief Michel delivered a short address in his native tongue to the assembled whites. The old warrior spoke with apparent eloquence. His gestures and his appearance were admirable. Finally, amid hand clapping, he stepped back and an interpreter repeated his remarks in English. The interpreter got as far as, "The chief says that he wishes that each one of you would put from five cents up into the hat to buy pop for the tom-tom players —"

At this point the Mission band, seated outside in a wagon and unconscious of the progress of affairs within the pavilion, began to play, and the rest of the speech was lost. It was unfortunate for Chief Michel, for the rest of the oration was undoubtedly less pragmatic.

Far more interesting than the dance was an inspection of the Indian village. It was grouped around the pavilion on the top of a knoll overlooking the town. Back of it lay the gigantic barrier of the Mission mountains, with no sign of civilization in sight. It took some imagination to overlook the n.....-baby and "ring-a-cane" booths which jostled the teepees, but with them out of the way, the inspection gave a glimpse into the real Indian life. There were 30 or more lodges in the village, each with its collection of lean hungry-looking dogs and plump, happy, little brown papooses. Inside, the Indians were to be seen at their ease; perhaps eating their noon-day meal from the family stove in the center, or resting in anticipation of the afternoon's excitement. Here a brave was decking himself in his finery or a pretty s.... was painting her face and hands. A walk around the camp was worth more than half a dozen war dances. Even here the jarring influence of civilization was apparent. Chairs and cots and shining trunks were in some of the teepees, and in one — it is hard to believe, but true — a young boy was washing his face and neck with soap and water.

But these little things were only incidents. The affair as a whole was splendid. Such performances are getting rarer and the staginess of them growing stronger every year. It would be hard to imagine a more satisfactory way of spending a holiday than that which St. Ignatius offered today.

Ball Game.

The Mission baseball team won a hard-fought battled from the Moiese valley crowd in the morning as a starter for the day. The score, 12 to 6, looks one-sided, but for seven innings the two teams fought neck and neck. In the eighth, with the score tied at 5 to 5, the Mission men made seven runs, and although the visitors tried hard, the best they could do was a single tally. The game was interesting throughout, and the big crowd was on its feet until the last man was put out. The team lined up as follows: Mission — Doty, third base, John Dishman, pitcher; Carney, second base; R. Dishmon, first base; C. Dishmon shortstop; Pierre, catcher; Gardipy, center field; Beachboard, left field; Gabin, right field.

Moiese Valley — Fullerton, second base; Aldrich, center field; R. Warnicott, third base; Hart, catcher; Ralph Warnicott, left field; Schoonover, shortstop; McManigall, right field; Handy, pitcher.

The Score by Innings.

Moiese Valley   0 1 2 0 2 0 0 0 1 — 6
Mission   1 0 1 2 0 0 1 7 x — 12

A fine program of races was held in the afternoon after the war dance and in the evening the Indians presented some of their tribal games and a historical pageant. The day ended with a big dance in the new hall.

The day was notable for the fact that there were no firecrackers nor other noise-makers in evidence anywhere. Especial credit for the success of the day is due the Mission band, which furnished good music throughout and to the following committees.

General — P. C. Thompson, G. H. Beckwith, V. A. McCormack.

Racing — W. H. Meglasson, Rube Dishmon, Sol Lemery, David Dowd, William Ducharme, D. Dorio.

Baseball — John Dismon, George Ketchum, Peter Lucier, Sol Gobin, J. C. Hoffman, Arsene Beauvais.

War dance — Chief Ki-Ki-She, Chief Lomie Joseph, Chief C. Mullmon, Frank Ashley, A. B. Beckwith, Frank Ducharme.

Judges — H. H. Goble, George Lindsay, Joseph Michaud, Joe Deschamps, Charles W. Donnally, Bert Lish, Gustave Dubrille.

Starters — George Ketchum, Ed Deschamps, George Buckhouse.
Clerk of course — Addison K. Lusk.

* * * * * * * *

At Jocko.

Flathead Agency, July 4. — (Special.) — There was a good dance of the agency Indians today at the Big Bend, where there are 40 teepees tonight and where there will probably be 60 tomorrow, as there are more coming all the time. The crowd was unexpectedly large and the dance is well managed. It will continue for several days. Thursday will probably be the best day and visitors from Missoula will then have a chance to see it at the best advantage. It is entirely managed by the Indians. Moiese and Leuisohn are at the head of management. Paul Charlie is in charge of the arrangements and preparation of grounds and is doing well. Three Heads is the dance leader and is a shining light; his work is specially good. Big Sam is assisting him in the dance direction.

* * * * * * * *

Ronan's Day.

Ronan, July 4. — (Special.) — Ronan today threw open its doors to the largest number of people ever seen in the town. A ball game, races, Indian dances, a boxing contest, a Fourth of July oration and all of the amusements incident to a real celebration were to be found in the city today.

John H. Tolan of Missoula delivered the speech of the day. Always a brilliant speaker, Mr. Tolan fairly eclipsed himself today and held his audience spellbound by his magnificent address. The ball game between the Missoula Assassins and the Ronan team was one of the most brilliant ever seen on the local diamond and was won by a score of 2 to 1. The visitors being the victors. The game was free from errors and was one that had the large audience on its feet the greater part of the time. Sensational plays were the feature. Eickmann and Kelley starred for the visiting team.

The Indian dances were better than usual and were largely attended. Attired in their full regalia, the Indians gave their famous dance in a manner that gave the audience a highly pleasing entertainment.

A pretty glove contest was put on by "Kid" Doyle of Butte and John Richards of Ronan. The local man won by the knockout route in the third round. He was the aggressor all the way and won handily, never being pushed by the Butte fighter.

Three dances were given in the evening. A dance was given by the Indians and both local dance halls were crowded to the utmost. The celebration was undoubtedly the best ever held in the town and passed without a single mishap to mar its success.

Document 68

Kootenais Complain About Government Control of Land Sales July – August 1911

Source: Chief Thomas Anties [Antiste] to Department of Indian Affairs, July 14, 1911, and Fred C. Morgan to Commissioner of Indian Affairs, August 17, 1911, from file 62,904/1911 Flathead 310, Central Classified Files, RG 75, National Archives, Washington, D.C.

Editors' note: In 1911, the government tried to control how the money from sales of tribal land was spent. The Kootenais lived a long distance from the agency in Jocko and resented the government controls. Some periods have been added to Antiste's letter.

C. E. Rakeman
Real Estate and Loans
And Music Dealer.
Polson, Mont. July 14, 1911.

Department of Indian Affarirs,
Washington, D.C.
Dear Sir:

I wish to ask for a permit to sell land. I am getting old and grey haired and not able to work and am poor and need money to live on. I would like to here from you as soon as possable. I cant wait any longer. I wish you would give me the right to sell ore trade my land. I cant wait any longer. I am getting plum tired and worn out. I am getting discusted. I go to the Indian Agent here and he promises me to do something but does nothing. That is why I am making this complaint to you as to how I am treated. I wish you would send me papers so I could sell my farm. I would be very glad to get it right a way from you. Our Indian agent make lots of promises but never does anything. we cant even get money for the leases ore rent of our land to live on ore from timber sold from it. The hole tribe of indians here are afraid of the agent here because he seems to be working agent [against] us. he is not a man of his word. we called to meet the Agent July 7 and when all the Cautney tribe came he skiped of then and could not be found and we never could find him. we made a date the next day with the clerk July 8 and called then but he to skiped out. I am back here to

Polson and must Depend upon you helping me out. something must be done at once as this is driving us mad the way things are done here. I hope to here from you soon askong you these favors I Remain Yours

Chief Thomas Anties [Antiste].
by H. E. Rakeman.

* * * * * * * *

Department of the Interior
United States Indian Service
Flathead Agency, Jocko, Montana,
August 17, 1911.

The Honorable,
Commissioner of Indian Affairs,
Washington, D.C.
Sir:

I have the honor to return herewith the letter transmitted by your Office on August 1, 1911, for report, of Chief Thomas Anties, by H. E. Rakeman, this letter being dated July 14, 1911. Relative to same I would advise that Chief Antiese Thomas had sometime previous to the writing of this letter (July 2, 1911) made certain complaints to your Office, and while the signature does not so show, yet because it is on the stationary of H. E. Rakeman, and the typewriter used seems to be the same as the one used for the letter dated July 14, 1911, I am of the opinion that both letters were written for Antiste by the same party. The letter of July 2, 1911, was transmitted for report under date of August 9, 1911, and copy of my reply is enclosed herewith.

As I understand it, H. E. Rakeman is the son C. E. Rakeman, deceased, and Matilda Rakeman. Mrs. Rakeman has advised me that prior to the death of her husband, who conducted a general merchandise store at the town of Polson, Antiste and other Kootenai Indians had secured credit in considerable amounts, and as they do but very little, if any work, have never made any settlement. From the fact that both letters seem to have been written for Antiste by Mr. H. E. Rakeman, and the principal, or, in fact, the only subject seems to be a desire to secure for Antiste, from some source or other, money to live on and to *"pay the merchants we owe for goods,"* I should judge that Mr. Rakeman has requested settlement from Antiste, or, perhaps, refused him further credit, and that Antiste, in order to secure further credit, or to prevent for a time Mr. Rakeman's calling his attention to the account, stated that the Agent would not allow the Indians to sell their lands — and insofar as this statement applies to selling without complying with Departmental regulations, it is correct. As shown in the letter of July 14, 1911, Antiste (and the same is true of many of the Kootenai Indians) wants to sell his allotment direct, and when he finds he cannot do so thinks that the Agent is to blame. We now have in the office the applications of Antiste and wife to sell parts of their allotments, and if he could secure in a lump sum the entire proceeds from such sale (when made) I think there would be no complaints from him for a short time.

Relative to Antiste's complaint that the Kootenai Indians came to the office to see the Agent and that they could not find him, and that next day (July 8th) they made a date with the clerk and when they called he skipped out. I have to advise that Antiste and several Kootenai Indians did come to the agency on July 7th, not so much because they had business to transact, but because the Indians in Jocko Valley, who were having a little celebration, had invited them to attend. In the afternoon of July 7th Antiste and a few other Kootenais came to the office and there found all four clerks and myself. As fast as possible the different matters which each had to present were taken up and disposed of, and it was about six o'clock before they were through for the evening. A few of the Indians who were anxious to get back to the camp grounds stated they would be in in the morning, and I told them, and also the other Kootenais present, including Antiste, that I would have to leave that evening, but that the clerks would attend to any business they wished to present in the morning. Mr. Allen, chief clerk, states that early next morning, Saturday, July 8th, the Kootenais came again to the office, and that the entire office force was busy with them all morning, through the noon-hour, and until about three o'clock in the afternoon, when they left, stating they wanted to get to St. Ignatius, a distance of about 25 miles, that evening. During the afternoon of the 7th Paul Martin, one of the Kootenais, informed me that he had sold his allotment for $3000, and when I told him such transaction was not valid he, and other Kootenais, became very much incensed. Mr. Allen states that on Saturday morning the Kootenais took up again this sale, and others which they stated they had made, and when attempt was made to explain to them that they could not sell in this manner, but would have to comply with the regulations, that Paul Martin told Mr. Lewis, lease clerk, who was trying to explain to him the regulations, that he lied, and he and two or three others refused to have any further dealings with the clerks.

On Saturday afternoon July 8th, the clerks inform me that Mr. Main, clerk, did not leave the office for dinner until about 1:30 P.M., but did not return to the office after that. Mr. Lewis lease clerk, and Mr. Brown, day school teacher (who was also assisting in the office) did not leave the office until after three P.M., and after the Kootenais had left. And Mr. Allen, chief clerk, and Mr. Hawley, stenographer, were at the office all afternoon.

It is my understanding that during the months of July, August and September that Saturday afternoons may be observed as half-holidays, but we have modified this at this agency that these half-holidays may be taken unless there is work that prevents, as was the case on July 8th.

Respectfully
Fred C. Morgan
Superintendent.

Thomas Antiste
Source: Photograph Archives, Montana Historical Society, Helena, Montana,
detail from photo 954-573

Document 69

Joseph Allard Chosen for Appraisal Committee

August 17, 1911

Source: "Joseph Allard Is Chosen," *The Daily Missoulian*, August 17, 1911, page 1, col. 6.

Editors' note: Joseph Allard was originally chosen to be the tribal representative on the committee to appraise those lands that were not covered by the first appraisal in 1908. See, however, the newspaper article from September 9, 1912, where Duncan McDonald was finally selected as the tribal representative on the appraisal committee.

Joseph Allard Is Chosen

St. Ignatius, Aug. 16. — (Special.) — Responsive to the call of Superintendent Morgan, the head men of the confederated tribes met here today in council for the purpose of selecting a representative to serve on the board which will appraise the unallotted lands not yet classified. Owing to the fact that most of the Indians are busy harvesting their crops, there were only 50 present at the council, but they were representative and the situation had evidently been carefully discussed with others. There was a thorough discussion at the council and Joseph Allard was selected as the choice of the council for the position on the appraising commission. He is well known on the reservation and in Missoula. He is the son of the late Charles Allard, partner of Michael Pablo in the ownership of the famous buffalo herd. He is a successful farmer, has a good home on the reservation and an excellent family.

Document 70

Indian Celebration and Tribal Member Run
Auto Stage
September 15, 1911

Source: Excerpts from *The Ronan Pioneer*, September 15, 1911, page 2, col. 1.

Editor's note: A tribal member was part owner of an automobile stage between Ravalli and Ronan in 1911.

About 200 Flathead Indians have been spending the week on their old camping grounds in the Bitter Root valley. A celebration lasting three days was given them at Stevensville. . . .

The Bateman & Stinger 16-passenger auto has commenced making regular trips between Ravalli and Ronan. The auto leaves Ravalli every day after the arrival of No. 41 and makes Ronan for dinner. Returning they leave Ronan at 2:30 and make connections at Ravalli with all evening east and west bound trains. . . .

Document 71

Harry Burland, Businessman

September 1911 — June 1917

Source: "Ronan Blacksmith Shop," *The Ronan Pioneer*, September 15, 1911, page 3, col. 5-6; "Central Garage," *The Ronan Pioneer*, May 19, 1916, page 2, col. 2-3; *The Ronan Pioneer*, June 1, 1917, page 8, col. 3.

Editors' note: Tribal member, Harry Burland, operated several businesses in Ronan between 1911 and 1917. He started with a blacksmith shop and then went on to automobile repairs and sales.

* * * * * * * *

Ronan Blacksmith Shop
HARRY BURLAND, Proprietor
HORSE SHOEING A SPECIALTY
Plow, Wagon and Wood Work in connection.   I have on hand everything in the blacksmith line.
Ronan, Montana

Source: "Ronan Blacksmith Shop," *The Ronan Pioneer*, September 15, 1911, page 3, col. 5-6.

* * * * * * * *

≈CENTRAL GARAGE≈

Equipped to do all kinds of repair work

HUPMOBILE SERVICE

FORD STATION

FORD PARTS AND AUTOMOBILE ACCESSORIES

Gasoline————Oil————Tires————Tubes

HENRY H. BURLAND, Proprietor

Source: "Central Garage," *The Ronan Pioneer*, May 19, 1916, page 2, col. 2-3.

* * * * * * * *

Harry Burland of the Central garage, announces that he has secured the agency for the Chevrolet and Reo cars for this territory and can make immediate deliveries. — adv.

— June 1, 1917

Document 72

Central Hotel

The Ronan Pioneer, September 22, 1911, page 3, col. 2.

Document 73

Salish Indians Return to Stevensville for Celebration September 24, 1911

Source: "Echoes of the Flatheads' Return," *The Daily Missoulian*, September 24, 1911, editorial section, page 9, col. 1-3.

Editors' note: On the twentieth anniversary of the final removal of the Salish from the Bitterroot, the white people in Stevensville had a celebration attended by a number of Salish people from the reservation.

Echoes of the Flatheads' Return

Perhaps one of the most pleasant features of the recent celebration by the Flathead Indians at Stevensville — a celebration to commemorate the 20th anniversary of their leave-taking from the Bitter Root valley — was the opportunity afforded the old-time white residents of the valley and the old-time Indians to discuss the old-time subjects and happenings in which they were both interested a quarter of a century ago. The meeting of some of the whites and some of the redmen at Stevensville was the first in 20 years — since the tribe moved over into the Jocko valley. During the days of the Indian's supremacy in the Bitter Root their relations with the few white people who had first discovered the wonders of the Bitter Root were closer than they have ever been since. Then they combined forces for protection against the Blackfeet; they traded horses and furs and together endured many of the same hardships. In many instances there grew up friendships which were warm and sincere. Although there are only a comparative few of the white men remaining in the valley who were there when the Indians made it their home, the Indians remember them all and the exchange of reminiscences included things which nearly all of the whites were connected.

Two of the old residents who spent an enjoyable day at the Indian camp were Mr. and Mrs. Perry McClain of Florence. They made a thorough visit around the circle of lodges and at each one they were warmly greeted. The Indians, usually so difficult to engage in conversation, talked without reserve to both Mr. and Mrs. McClain; they discussed the things of serious nature and the also remembered and laughed over circumstances which had a humorous side.

Major Catlin of Missoula was another of the old-timers who enjoyed meeting the Indians at Stevensville, and he and Artist E. S. Paxson spent a couple of jolly days at the celebration. Every little while something would call to Major Catlin's mind happenings of the old days and he told many a good story to the great delight of those who happened to be in his crowd. Among the stories was one concerning the wife of Major Owen, who built the fort at Stevensville which bore his name.

"I well remember Major Owen's s....," said Mr. Catlin. "She was a Snake, I think, but she was fair of feature and form and had a most aristocratic air and manner. She loved fine togs. In the attempt to please her one year the major, at great trouble and expense, secured for her a very fine specimen of the then fashionable hoopskirt. It was a beautiful creation, made up of flashing red goods, and if ever you saw a proud woman in her life, that s.... was it when fully togged out in the new rai[n]ment. She was in the habit of making a weekly visit to some friends who lived up Mill creek, and on these occasions always went horseback. She also always wore her new skirt. Talk about the new sensation of the harem skirt — it simply was nothing compared with Major Owen's s.... riding forth in her hoops. It was a great sight and people used to come miles to witness her weekly excursions."

Document 74

White Hunter Kills Flathead Reservation Buffalo

October 1911

Source: Lincoln Ellsworth, *The Last Wild Buffalo Hunt* (New York: Privately Printed, 1916), pages 13-28.

Editors' note: Ellsworth left a detailed description of his 1911 hunt for one of Pablo's outlaw buffalo on the Flathead Reservation. Many of the Indians he dealt with on his hunting trip were not named, but his guide may have been August Finley. Ellsworth enjoyed the hospitality of the family of Alicott, a Nez Perce Indian who was rich in horses, and Ellsworth attended a mixed blood fiddle dance.

The Last Wild Buffalo Hunt

One late fall day, as the evening train on the Northern Pacific passed through a rocky gorge in the Bitter-Root Mountains of Montana, an observant traveller could have seen a tipi pitched on a small flat across the Pend d'Oreille River, and before it, cooking over a little fire, an Indian and a white man. The Indian was a French half-breed and the white man myself. Little did the traveller dream that on the heavily timbered tops of those high, rugged hills, deeply gorged and running in "hog-backs" down to the river, roamed the last herd of wild buffalo in the United States. They had been driven to seek there their last refuge again man. The two men cooking over the little tipi fire were hunting buffalo.

The story of these buffalo is interesting. In 1873 or '74 Michael Pablo, a Mexican living in the Flathead Valley, bought from Walking Coyote, an Indian, twelve calves which he had captured on the Milk River in Canada. Walking Coyote was married to a Cree woman, and one day in anger he shot her in the arm. He fled to Canada and made his home among the Piegan Indians, but, like all Indians, soon became homesick. It occurred to him, Indian-like, that by returning home with some captured buffalo it might appear as an excuse for his having left. He captured fourteen calves, killing two for meat. Pablo turned these twelve calves loose on what is now known as the Flathead Reserve, a rugged country fifty miles long by forty wide and hemmed in on all sides by the Bitter-Root Mountains except on the north, where lies Flathead Lake.

Within this boundary lie three parallel valleys, the Flathead, the Bitter-Root, and the Camas, separated from each other by the rugged hills of which I have spoken.

The buffalo made this their home and did not leave, for the valleys so lie that the winters are mild and on the hills the food abundant. Four years ago the reserve was opened up for settlement, and Pablo negotiated the sale of his buffalo to the Canadian Government, and in the great round-up, which lasted nearly four years, seven hundred head have been delivered and still there are some left, the outlaws of the herd, unconquerable old veterans who live high up in these timbered fastnesses. Many tales of the round-up have been told: of how the cowboys drove old bulls from brush thickets where they had taken refuge only by setting fire to their fetlocks with burning brush tied to a long pole; of how once when a rider was driving a cow toward the corral she turned and charged him, and, lifting the horse and rider onto her head, carried them a hundred yards at top speed, when she struck the corral fence and the rider was tossed over unhurt. Again when an old bull was being driven up a chute into the car and he found he could not turn back, he charged straight ahead, going through the opposite side as though it were paper. (Two of them did this, one breaking his neck.) One of the largest bulls of the herd, who was unconquerable, they left in a crate overnight. In the morning they found him dead without a bruise or a scratch on him; he had died from a broken heart.

I could tell many stories of the chase, but the last I shall tell is of two old bulls who broke out of the car near Edmonton, Alberta. They found their way back to Great Falls, Mont., a distance of over twelve hundred miles. They were both on the fight, one breaking into a farmer's field and ruining his grain, for which he was shot. The other found his way back to his native range.

These outlaws that live high in the mountains generally lie on the edge of the timber among the rocks. The old bulls are solitary animals, and one will find them in the rockiest and most inaccessible places imaginable. When they scent danger they will start travelling, or dive down into the brush and stand perfectly still. It is impossible to track them except in winter-time, and this winter Pablo says he will kill what remain, for settlers will shoot at them and many make away wounded and die.

It was one of these outlaws that I came down to hunt with a letter from the Canadian Commissioner to Mr. Pablo. I left Kalispell on October the 17th, took a small steamer down Flathead Lake thirty-five miles, then a four-horse stage eleven miles to the settlement of Ronan, Mr. Pablo's home. He was pessimistic about my getting a buffalo before the snow fell, saying I would have first to find them, and that he hoped I had plenty of time. He supplied me with a horse and blankets, and sent me out with a French half-breed, an old-time buffalo-hunter of the plains, who spoke English only when he felt disposed, and that generally after the inner man had been well warmed with "whiskey blanc"; when his tales of the buffalo chase would exceed my wildest fancies and a thrilling story of adventure come to a sudden end only for his lack of expression in the English language, when he would continue in French. Then when the fire had burned itself out he would sink into a fathomless taciturnity, and to all questions his only answer was "Maybe" or "I dunno." He was tall, lean, and withered, and his eyes were always watery, for he had sat over the smoke of too many camp-fires. His outfit was abominable, the tipi had one side burned out of it, and we got caught in the worst rain-storm of the season. The water and tea pail (we had only one) had a hole in one side, and when you forgot and turned that side to the fire the canvas plug would burn out, and it was always dark when we cooked supper, and the creek was always down in some brush-tangled bottom. The dishes I don't believe had ever been washed, for they were caked with rust. His name was August, and he said he would be ready to start early in the morning, but it was well in the afternoon before I could get him out of town, and as a consequence we pitched camp that night in the dark, eighteen miles up the Bitter-Root Valley. We carried our stuff in a democrat, with saddles and an extra horse, for we intended camping in a good place and hunting the hills on horseback.

The following day we crossed over the hills into the Camas Valley, twelve miles. It was a glorious fall day and the bare, rugged hills stood out clear and bold against a translucent blue sky. High up bands of wild horses looked down upon us — lean, wiry individuals, tails and manes blowing with the wind and heads thrown up, ready to start should we approach too close. It was a fair sight to look down upon the broad Camas dotted over with the cabins of Indian and white settlers and waving fields of grain, after travelling through the bad lands of the narrow Bitter-Root. We stopped at an Indian's cabin to inquire if they had seen buffalo. We both went inside to warm ourselves, and had been there but a few moments when we heard a crash outside and jumped up to see our team running away. They struck the heavy rail fence, going through it as the buffalo did through the car, the rails flying in all directions. The wagon never upset, but one horse broke his nose in striking. After the team had been rounded up by Indians from all directions and, after August had administered a kick to the uninjured horse and looked to see that the axles had not been broken, his only remark was: "Good wagon."

We stayed with this family for two days, hunting the hills about. They included our stock of provisions among theirs and cleaned us out of everything except coffee and rice. They didn't use coffee (I have seen few Indians that do when tea is obtainable) and the rice we had *cached* among our blankets. They didn't use a table, but sat about on their blankets on the floor to eat. Generally at meal-time a couple of other families would join them. One old s...., so old and withered, would not say a word until she had finished eating, and after she had lighted her pipe and had it drawing well, through the heavy clouds fragrant with kin-ic-i-nic she would become very talkative, using many gestures, and her voice was low and soft as were those of all the others. A young girl was busy with bead work. They were Mission Indians and they called themselves good Catholics, even if they did rustle horses at times.

In these hills are countless wild horses, many that have never felt a branding-iron, so naturally there are many "rustlers," men whose past is questionable. I had many such pointed out to me before leaving town. "There's a man who has just been in three years for rustling, best rider in western Montana." And again: "That fellow over there held up the station agent at Ravalli by pointing his finger at him, and he got all the cash, too." I noticed that these men looked anything but desperate, in fact *quite* the contrary. The man who takes desperate chances and "makes good" in this country is generally the quietest, most inconspicuous-looking individual imaginable; yet he looks you straight in the eyes, and in their quiet depths you notice a steely, hardy purpose. Outside of his profession you would probably never find a stauncher friend. Such is the way of the West.

Having found only one track, and that going south, we packed up and went down the valley fifteen miles. We camped in a deep gulch among the hills, and for nine days followed fresh tracks, the tracks of eleven wild buffalo in one bunch and three in another, a bull, a cow, and a calf. Our first day in these hills we saw five "black-tail" deer, but over the bare hillsides they saw us long before we could get within range. Again and again blue-grouse would rise with a whirr from under our very feet and sail down to some covert of brush below. In the evening of the second day we ran onto a black-tail in the timber's edge. I told August to shoot, and after an indefinite aim the hammer clicked on an empty shell, for he had shot at an eagle that morning from camp and forgotten to remove the shell. I asked him if that was the way he hunted buffalo. We saw hundreds of wild horses. Looking down into the gulches from far above we would startle a band with our yell. They throw up their heads with a start and were off at a gallop, never stopping till out of sight. Generally they saw us first. Their footing on the steep, rocky slopes was marvellous, for I never saw one stumble. We rode steadily all day long, never stopping to eat at noon, dropping down five hundred feet to examine the bare hillside for tracks, only to climb again to search the timber above. Our horses were dripping with sweat, and their flanks heaved with laboured breathing as they climbed and dropped. We were never discouraged for always just ahead, around some rocky bluff or behind some thicket of brush, we expected to come upon buffalo.

As we struck the bottom, going to camp on the evening of the eighth day, the breed turned in his saddle and silently pointed to the top of the hills, and there, plainly silhouetted against the evening sky, stood four buffalo in single file, motionless and, it seemed to me, watching us; darkness settled and the four forms became four shaggy shadows. My first thought as I drew my head from underneath the blankets in the morning was, would we find those buffalo? The blankets were wet, and I looked out to see a slow drizzle coming down. The hills were hidden in mist. Nevertheless we climbed to the top to find them covered with snow and the tracks of the night before blotted out.

The following morning, after eleven days out, we started for home utterly discouraged. In town I met one of the old round-up men who said he was sure we could find buffalo in three days. So we started again taking only our saddle horses and relying on some rancher for food and shelter. For five days we rode the hills in vain. Indians were chasing wild horses, which kept the buffalo always on the move. On the evening of our fifth day, as we were returning to camp, the clouds that had been threatening all day broke and a heavy snow-storm set in. We were in a valley running parallel to the one in which our camp was, and as we started to climb the thousand-foot divide my hunter's horse suddenly and without any warning played out and refused to move another step. With one end of a rope around his lower jaw and the other tied to the cantel of my saddle we dragged and coaxed him foot by foot and reached camp just before midnight. Only one with the instinct born to the hills could have found his way on such a night. We let down the corral bars but the animal refused to step over them, so we left him, and in the morning he had not moved. We were now in the grip of a bad storm, and we started to town for fresh horses. Fourteen flocks of wild geese passed over us, heading south. Shortly after they had passed we again heard honking and looked up to see them returning. They had become confused or lost in the heavy mist above. The flocks separated, some bolder ones wanting to return; the others wavered, then turned and followed the bolder; and the last stragglers were headed south again.

We made town by noon, and shortly after started out again and got to the river, fourteen miles away, just at dark. We found the ferryman had gone to town, and his wife, an enormously fat s...., said the river was frozen along the banks and we couldn't cross. There was no room in the squalid little shack and, still worse, no feed for the horses, so in the darkness we struck down-stream looking for a place to stay. Four miles down we came to Alicott's ranch. He was a rich Indian who had made his money in horses. Seventeen years ago he sold nine hundred horses for nine hundred dollars. His wife and two daughters were just preparing for a dance and they welcomed us. A breed dance would be a comic affair if it wasn't always made so tragic. Around the bare room, seated on packing boxes, are a motley congregation of men, women, and babies, for the most part hidden behind clouds of tobacco-smoke, while in the centre the dancers, shod in moccasins or high-heeled riding-boots, bow, advance, and swing in the most solemn manner. A fiddler seated in the corner scrapes off tunes to the beat of his foot, while an important-looking individual, seated on a box on the table, calls off the dances. I learned afterwards that I had caused great amusement when I danced because I had forgotten to remove my huge skinning-knife. At three o'clock in the morning we threw our blankets down on the ballroom floor and were soon sound asleep.

There was no alternative but to return to town again next day. Not discouraged, I started again by stage twenty-two miles up the Camas Valley, then with only my gun started over the hills twelve miles to a half-breed's cabin that I knew of in Garceau Gulch. He gave me a raw-boned pinto to ride, and together we started out, which made my seventeenth day after buffalo. We hunted a range I had not been on before, and, as we saw nothing, headed again for the hills I knew so well. My guide was a hard rider, and I shall not forget the steep hillsides we took on the lope, when each moment it seemed as though the horses might stumble or slip on the frozen ground where it meant a drop of three or four hundred feet. In the afternoon of the first day the breed's animal struck an old horseshoe lying on the ground, and it wasn't twenty minutes before we ran onto two "black-tails" on the edge of the timber, both of which we killed. That night we camped at a trapper's cabin, and the next afternoon, as we rode the wind-swept top of a high ridge, we saw a buffalo-track, going down into the heavy brush. The snow lay a foot deep and the slope was so steep that we left our horses on the top and followed the track on foot. It was only by chance that, looking ahead through the brush, I caught the movement of a dark, shaggy form against a clump of spruce in front of which it stood. I could see it was a large bull, and he must have seen or scented us, for he stood with his head raised and well forward, listening, and I could see his nostrils dilating. I felt sorry for the lonely old fellow as he started down through the brush, only to stop again shortly and listen. We climbed back out of sight, then made for the top, and went along until we thought we were well ahead of him, and again started down through the brush. Suddenly a dead tree crashed and he came running out into a small opening and stopped, for he had seen us but wasn't sure what it was. He stood not much over a hundred yards below us, and we both fired. At the seventh shot he fell to his knees, then tried hard to regain his feet again, but could not. As he sank he lost his footing and started rolling down the steep slope, a huge boulder finally stopping him. We went down to him and as I stood looking at the great shaggy form that had weathered the storms of many years the elation that I imagined I must feel when I had killed a buffalo did not come to me; instead, a deep regret welled up in me as I looked upon that rugged old fellow whose life I had taken. Hounded by man and forsaken by his kind, seeking a last refuge high in that rocky fastness, each morning and evening watering at a little spring below, to which we found his trail leading, then climbing to the rocks above to gaze down upon the peaceful valleys and across to the hills beyond, where maybe he could see others of his kind whom he dare not join.

As we finished skinning him I looked across the Bitter-Root and, through a rent in the hills to the Flathead beyond, saw where the snowy peaks of the Mission Range were bathed in lurid vermillion, the colour of blood upon the white snows, and watched until the shadows from the valley crept up and tarnished the vermillion to deep purple. We covered over the carcass with our saddle blankets to keep off the coyotes, and in the quiet of evening felt our way down to the valley below and to our camp, leaving the hardest part of the work for the morrow.

With the old trapper and two other ranchers to help it took us five hours to drag the hide and head down, and alternately drag and roll down the meat to where we could load it on packhorses. In town the news of the hunt had preceded, and the boys wanted to see the gun that had killed a buffalo and to hear the story of the hunt.

Missoula, Mont.
November, 1911.

Document 75

Reservation Indians Hire
Indian Claims Attorney
October 22, 1911

Source: "Noted Chiefs Come Before Court," *The Daily Missoulian*, October 22, 1911, page 8, col. 3.

Editors' note: In the first half of the twentieth century the Flathead Reservation Indians made repeated attempts to have their claims heard against the government. The claims cases were not actually settled until the second half of the century. Richard C. Adams was a member of the Delaware Tribe in Oklahoma and one of the founders of the Brotherhood of North American Indians, a short-lived Indian lobbying organization. Adams had a controversial history which may have included graft. See also the 1912 documents about the Brotherhood on the Flathead Reservation in volume six of this series, 1912-1920.

Noted Chiefs Come Before Court
Flathead and Pend d'Oreille Tribes Make Out Power of Attorney.

Stolid, blanketed Indians, representing the blue blood of the Flathead and Pend d'Oreille tribes, gave Judge Webster's courtroom an unusual appearance yesterday morning. Five head men from each tribe and two interpreters comprised the Indian delegation that appeared before the judge and officially gave power of attorney to Harve H. Phipps, who, with his associate counsel Richard C. Adams, will endeavor to secure a settlement of many Indian claims. On October 19, the Flatheads held a meeting and appointed five of their chiefs to come to Missoula and legalize the appointment of Mr. Phipps. On October 20, the Pend d'Oreille tribe took the same action and appointed five of its leaders to accompany Mr. Phipps. Yesterday morning they arrived here and signified to the judge their willingness to have Mr. Phipps appear in their behalf. Speaking of the action and its ultimate aims, Mr. Phipps said:

"The action taken today by the Flathead and Pend d'Oreille Indians is the same as that of the Cayuse, Walla Walla, Umatilla, Nez Perce and Colville tribes. Mr. Adams and myself will represent the various tribes in an endeavor to secure a settlement of the Indians' claims against the government. In 1910 there was $73,000,000 in Washington, the greater part of which rightfully belongs to the Indians. They have many claims against the government and the work of getting them adjusted will be tremendous. We have a force of men in Washington and it will take us about four years of time and $20,000 to get these cases into shape for presentation. The government has not been giving the Indian the proper encouragement. They talk of trying to make him more like the white man, but he is discouraged in his endeavors at every turn in the road. Every time that an Indian wants to do something, it is necessary for him to ask somebody's permission. The money that should go to him, such as is derived from the rental of land and the sale of timber, is handled by Washington and it gives the red man no incentive to better himself.

"I want to emphasize the fact that we are not attempting to cause any hard feelings between the Indians and the government. Just the opposite. We are doing our best to get the Indian claims settled in a manner satisfactory to both sides and we believe that when we accomplish this end, we will make the Indians more satisfied and more friendly to the government than they have ever been before. Much of the money that is due to the Indians comes from the fact that some would die and leave their heirs in another tribe. The government would fail to notify the heirs that they had any money coming on account of a relative's death and the amount due would simply lie in Washington drawing interest.

"While the Indian is not by any means the hardest working class, still, he is fairly industrious and is trying to do the best he can. The government has failed to teach them what they ought to know in order to run their business. If the government would encourage and organize the Indians it would not be long before a big improvement could be noticed.

"The Indian has been moved from place to place and has not received the proper consideration. He has not received the proper compensation for his land. In the states of Oregon, Idaho, Montana and Wyoming the India[n]s have a total acreage of about 316,147,000 acres. The Indian has received about three cents an acre for this land, none of which the government has sold for less than $1.25 an acre. The Indians are supposed to have 93,491,200 acres of land in Montana. We are going to try and get some legislation this winter that will release a great deal of this money to the Indians and we will attempt to have congress authorize the bringing of actions in the court of claims that will adjust these tribal claims. We intend to take up the Indians' case like we would that of a white man and want their cases settled by the same law that would apply to you and me. I think the time is coming when the Indian will want to vote. Some of them want the ballot now. When the time comes that they are given the privilege of voting, the Indian vote will have to be taken into consideration, particularly in states like Wyoming. At the recent tribal meetings of the Pend d'Oreille and Flathead Indians, they had me prepare a memorial to congress asking that their claims be given consideration."

Mr. Phipps is a prominent Spokane attorney and is a member of the legislature in that state at the present time. He will leave Missoula at once and visit some of the other Indian tribes.

The following are the Indian chieftains present in the courtroom yesterday morning:

Pend d'Oreilles — Baptiste Kakashi, Sophiel Michael, Cooloostapa Clarlowain, Marcial Three Heads and Alex Bigknife.

Flatheads — Martin Charlot, Antoine Moiese, Louis Vanderburg, Pierre Bighawk and John Lumphrey.

Document 76

The St. Ignatius Pool Hall

The Ronan Pioneer, November 17, 1911, page 3, col. 2.

THE ST. IGNATIUS

POOL HALL

ED. DESCHAMPS, Proprietor.

First Pool Hall on the hill
above the Mission Hotel

Four Good Tables, Soft Drinks
Candies, Cigars, Tobacco.

Courteous Treatment to All.

Document 77

Michel Pablo Was Partner in Ronan Store

December 17, 1911 — April 5, 1912

Source: "Pablo & Potvin," *The Daily Missoulian*, December 17, 1911, West-end Section, page 3, col. 6-7; *The Ronan Pioneer*, February 9, 1912, page 2, col. 3; "Our New Spring Invoice of Dry Goods," *The Ronan Pioneer*, April 5, 1912, page 3, col. 5-6.

Editors' note: Michel Pablo invested in a Ronan store in the early 1910s. He made improvements in the store, but it was burned down in the August 1912 fire in the Ronan business district. Pablo was originally going to rebuild the store after the fire, but then decided to not run the risk of another fire loss. See the *Ronan Pioneer's* August 30, 1912 article on the fire and also the October and December 1912 articles about the Pablo & Potvin store.

Pablo & Potvin

Dealers in
General Merchandise

Our stock is complete and fresh, selected with careful attention to quality and to suit the needs of Ronan and vicinity.

An investigation of our goods and our prices will convince you we are right.

M. Pablo—   —Fred T. Potvin

Pablo & Potvin

RONAN MONTANA

Source: "Pablo & Potvin," *The Daily Missoulian*, December 17, 1911, West-end Section, page 3, col. 6-7.

* * * * * * * * *

Pablo & Potvin have had wires strung and pipes laid from the Central hotel and will soon have steam heat and electric light in all parts of their general store and warehouse. Modern improvements such as these will soon be installed all over town, or just as soon as same are available.

— February 9, 1912

* * * * * * * * *

Our New Spring Invoice of Dry Goods

Have arrived and here you will find many novelties which will please. Also our spring shipment of Ladies', Men's and Children's Shoes. Large assortment of the best shoes made.

A Car of Barbed Wire
At Lowest Prices

5 Tons of Seed Potatoes

Remember the Grocery Department when buying. Always complete and fresh, and prices the lowest.

THE STORE OF QUALITY **PABLO & POTVIN** **THE STORE OF QUALITY**

Source: "Our New Spring Invoice of Dry Goods," *The Ronan Pioneer*, April 5, 1912, page 3, col. 5-6.

Document 78

Flathead Indians Complain of Indian Policies

December 1911

Source: "Indians Back from Pow Pow," *The Helena Independent* (daily), December 27, 1911, page 8, col. 1-2; "The Wrongs of the Flathead," *The Daily Missoulian*, January 6, 1912, page 4, col. 3-4.

Editors' note: Henry Matt and other delegates from the Flathead Reservation complained about government policies that they thought were robbing the tribes. Joseph Dixon had pushed through an allotment bill for the reservation without the consent of the tribal members. Dixon had also supported a reclamation project on the reservation that was being built with tribal money and mainly served the white homesteaders. Many tribal farmers had their own irrigation ditches that were being destroyed during the construction of the Flathead Irrigation Project. In place of their water rights, tribal farmers were promised a bill for irrigation water. Some tribal farmers were located on land that had been naturally watered by drainage from the mountain water pack. Tribal money was also being used to pay for the salaries and expenses of the Flathead Indian Agent and other agency employees. The *Missoulian* ridiculed the complaints of the tribal members, but the paper was owned by Joseph Dixon who had pushed through the allotment, homesteading, and irrigation on the reservation as political return for white votes. Dixon built his political career on transferring Flathead, Crow, and other Indian assets to white voters at bargain prices. The tribal members were looking to the Brotherhood of North American Indians headquartered in Washington, D.C., to support their grievances against government policy.

Indians Back from Pow Pow
Three Montana Chiefs Return From Conference with
"Great Paleface Chief."
Pleased at Reception
Made Trip to Washington to Protest Alleged Mistreatment and Return
After Being Promised That All Abuses Will Be Speedily Remedied —
Submit Written Report Indians.

Much satisfied with the result achieved at their recent great council with the "big chief of the white house" senators and congressmen, Henry Matt, of the Flatheads, Chief Baptiste [KaKaShe] and Chief Antoine Moiese returned from their trip to Washington, where they went to complain of the treatment being offered them by the Indian bureau. While at Washington, the three representatives met some of the big men of the country, who, it is stated in the report offered by the chiefs to the Flathead Indians, were sorry that the Flathead Indians and the other Indians of Montana had not been treated right but that they would see that they were better cared for.

The Indians in their written report which they will submit to Montana tribesmen at a coming grand council, state that the eastern people are utterly unaware of the treatment that is being offered the Indians of Montana, and as fast as they learned the facts, they one and all extended their sympathy and promised to help in what ever way they could. The success of their trip to Washington is given in full in their report to the chiefs and members of the Flathead Indian council, which, in part, is as follows:

"I have the honor to make the following report of our visit to the city of Washington:

"We arrived there on December [4?] and spent the day visiting and seeing the sights.

"On Monday following we had a visit with our Senator Myers and Congressman Pray. They said that they were sorry to see that the Flatheads were not treated right since the republicans had been in power and promised that they would do all in their power to help these poor and unfortunate Indians. Senator Myers afterward presented himself at one of the sessions and gave an address and before he left became an honorary member of our order.

"What surprised me beyond measure was the fact that nine-tenths of the people of Washington, and of the east are absolutely ignorant of the treatment the Indians receive from the Indian bureau. As fast as they learned the facts they, one and all, extended their sympathy and promised to help us in every way possible. The matters and things made known to the people here through memorials to both the president and congress, by the Brotherhood of North American Indians was a revelation.

Organize Brotherhood.

"We were in daily attendance and helped to organize a society of the Brotherhood of North American Indians. We were able to learn a great deal about the grievances, not only of our tribes, but all other tribes. We had a great many influential men, such as congressmen, senators and other men of note to join our association and make speeches to us and advise our organization and praise its purpose and the sincerity of its members. We were more interested in our Indian senators, whom we found in congress, representatives and delegates of Indians tribes who were very smart and discussed all evils and oppressions of our race. We learned a great deal from these, and fell [felt] that we are better able to tell our people of the great uplift that we have undertaken for the Indian race. One man in particular we were interested in by the name of Un-a-Qua (August A. Breuninger), who is fighting for the Indian rights. He seemed to us to be the only man that thoroughly understood the history and proper standing of each Indian and what they are entitled to.

"The organization was formed and Mr. Richard C. Adams was elected great sachem of the order. He is a very nice man and has the welfare of the North American Indians at heart.

Prepare a Memorial.

"We prepared a memorial and was invited up to the white house to visit the president, and during this visit we presented this memorial to the great white father. He stood there with a grand smile on his face and welcomed all his Indian brothers, and afterward said our organization was a grand work on the part of the Indians. He will probably recommend to congress in his next message to take some action upon this matter that we called attention to. In this memorial we asked that we be given control over our individual moneys and control of our affairs. We have come home to report to the tribe and ask that they draw up a tribal memorial containing all of their grievances to be presented to the head organization at Washington so that they can recommend that the matter be taken up by congress. All the Indians that were in attendance were very glad and thankful for the meeting and the prospects of the organization. It was grand because the old Indian chiefs had a chance to stand up and tell their troubles and these were written down, so that their tribe will know later what they had to say for their people. Something that has never happened before. Again it was good for these Indians representing about 40 tribes had a meeting place, where they all joined together as brothers and departed happy.

"Father Ketcham, the head of the Indian bureau of Catholic missions took all the Indians who wished to accompany him to St. Paul's church Sunday where, during the services, he welcomed the Indians to Washington and praised the work that they were doing and expressed his belief that the organization

Henry Matt
Source: Virginia Matt Brazill, Arlee, Montana

of the Brotherhood of North American Indians would be a great factor in obtaining for the Indians many of the rights they were entitled to, but now denied.

"In the course of his remarks he said that he could not refrain from expressing his great pleasure over the way the Indians, one and all, conducted himself [sic] since he came to Washington; that their conduct was such that it reflected great credit on the Indian race.

"Mr. Henry Matt says that he has learned more in one minute while on his trip from the Indian leading men and leading men in Washington than ever before in his life. It certainly was a great education to him. He said that he believes that the democrats will soon come into power in congress and he hopes they will and [then?] change the political conditions there. The democrats are doing all they can the help the Indians.

"Thanking you one and all and hoping that we get together an organization of a local brotherhood. The next congress will thoroughly look into our case and change the conditions now existing. Very respectfully submitted,

"Chief Baptiste.
"Henry Matt.
"Chief Antoine Moiese."

* * * * * * * *

The Wrongs of the Flathead

According to current reports, some Washington claim agents and lawyers have recently been instrumental in organizing "The Brotherhood of North American Indians." Under the plea of "getting them their money," various and sundry "delegations" of "war chiefs" from western communities were persuaded to come to Washington to perfect the organization of "The Brotherhood." In the prospectus of the brotherhood, just issued, the name of a Washington lawyer appears as "Grand Sachem" of the order.

Judging from the power conferred upon the "Grand Sachem," it seems that he is the chief cook and bottlewasher of the whole propaganda.

It appears that three or four of our Flathead friends, with varying degrees of claim to the title and dignity of war chiefs, were persuaded to invest their hard earned dollars in making a trip to Washington to give aid and comfort to the organization of the brotherhood and in the hope of "getting their money."

According to current newspaper reports, the great War Chief of the Flatheads, Henry Matt, and his co-laborers in the Brotherhood, Moiese and Baptiste, on their return from the capital, issued a manifesto. In a recent number of the Helena Independent, War Chief Henry Matt says he "learned more in one minute while on his trip than ever before in his whole life." The great chieftain of the Flatheads also discovered, while thus engaged in "getting the money for the Indians," that "the democrats are doing all they can to help the Indians["] and that it was apparent to him "that the democrats will soon come into power in congress and he hopes they will change the conditions," so the Indians will "get the money."

The one chief cause of complaint seems to be that instead of "getting the money" as soon as it is paid into the Flathead fund from the sale of land, timber, townsites, etc., the government is now foolishly spending the same in the irrigation of Indian allotments and white settlers' homesteads, the Indian of course having his land irrigated free of any individual cost to him; the white homesteader paying back the actual cost of the irrigation of his homestead, during a term of years.

The great Flathead war chiefs are indignant that the government should dare in this high-handed manner deprive the poor Indian of his "rights" and prevent him from "getting his money" at once and instanter. Why should a despotic government thus divert the money from the immediate purchase of tobacco, grub and firewater and phonographs, into the useless construction of irrigating ditches? Why not let future generations devise ways and means for the irrigation of Indian lands and white homesteads on the Flathead? Why compel these great war chiefs and their vassals to forego these pleasures of life when the money is available for supplying their every want and desire? It is outrageous that such things are permitted in this age of freedom. The great war chief further says in his interview: "What surprised me beyond measure was the fact that nine-tenths of the people at Washington are absolutely ignorant of the treatment the Flatheads have received. As fast as they learned the facts, they, one and all, extended their sympathy and promised to help us. They were sorry to see that the Flatheads were not treated right since the republicans had been in power."

Stop the steam shovels on the Flathead canals. Banish Savage and Tabor with their mule teams and Fresno scrapers. Fill up the reservoirs. Stop marring the beautiful Flathead landscape. Let the Jocko, Mission, Mud, Post, Little Bitter Root and the beautiful Pend d'Oreille run untramelled to the sea.

Down with the tyrants, the wicked republicans, the Indian bureau and the reclamation service. Give Henry his "rights and the money." Supply Moiese with free tobacco and repeal the twenty-five-year prohibitory clause so that Sam Resurrection may purchase firewater to his heart's content and untrammelled by all sumptuary laws that now vex and harass him.

Colonel Sam Gordon, in a recent issue of the Yellowstone Journal, comments on the Brotherhood and the demands of its organizers:

"The Brotherhood of North American Indians" is the high-sounding appellation given, by a bunch of Washington claim attorneys, to an organization consisting of themselves, and designed to look after the interests of the poor Indian in matters before congress and the departments.

Looking after the interests of the poor Indian is about the richest graft connected with the government, if one gets properly located as the authorized attorney for a tribe, or even a subdivision of a tribe, that still has landed interests. That was demonstrated in the exposures connected with the Oklahoma Indians a year or so ago, when it was found that these Indians — immensely wealthy in oil and coal lands — had one special attorney who stood to grab off three million dollars, if a job he was engineering had gotten through. In addition to this enterprising attorney these same Indians had other "attorneys" by the dozen, appointed by the government to "protect their interests" and paid handsomely out of the Indian purse, who sat absolutely still and somnolent while this big steal was being pushed through.

This is stated merely as an exemplification of what kind of an animal the Indian attorney usually is. The point that interests Montana is that a few days ago "The Brotherhood of North American Indians," as represented by this bunch of Washington claim agents, addressed a formal notice to Senator Dixon stating that it was the desire of the "the brotherhood" that the bill now in progress through congress for the opening of the Crow Indian reservation, be "held up," until "the brotherhood" could communicate with its other brothers, the Crow Indians, and agree upon what was the best to be done in the premises. It is pleasing to be able to state that Senator Dixon lost no time in telling the Washington "brothers" exactly where they get off as the following excerpt from the letter he wrote them in reply to their impudent demand, with [will] testify:

"I have, from the beginning, been a little suspicious of the movement to 'organize' the North American Indians into 'one brotherhood.' To be frank with you, many members of congress are of the belief that it is more of a movement by certain Washington attorneys, who hope to reap financial reward, in having themselves appointed attorneys for poor, helpless Indians with good, fat salaries attached thereto. * * * It is needless for me to say that the entire Montana delegation resents any assumed activity by Washington lobbyists to attempt to regulate the internal affairs of our Indians, whose representatives we are. * * * I shall not, of course delay action on the bill that so vitally affects the welfare of the Crow Indians as well as the people of Montana and the Montana delegation will reserve to itself the right to specifically inform the Crow Indians of any and all efforts that may be made to induce them to give up their money to self-constituted guardians under the specious plea of the 'Brotherhood of North American Indians.'"

Index